Bien dit!

Grammar Tutor
for Students of French

HOLT McDOUGAL

HOUGHTON MIFFLIN HARCOURT

Table of Contents

French 1

Table of Contents (continued)

French 2

Table of Contents (continued)

French 3

To the Teacher

Many students do not have a clear understanding of their own language and cannot, therefore, build on that understanding as they learn a second language. The intention of this *Grammar Tutor for Students of French* is to explain the basic grammar concepts introduced and practiced in *Bien dit!* first in English, with English examples and activities, and then in French. Students can then relate the targeted grammar concept to something they do everyday in English and thereby gain insights about how the grammar works before they attempt to learn it in the context of an entirely new language.

The *Grammar Tutor* presents in sequential order the main grammar points introduced in *Bien dit!* Levels 1, 2, and 3. These grammar points are compared to English as appropriate, so that students can readily see the many similarities between the two languages. In some cases, they will, of course, see differences; however, as they compare and contrast the structures of French and English, they will no doubt accomplish one goal: they will increase their understanding of language in general and become better able to use it to communicate.

The explanation of each grammar concept is accompanied by examples, and each presentation is followed by an activity that allows students to verify that they have understood the explanation of the grammar concept. The concepts are presented first in English and then in French; the activity immediately following each presentation has the same format in both languages, to enable students to quickly see the comparison between the two languages. Following this basic introduction, students are asked to apply the grammar concept to simple, structured activities in French. The final activity on most of the Activity Masters encourages students to think both about the target language and their own.

On the following pages is a glossary of the grammar terms that are covered in this book. This "Grammar at a Glance" can serve as a quick reference to the more detailed material covered in the body of the *Grammar Tutor for Students of French*.

Grammar at a Glance

adjective An adjective modifies a noun or a pronoun. (See also **adjective, interrogative adjective,** and **possessive adjective.**)

> **EXAMPLES** The Duponts have a **beautiful, red** car.
> *Les Dupont ont une **jolie** voiture **rouge**.*

adjective agreement (See **agreement.**)

adverb An adverb modifies a verb, an adjective, or another adverb.

> **EXAMPLES** When it is **very** cold, I **often** take the subway.
> *Quand il fait **très** froid, je prends **souvent** le métro.*

agreement Agreement is the correspondence, or match, between grammatical forms. Grammatical forms agree when they have the same number and gender.

> **subject-verb agreement** refers to the form of the verb that goes with its subject.

> > **EXAMPLES** This package **is** a gift for my mother.
> > *Ce paquet **est** un cadeau pour ma mère.*

> **adjective agreement** Adjective agreement refers to the form of an adjective that matches the number and gender of the noun it modifies. English has no adjective agreement, but French adjectives must match the nouns they modify.

> > **EXAMPLES** My sister is **short**. My brother is **short**, too.
> > *Ma sœur est **petite**. Mon frère est **petit** aussi.*

article An article refers to a noun. Articles are the most frequently used type of adjectives.

> **definite article** refers to a specific noun.

> > **EXAMPLES** **The** kitten won't come down from **the** tree.
> > *Le petit chat ne veut pas descendre de l'arbre.*

> **indefinite article** An indefinite article refers to a noun that is not specific.

> > **EXAMPLES** They ordered **a** pie and **a** cake.
> > *Ils ont pris **une** tarte et **un** gâteau.*

> **partitive article** A partitive article refers to some or part of something. English uses "some" to express the partitive.

> > **EXAMPLES** Martha bought **some** bread, **some** jam, and **some** mineral water.
> > *Marthe a acheté **du** pain, **de la** confiture et **de l'**eau minérale.*

command (See **imperative mood.**)

conditional The conditional verb form is used to tell what you would or would not do under certain conditions.

> **EXAMPLES** If I had the money, I **would buy** this book.
> *Si j'avais de l'argent, j'**achèterais** ce livre.*

contraction A contraction is a shortened form of a word, numeral, or a group of words. Apostrophes in contractions indicate where letters or numerals have been omitted.

> **EXAMPLES** I'm thirteen years old.
> *J'ai treize ans.*

definite article (See article.)

demonstrative adjective A demonstrative adjective points out a specific person, place, thing, or idea.

> **EXAMPLES** Do you prefer this coat or that jacket?
> *Tu préfères ce manteau ou cette veste?*

demonstrative pronoun A demonstrative pronoun stands for a specific person, place, thing, or idea.

> **EXAMPLES** I like these.
> *J'aime ceux-là.*

direct object A direct object is a word or word group that receives the action of the verb or shows the result of the action. A direct object answers the question *Whom?* or *What?* after a verb of action.

> **EXAMPLES** My parents rarely watch television.
> *Mes parents regardent rarement la télévision.*

direct object pronoun (See pronoun.)

imperative mood An imperative sentence gives a command or makes a request.

> **EXAMPLES** Do your homework! And then, let's go to the movies.
> *Fais tes devoirs! Ensuite, allons au cinéma.*

imperfect The imperfect tense refers to actions or conditions in the past that were ongoing, that occurred regularly, or that were going on when another event occurred.

> **EXAMPLES** I was watching television when the phone rang.
> *Je regardais la télé quand le téléphone a sonné.*

indefinite article (See article.)

indirect object An indirect object is a word or word group that tells *to whom* or *to what* or *for whom* or *for what* the action of the verb is done.

> **EXAMPLES** The teacher gave the students their assignments.
> *Le prof a donné les devoirs aux élèves.*

indirect object pronoun (See pronoun.)

interrogative adjective An interrogative adjective introduces a question.

> **EXAMPLES** Which class do you like?
> *Quel cours aimes-tu?*

interrogative pronoun An interrogative pronoun is a word that stands for a noun and introduces a question.

> **EXAMPLES** Which one do you like?
>
> *Laquelle aimes-tu?*

interrogative sentence An interrogative sentence asks a question and is followed by a question mark.

> **EXAMPLES** Are you coming with us?
>
> *Tu viens avec nous?*

irregular verb An irregular verb is a verb whose forms do not follow a regular, predictable pattern.

mood Mood is the form a verb takes to indicate the attitude of the speaker. (See also **imperative mood**, **conditional**, and **subjunctive mood**.)

noun A noun names a person, place, thing, or idea.

> **EXAMPLES** Carol brought the music to the party.
>
> *Carole a apporté de la musique à la boum.*

partitive article (See **article**.)

possessive adjective A possessive adjective is an adjective that indicates to whom or what something belongs.

> **EXAMPLES** This is my pencil. These are their friends.
>
> *C'est mon crayon. Ce sont leurs amis.*

preposition A preposition shows the relationship of a noun or a pronoun to another word in a sentence.

> **EXAMPLES** Michael is going to the swimming pool with Sophie.
>
> *Michel va aller à la piscine avec Sophie.*

pronoun A pronoun is used in place of one or more nouns. (See also **demonstrative pronoun** and **interrogative pronoun**.)

> **EXAMPLES** Francine is going with her cousins. She likes them a lot.
>
> *Francine va avec ses cousins. Elle les aime beaucoup.*

direct object pronoun A direct object pronoun is a pronoun that stands for the direct object of a sentence.

> **EXAMPLES** Do you like this dress? I like it a lot.
>
> *Tu aimes cette robe? Je l'aime bien.*

indirect object pronoun An indirect object pronoun is a word that stands for the indirect object of a sentence.

> **EXAMPLES** Lisa sent us a letter.
>
> *Lisette nous a envoyé une lettre.*

subject pronoun A subject pronoun stands for the person or thing that performs the action of the verb.

> **EXAMPLES** They (Mary and Jean) are going to the mall.
>
> *Elles (Marie et Jeanne) vont au centre commercial.*

reciprocal verb A reciprocal verb generally expresses *each other*. Because the action of reciprocal verbs takes place between two people or things, they are always plural. In English, we don't have reciprocal verbs – just reciprocal pronouns.

> **EXAMPLES** Melinda and Robyn talk (to each other) on the phone often.
>
> *Elles se parlent souvent au téléphone.*

reflexive verb A reflexive verb indicates that the action of the verb is done to, for, or by oneself. It is accompanied by a reflexive pronoun. In English, we do not have reflexive verbs, only reflexive pronouns.

> **EXAMPLES** Let's make ourselves an ice cream sundae.
>
> *Il se brosse les dents.*

regular verb Regular verb forms follow a regular, predictable pattern.

> **EXAMPLES** Marie likes French.
>
> *Marie aime le français.*

relative pronoun A relative pronoun is used to join two or more related ideas in a single sentence. They can be subjects, objects, or objects of prepositions, and they can refer to people or things.

> **EXAMPLES** That's the boy who lives beside us.
>
> *C'est le garçon qui habite à côté de chez nous.*

subject A subject is a word, phrase, or clause that performs the action of the verb.

> **EXAMPLES** Their children are cute.
>
> *Leurs enfants sont mignons.*

subjunctive mood The subjunctive mood is used to express a suggestion, a necessity, a condition contrary to fact, or a wish.

> **EXAMPLES** If I were you, I would tell the truth.
>
> *Il faut que tu dises la vérité.*

tense The tense of verbs indicates the time of the action or state of being that is expressed by the verb.

> **EXAMPLES** She is singing. She sang. She will sing.
>
> *Elle chante. Elle a chanté. Elle chantera.*

verb A verb expresses an action or a state of being.

> **EXAMPLES** Lawrence plays basketball. He is French.
>
> *Laurent joue au basket. Il est français.*

Level 1
Grammar Tutor Activities

Subjects and verbs

In English Sentences have a subject and a verb. The subject is the person or thing doing the action or being described. The verb is the action word like jump or sing, or a linking word, like am or is, that links the subject to a description.

 Denise sings well.

 Simon is blond.

Sentences always have a subject. The subject can be a noun or a pronoun. A noun refers to a person, a thing, or a place. A noun can be replaced with a pronoun, which is a word that stands for the noun. Examples are he, she, you, and they.

 Denise is a friend.

 She is fifteen years old.

A Underline the subject and circle the verb in each sentence.

Nicole	Hello, I am Nicole.
Paul	Hi, my name is Paul. Are you the new student?
Nicole	Yes, I am from Belgium.
Paul	Who is your English teacher?
Nicole	Mrs. Paterson is my teacher. I like her a lot. She is very funny.
Paul	Yes, she makes English fun.
Nicole	But, we have a lot of homework in her class.
Paul	Would you like to study together?
Nicole	Sure, you can help me with English grammar.

In French Sentences also have a subject and a verb.

 Denise chante bien.

 Simon est blond.

The subject can be a noun or a pronoun. Some examples of French pronouns you have already seen are je, tu, il, elle, nous, and vous.

 Je te présente Denise.

 Elle a quinze ans.

SUBJECTS AND VERBS CHAPITRE **1**

B Underline the subject and circle the verb in each sentence.

Laurent Salut, je m'appelle Laurent Humbert.

Corinne Salut, je m'appelle Corinne Thibaut. Je te présente Nathalie.

Nathalie Tu as quel âge, Laurent?

Laurent Moi, j'ai quatorze ans.

Corinne Nathalie a dix-sept ans!

Laurent Eh bien, mon ami s'appelle Marcel. Il a vingt ans.

C Find the subject in each sentence and write it in the correct column.

	Noun	Pronoun
1. Je m'appelle Quentin.		Je
2. Marine est une amie.		
3. Le professeur a trente ans.		
4. Comment allez-vous?		
5. Tu as quinze ans?		
6. Elle s'appelle Camille.		
7. Mon ami parle français.		
8. M. Lemaire présente Mme Dufont.		

D Complete each sentence with the appropriate verb from the box. Some verbs can be used more than once.

a	est	s'appelle	va	présente	as

1. Il _____va_____ bien?

2. Je te _____ mon ami.

3. Lucas _____ mon ami.

4. Comment elle _____?

5. Eva _____ quel âge?

6. Tu _____ seize ans.

Subject pronouns

In English Subject pronouns refer to a specific person or people and act as subjects of a sentence or clause. The subject pronouns in English are I, you, he, she, it, we, and they. Notice how the pronouns below are used to avoid repeating the subject once it has been made clear.

Thomas lives next door. He is from Louisiana.
My friends met Thomas and they really liked him.

A Complete the sentences with the correct subject pronouns.

1. Yolanda plays tennis, but _____**she**_____ prefers to skate.

2. Henry and I like pizza._____ eat it every day.

3. My parents wake up very early because _____ both work.

4. Marie looks great today! Did _____ get a haircut?

5. Mr. Mallet is very happy. _____ just got a promotion.

6. Tom, Arthur, Alice, and you are invited to my party. _____ don't need to bring anything.

In French The subject pronouns are je or j' (I), tu (you), il (he), elle (she), on (one), nous (we), vous (you), ils (they), and elles (they).

Je changes to j' before a verb beginning with a vowel sound.
   J'ai dix-sept ans.

To say *you*, use tu to talk to a friend, a family member, or someone your age. Use vous to talk to more than one person or to an adult who is not a family member.
   Monsieur et madame, comment allez-vous?
   Tu as quel âge, Eva?

To say *they*, use elles when you are talking about two or more females. Use ils when talking about a group of males or a mixed group of males and females.
   Clara et Émilie? Elles ont treize ans.
   Hugo et Julie? Ils ont quinze ans.

The pronoun on has no direct equivalent in English. It can mean *one, we,* or *people in general.*
   En France, on parle *(speak)* français.

SUBJECT PRONOUNS

B Complete the sentences with the correct subject pronouns.

1. Comment _____**tu**_____ t'appelles?

2. Monsieur Guillaud, comment allez- _____?

3. C'est un ami. _____ s'appelle Mathieu.

4. Sarah et Laura? _____ ont quel âge?

5. _____ ai quinze ans.

6. En France, _____ parle *(speak)* français.

7. Et toi? _____ as quel âge?

8. Bonjour, mademoiselle. _____ m'appelle Alexis.

C Underline the subject in each sentence. Then write the subject pronoun that could replace each subject.

1. <u>Michel</u> est mon ami. _____Il_____

2. Valentin et moi parlons français. _____

3. Le professeur s'appelle M. Cartier. _____

4. Charlotte a dix-huit ans. _____

5. Mme Lambert et Mme Gidon sont professeurs. _____

6. Nicolas et Benjamin adorent le tennis. _____

7. Nathan et Amandine ont vingt ans. _____

D Look again at the subject pronouns you wrote in the last three items in Activity C. In your own words, explain why you chose each pronoun.

1. Mme Lambert et Mme Gidon

_____

_____

2. Nicolas et Benjamin

_____

_____

3. Nathan et Amandine

_____

_____

Indefinite articles

In English Indefinite articles are used to introduce unspecified nouns. The indefinite articles in English are **a** and **an**. The article **a** is used to introduce nouns beginning with a consonant or consonant sound, and **an** is used to introduce nouns beginning with a vowel or vowel sound.

    I need **a** backpack for school.   Julie brings **an** eraser to class.

Adjectives such as *some, few,* or *several* can be used to introduce plural, unspecified nouns.

    I need **some** books.   Julie has a **few** erasers left.

A Circle the indefinite article in each sentence, and underline the noun the article introduces.

    1. Lucy is carrying a heavy <u>suitcase</u>.

    2. Did you mail a card to Aunt Ruthie?

    3. I don't have a calculator in my backpack.

    4. Victor has an iguana in his bedroom.

    5. I want a new mp3 player for my birthday.

    6. Do you have an e-mail address?

    7. My friends and I bought a DVD and some CDs.

In French The French indefinite articles are **un**, **une**, and **des**. While the use of **a** or **an** in English is determined by whether the noun that follows begins with a vowel or a consonant sound, in French, the indefinite article used is determined by the gender of the noun and whether it is singular or plural.

Use **un** with masculine singular nouns and **une** with feminine singular nouns.

    un livre   **une** fenêtre

Use **des** with plural nouns whether they are masculine or feminine.

    des chaises   **des** tableaux

In negative sentences, **un**, **une**, and **des** change to **de**.

    Il y a **une** carte dans la classe.   Il n'y a pas **de** carte dans la classe.

    Il y a **des** fenêtres.   Il n'y a pas **de** fenêtres.

INDEFINITE ARTICLES   CHAPITRE **1**

B Circle the indefinite article in each sentence, and underline the noun the article introduces. Then check the appropriate columns to indicate whether the noun is singular (S) or plural (P), masculine (M) or feminine (F).

	S	P	M	F
1. Oui, il y a des CD.		✓	✓	
2. Est-ce qu'il y a des posters?				
3. Il n'y a pas de lecteur de DVD.				
4. Est-ce qu'il y a une fenêtre?				
5. Non, il n'y a pas de filles.				
6. Il y a des ordinateurs.				
7. Il y a un tableau dans la classe.				

C Complete the following sentences with the correct indefinite articles.

1. Je te présente Axel. C'est _____**un**_____ ami.

2. Il y a _____ bureaux dans la classe.

3. Il n'y a pas _____ tableaux dans ma classe.

4. Est-ce qu'il y a _____ carte?

5. Je te présente Jade. C'est _____ amie.

6. Il y a _____ élèves et _____ professeurs.

7. Non, il n'y a pas _____ télé dans la classe.

D Rewrite the following negative sentences so they are positive. Change the indefinite articles as necessary.

1. Il n'y a pas de cahiers.

    ____ **Il y a des cahiers.**_____

2. Il n'y a pas de garçons.

    _____

3. Il n'y a pas de bureau.

    _____

4. Il n'y a pas de livres.

    _____

5. Il n'y a pas de fenêtre.

    _____

Avoir and negation

In English The verb **to have** has only two different forms in the present tense: **have** and **has**.

I **have** two older brothers.

Lucie **has** a new backpack.

We always **have** math homework.

To contradict or make a statement negative, you add the words **do** or **does not** or its contractions **don't** or **doesn't**. The verb forms "to be" simply add the word **not**.

I **don't** have a cell phone.

They are **not** French.

A Circle the form of the verb **to have**. Then check the appropriate column to indicate whether the sentence is affirmative or negative.

	Affirmative	Negative
1. My cousins don't have a DVD player.		
2. Beatrice has a French uncle.		
3. I don't have your e-mail address.		
4. Our classroom has four computers.		
5. My friends and I don't have a car.		
6. Sarah has a cell phone.		
7. We have too many things to do.		

In French The verb **avoir** *(to have)* has six different forms. The form used depends on its subject.

j'	ai	nous	avons
tu	as	vous	avez
il/elle/on	a	ils/elles	ont

Nous **avons** un prof de français super.

Dominique **a** trente ans.

Tom et Hugo **ont** vingt-huit posters.

To make a sentence negative, add **ne** in front of the verb and **pas** after it. If the verb begins with a vowel sound, **ne** becomes the contraction **n'**.

Je **ne** m'appelle **pas** Enzo!

Marie **n' a pas** douze ans.

AVOIR AND NEGATION

B Circle the form of the verb avoir. Then check the appropriate column to indicate whether the sentence is affirmative or negative.

	Affirmative	Negative
1. Je n'ai pas quinze ans.		✓
2. Vous avez un lecteur de DVD.		
3. Mon ami Romain a dix-sept ans.		
4. Nous n'avons pas de carte.		
5. Pauline n'a pas d'ordinateur.		
6. Jeanne et moi, nous avons dix livres.		
7. Tu n'as pas de cahiers?		

C Complete the following sentences with the correct form of avoir.

1. Le prof de maths _____a_____ vingt-neuf ans.

2. Tu n'_____ pas seize ans?

3. Nous _____ un ami français: Jean-François Rivière.

4. Je n'_____ pas de bureau.

5. Thomas et Claude _____ l'adresse e-mail d'Agathe.

6. Vous _____ une télévision et un lecteur de DVD?

7. Le professeur _____ vingt-trois élèves.

D Rewrite the following sentences as negative sentences.

1. Ça s'écrit d-i-x.

   _____ Ça ne s'écrit pas d-i-x._____

2. Lucas a vingt-deux ans.

   _____

3. Je présente l'élève.

   _____

4. Nous avons quatorze ans.

   _____

5. Ça va?

   _____

Definite articles

In English The definite article *the* introduces a specific noun. *The* is used with all nouns: both singular and plural nouns, nouns that refer to the masculine gender (like *man*), nouns that are clearly feminine (like *actress*), and those that have no gender (like *table, car,* and most nouns in English).

> I went to the party with Paul. (*party* is a singular noun with no gender)
> The girl ran a good race. (*girl* is a singular noun with feminine gender)
> I gave the boys a snack. (*boys* is a plural noun with masculine gender)
> She returned the books to Marion. (*books* is a plural noun with no gender)

A Circle the definite article in each sentence and underline the noun that the article introduces. Then check the appropriate boxes to indicate whether each noun you underlined is singular (S) or plural (P) and whether it can be classified as masculine (M), feminine (F), or whether it has no gender.

	S	P	M	F	no gender
1. They bought the house next door.	✓				✓
2. She made cookies for the boys.					
3. The businesswoman is wearing earrings.					
4. The ship sailed to Martinique.					
5. John painted the chairs in one day.					
6. The girls love to play with my cat.					

In French There are four forms of the definite article: le, la, l', and les. The form that is used depends on the gender (masculine or feminine) and the number (singular or plural) of the noun it introduces. While only some nouns in English have a gender, all French nouns are either masculine or feminine.

Use la with feminine nouns: la musique   la glace

Use le with masculine nouns: le chocolat   le roman

Use l' with any singular noun
that begins with a vowel whether
the noun is masculine or feminine: l'école *(feminine)*   l'anglais *(masculine)*

Use les with all plural nouns
whether masculine or feminine: les filles *(feminine)*   les garçons *(masculine)*

When you say that you like something, you must always use the definite article before the noun.
> J'aime la musique. *(I love music.)*

DEFINITE ARTICLES

B Circle the definite article in each sentence and underline the noun that the article introduces. Then check the appropriate boxes to indicate whether each noun you underlined is singular (S) or plural (P), masculine (M) or feminine (F).

	S	P	M	F
1. Sophie adore la glace.	✓			✓
2. Ils aiment bien l'école.				
3. Tu n'aimes pas les mathématiques?				
4. Je déteste le chocolat.				
5. J'aime bien les animaux.				
6. Vous aimez la voiture de sport?				
7. Alexandre adore les romans.				

C Complete the following conversation with the correct definite articles.

Antoine Tu aimes _____ l' _____ école?

Monique J'aime _____ maths, mais je n'aime pas

_____ anglais. Et toi?

Antoine Moi, j'adore _____ classe de musique. M. Panier

est _____ professeur et il est super.

Monique Moi aussi, j'aime bien _____ musique, mais je préfère

_____ vacances!

D Write four sentences telling what you like, using **J'aime**. Circle the definite article in each sentence and explain why you chose that form.

1. **J'aime regarder la télé.**

    Télé is a singular, feminine noun.

2. _____

    _____

3. _____

    _____

4. _____

    _____

5. _____

-er verbs

> **In English** Verbs are words that express actions or states of being. The endings of most present-tense verbs do not change unless the subject, or doer of the action, is *he, she, it,* or a proper name like *Pierre*. With these subjects, an **-s** is added at the end of the verb.
>
> | I sing | we sing |
> |---|---|
> | you sing | you sing |
> | he, she, it sings | they sing |

A Underline the subject and the verb in each sentence. Two of the verbs end in **–s**. Circle those two endings.

1. We ride our bikes to school sometimes.

2. Gary rides his bike to school always.

3. Jeannette and Sandra like football.

4. Sandra likes tennis, too.

5. You and Peter go to the movies on Fridays.

6. I play sports after school.

> **In French** French verb forms vary much more than English verb forms, but they follow predictable patterns. Once you learn the pattern of a group of verbs, you'll know how to form other verbs within that group. For example, to form regular verbs that end in **-er**, drop the **-er** and add the appropriate ending that goes with each subject as shown below.
>
> **aim**er *(to like)*
>
> | j' aime | nous aimons |
> |---|---|
> | tu aimes | vous aimez |
> | il, elle, on aime | ils, elles aiment |
>
> Ils téléphonent à des amis.
> Nous ne regardons pas la télé.

B Underline the subject and the verb in each sentence. Then go back and circle the ending of each verb.

1. Tu aimes bien l'école?

2. Micheline adore l'anglais.

3. Les amis surfent sur Internet.

4. J'étudie les maths.

5. Nous adorons les vacances.

6. M. et Mme Blanchard, vous regardez la télé?

-ER VERBS

C Circle the subject that matches the verb form in the following sentences.

1. (Tu / Elle / Nous) adore surfer sur Internet.

2. (Paul / Vous / Ils) aimez étudier le français?

3. (J' / Tu / Nous) écoute de la musique moderne.

4. (Mathieu / Elles / Tu) détestes la glace?

5. (Je / Marie et Jade / Nous) préfère lire des magazines.

6. (Mes amis / Vous / Agnès) aiment écouter la radio.

7. (Je / Nous / Elles) parlons anglais et français.

8. (Tu / Claudie / Vous) dessines aussi.

D Complete the following sentences with the correct form of the –er verb in parentheses.

1. Oui, j'_____ adore _____ (adorer) les maths.

2. Ils _____ (regarder) la télé.

3. Tu _____ (écouter) de la musique classique?

4. Nous _____ (téléphoner) à des amis.

5. Paul et Sandrine, vous _____ (étudier) le français.

6. Mme Bertrand _____ (aimer) envoyer des e-mails.

7. Tu _____ (adorer) dessiner?

8. Elle _____ (détester) dormir.

9. Tu _____ (préférer) les romans?

10. Non, je ne _____ (travailler) pas.

11. Est-ce que vous _____ (aimer) la musique moderne?

12. Hélène et moi, nous _____ (chanter) bien.

E Explain how you would know what form an **-er** verb has even if you're not sure of its meaning. Use the verb **penser** and the subject **nous** as an example.

_____

_____

_____

_____

Irregular plurals

In English The plural of most nouns is formed by adding **-s** to the singular form: book → book**s**. However, there are some nouns that have unusual or **irregular plurals**.

Some nouns that end in **-f** or **-fe** change to **-ves** in the plural.

    calf → calves   knife → knives

Some nouns change the vowel sound in the plural.

    foot → feet   man → men

Some nouns do not change at all to form the plural.

    deer → **deer**   sheep → **sheep**

A Circle the plural noun in each sentence. Then check the appropriate column to indicate whether it is a regular or irregular plural.

	Regular	Irregular
1. The firemen came fast.		✓
2. How many scarves do you have?		
3. The school will buy new computers.		
4. Canadian geese migrate every year.		
5. Please buy two loaves of bread.		
6. I am reading about pioneer women.		
7. Do you recycle newspapers?		
8. Gray wolves are still endangered.		

In French To form the plural of most nouns, you add **-s** to the end of the singular form: le magazine → les magazine**s**. Some nouns have **irregular plurals** that are formed differently.

If the singular noun ends in **-eau** or **-eu,** add **-x** to form the plural. The pronunciation of the word does not change.

    le tabl**eau** → les tabl**eaux**   le **jeu** *(game)* → les j**eux**

If the singular noun ends in **-al,** replace **-al** with **-aux**.

    le journ**al** → les journ**aux**   l'anim**al** → les anim**aux**

The singular and plural forms of some nouns are the same.

    le CD → les **CD**   le DVD → les **DVD**

B Circle the plural noun in each sentence. Then check the appropriate column to indicate whether it is a regular or irregular plural.

	Regular	Irregular
1. Il y a deux [tableaux] dans la classe.		✓
2. J'aime lire les journaux.		
3. Georges préfère lire des magazines.		
4. Est-ce que tu aimes les animaux?		
5. Nous n'aimons pas les bandes dessinées.		
6. J'ai trente-six DVD.		
7. Il n'y a pas de bureaux dans la classe?		
8. Mon ami a des CD de musique classique.		

C Complete the following sentences with the plural form of the noun in parentheses.

1. Les garçons aiment les _____**jeux**_____ (jeu).

2. Vous avez des _____ (bureau) dans la classe?

3. Samir n'a pas de _____ (journal). Moi non plus.

4. Est-ce qu'il y a des _____ (animal)?

5. Moi, j'aime bien les _____ (CD) de musique classique.

6. Il y a des cartes et des _____ (tableau) dans la classe.

D Rewrite the following sentences, changing the underlined words with the cues in parentheses.

1. Il y a <u>une</u> élève dans la classe. (dix-neuf)

    ____Il y a dix-neuf élèves dans la classe._____

2. Il y a <u>un</u> animal dans la classe. (trois)

    _____

3. Il y a <u>un</u> bureau dans la classe. (deux)

    _____

4. Il y a <u>un</u> journal dans la classe. (vingt)

    _____

5. Il y a <u>quatre</u> tableaux dans la classe. (un)

    _____

Contractions with à

In English A **contraction** is a shortened form of a group of words: we will → we'll.
In English, contractions are usually negations or combinations of pronouns with
helping verbs. They always include an apostrophe in place of the missing letter or
letters.

   don't   isn't   I'm   he's   they've

Contractions are optional and rarely used in formal writing.

   You're coming to the party, **aren't** you?

A Circle the contraction in each sentence. Then rewrite the contraction as a group
of individual words.

   1. This isn't my backpack._____ **is not** _____

   2. You don't like to dance? _____ _____

   3. How come she's always late? ___ _____

   4. How's it going, Bob?_____ _____

   5. We've come a long way. _____ _____

   6. Sam, you're a great friend._____ _____

   7. I haven't done my homework. _ _____

In French A **contraction** is also the formation of a new word from two or more
individual words. While contractions in English are optional, in French,
contractions are required. The preposition **à** *(to, at)* never appears in combination
with the articles **le** and **les**. Instead, the contractions **au** and **aux** occur.

   à + le → au   J'aime aller **au** cinéma.
   à + les → aux   Tu aimes parler **aux** professeurs?

However, contractions do not occur when the preposition **à** is used before the
articles **la** and **l'**.

   à + la → à la   J'aime aller **à la** piscine.
   à + l' → à l'   Tu aimes aller **à l'**école?

B Circle the contraction in each sentence. Then write the two words that make up
the contraction.

   1. M. Baubeau travaille à l'école. _____ _____ **à + l'** _____

   2. Jacques adore aller au cinéma._____ _____

   3. Abdul n'aime pas aller au café. _____ _____

   4. Tu aimes jouer aux cartes?_____ _____

   5. Nous allons au parc souvent. _____ _____

CONTRACTIONS WITH À

C Check the correct box to tell which preposition completes each sentence.

	au	aux	à la	à l'
1. Mes amis jouent _____ base-ball.	✓			
2. Nous aimons aller _____ piscine.				
3. Zoe travaille _____ café.				
4. Tu études _____ école.				
5. Je n'aime pas jouer _____ échecs.				
6. Vous allez _____ stade?				
7. Jean et Célia dansent _____ MJC.				

D Write four sentences using one item from each of the boxes below. Be sure to include the correct preposition in each sentence.

Je/J'	travaille	école
Tu	manges	piscine
Nous	aimons aller	échecs
Camille	aime aller	parc
Mes amis	jouent	café

1. J'aime aller à la piscine.

2. _____

   _____

3. _____

   _____

4. _____

   _____

5. _____

   _____

E Explain two differences between English contractions and French contractions with **à**.

_____

_____

_____

_____

_____

Est-ce que

In English You can change a statement into a yes-no question by adding **do, does,** or **did** to the beginning of the question. With the verb "to be" or helping verbs, you can change a statement into a yes-no question by reversing the order of the subject and verb.

Statements	Questions
She skates.	**Does** she skate?
I like baseball.	**Do** you like baseball?
He is French.	**Is he** French?

You can also ask a question by raising the pitch of your voice. Asking a question in this way can express surprise or doubt.

| She's leaving for Paris. | She's leaving for Paris? |

A Rewrite the following statements as yes-no questions.

1. You're going to lunch at noon.

   _____ Are you going to lunch at noon? _____

2. Bernard likes ice skating and skiing.

   _____

3. It's cold outside.

   _____

4. They live in Miami, Florida.

   _____

5. You will play tennis with me.

   _____

6. Simone likes to go to the movies.

   _____

In French You can change a statement into a yes-no question by raising the pitch of your voice at the end of a sentence. You can also add **Est-ce que** (or **Est-ce qu'** before a vowel sound) to the beginning of a statement.

Statements	Questions
Tu aimes sortir.	**Est-ce que** tu aimes sortir?
Ils aiment nager.	**Est-ce qu'**ils aiment nager?
Odette joue aux cartes.	**Est-ce qu'**Odette joue aux cartes?

EST-CE QUE

B Rewrite the following statements as yes-no questions with **est-ce que.**

1. Tu aimes lire.

   _____Est-ce que tu aimes lire?_____

2. Océane aime faire du sport.

   _____

3. Lucie joue au golf.

   _____

4. Ils écoutent de la musique.

   _____

5. Vous aimez faire la fête.

   _____

6. Tu préfères discuter avec des amis.

   _____

7. Elles regardent la télé.

   _____

8. Bruno parle anglais.

   _____

C How is question formation similar in French and English? How is it different?

Similarities:_____

_____

_____

_____

Differences:_____

_____

_____

_____

Adjective agreement

In English An **adjective** is a word that describes a noun or a pronoun. It tells what someone or something is like. The spelling of an adjective does not change when describing masculine and feminine nouns, or singular and plural nouns. Adjectives usually come before the noun.

> Paul is a **kind** man. His wife Carol is **kind**, too.
> We met our **new** neighbors yesterday. They have a **new** car.
> I bought a pair of **black** jeans.

A Circle the adjectives in the following sentences and underline the nouns they describe.

1. Donna has a cute brother with big, blue eyes.
2. The huge locomotive made a loud noise.
3. The server spilled icy beverages on the clean floor.
4. Does Sophie know the secret code?
5. He reads a lot of exciting mysteries.
6. The campers were tired and hungry after the long hike.

In French The spelling of most **adjectives** changes according to the gender (masculine or feminine) and number (singular or plural) of the nouns they describe. Compare the adjective **noir** in the following sentences:

masculine singular	J'ai un crayon noir.
feminine singular	La porte est noire.
masculine plural	J'ai des crayons noirs.
feminine plural	Les portes sont noires.

Unless they ends in unaccented **-e**, to make most adjectives feminine, add **-e**:

> grand →grande   noir→ noire   jeune →jeune

To form the feminine of adjectives ending in –**eux** or –**if**, change **-eux** to **-euse** and **-if** to **-ive**:

> sérieux → sérieuse   sportif → sportive

These adjectives have irregular feminine forms:

> long → longue   gros → grosse   bon → bonne
> blanc → blanche   gentil → gentille   mignon → mignonne

Unless its singular form already ends in **-s**, to make an adjective plural, add **-s**:

> noire →noires   intelligent → intelligents   gros →gros

Adjectives come after the noun unless they describe beauty, age, goodness, or size.

> Martin est un **bon** ami et un étudiant **sérieux**.

ADJECTIVE AGREEMENT

B Circle the adjectives in the following sentences and underline the nouns they describe.

1. Thérèse est une bonne amie.

2. J'ai les yeux verts.

3. Est-ce que tu aimes les grands magasins?

4. Didier a un long nez et une petite bouche.

5. D'après moi, elle est mignonne et marrante.

6. Vous préférez les vieux films?

7. Émile déteste les animaux méchants.

C Circle the appropriate adjectives to complete the following sentences.

1. Mon ami Frédéric est (sérieux / sérieuse).

2. Tristan et Robert sont (marrant / marrants).

3. Monique a une voiture (blanc / blanche).

4. Mme Pendraud est une (bon / bonne) professeur.

5. J'aime mieux les cahiers (noirs / noires).

6. Lorraine est très (gentil / gentille).

7. Mes amis sont super (sportifs / sportives).

8. Florence est (créatif / créative) et (timide / timides).

D Rewrite the following sentences, replacing the underlined words with the words in parentheses. Make any necessary changes to the adjectives.

1. Inès est assez grande. (Luc)

   Luc est assez grand. _____

2. Pénélope est très généreuse. (Pascal)

   _____

3. Le tableau est noir. (La porte)

   _____

4. Mes amis sont gentils. (Julie et Edith)

   _____

5. Les animaux sont mignons. (Les filles)

   _____

Irregular adjectives

> **In English** Adjectives are invariable. They never change form, no matter whether they describe a noun that is singular or plural, masculine or feminine.
>
> Robert is **tall** and **handsome**. His children are **tall**, too.
>
> That **pretty** girl is also **tall**.
>
> Mrs. Belleview is very **nice**.

A Circle each adjective and underline the noun it describes. Then check the appropriate column to indicate whether each noun is singular (S) or plural (P).

	S	P
1. Patricia is brown-haired.	✓	
2. I bought a very cool shirt.		
3. These shoes are old.		
4. We went to an expensive restaurant.		
5. The Hinaults live in a beautiful house.		
6. Have you met my new neighbors?		

> **In French** A few adjectives, like **cool**, **chic**, and **marron** are invariable. They never change form.
>
> Mes amis sont **cool**.
>
> Mme Maigret est très **chic**.
>
> Marcel a les yeux **marron**.
>
> The adjectives **beau**, **nouveau**, and **vieux** are irregular. They do not follow the general rules for forming feminine and plural forms. They come before the nouns they describe.
>
> | | | | |
> |---|---|---|---|
> | **Masculine singular** (before a consonant) | **beau** | **nouveau** | **vieux** |
> | **Masculine singular** (before a vowel or vowel sound) | **bel** | **nouvel** | **vieil** |
> | **Masculine plural** | **beaux** | **nouveaux** | **vieux** |
> | **Feminine singular** | **belle** | **nouvelle** | **vieille** |
> | **Feminine plural** | **belles** | **nouvelles** | **vieilles** |
>
> Elle a de **beaux** yeux.
>
> Alain a un **vieil** ordinateur.
>
> C'est une **nouvelle** école.
>
> C'est un **nouvel** élève.

IRREGULAR ADJECTIVES CHAPITRE **3**

B Circle each adjective and underline the noun it describes. Then check the appropriate boxes to indicate whether each noun is singular (S) or plural (P) and masculine (M) or feminine (F).

	S	P	M	F
1. <u>Élisabeth</u> est belle.	✓			✓
2. Il n'y a pas de nouveaux élèves.				
3. J'aime bien les vieilles fenêtres.				
4. Olivier a une voiture marron.				
5. C'est un vieux stade.				
6. Tu trouves le magasin chic?				

C Complete each sentence with the correct adjective from the box.

bel	**vieille**	**nouvelles**	**nouveau**
marron	**nouvel**	**beaux**	

1. Jules a de _____beaux_____ posters.

2. Je te présente un _____ professeur.

3. Il y a de _____ chaises dans la classe.

4. Isaac est mon _____ ami.

5. J'ai trois crayons _____.

6. Constance a une _____ voiture.

7. C'est un _____ animal!

D Translate the following English sentences into French. Then answer the questions in item 3.

1. Colette is a beautiful girl and Gaston is a beautiful boy.

   _____

2. I have brown eyes and a brown car.

   _____

3. What is one difference and one similarity between the adjectives *beautiful* and *beau*? What is one difference and one similarity between the adjectives *brown* and *marron*?

   _____

   _____

Nom _____ Date _____ Classe _____

Possessive adjectives

In English Possessive adjectives (**my, your, his, her, its, our,** and **their**) indicate to whom or to what something belongs. They do not change form, regardless of whether they modify singular or plural nouns. The distinction between **his** or **her** tells us whether something belongs to a male or a female.

> **Your** uncle is taller than **our** uncle.
> Sam eats dinner with **his** grandparents. **Their** house is nearby.
> **My** sister Susan drives to school in **her** car.

A Underline the possessive adjectives in the following sentences, then circle the noun they modify.

1. The Smiths bought their first house last month.
2. His hamster is sleeping in its nest.
3. My parents have their 25th wedding anniversary tomorrow.
4. Where did I put my keys?
5. It's great to hear that our soccer team won.
6. Your sister left her backpack on the playground.

In French You can also show to whom or to what something belongs by using **possessive adjectives.** French possessive adjectives agree in gender (masculine or feminine) and in number (singular or plural) with the noun that is possessed.

	Masculine **Singular**	**Feminine** **Singular**	**Plural**
my	mon	ma	mes
your (tu)	ton	ta	tes
his/her/its	son	sa	ses
our	notre	notre	nos
your (vous)	votre	votre	vos
their	leur	leur	leurs

Mon père est grand. (**père** *is masculine and singular*)
C'est **ma** tante. (**tante** *is feminine and singular*)
Mes frères sont sportifs. (**frères** *is plural*)

Use the masculine singular forms **mon, ton,** and **son** before nouns that begin with a vowel or a vowel sound.

> Voilà **mon** amie Claudine.
> Quelle est **ton** activité préférée?

POSSESSIVE ADJECTIVES

B Underline the possessive adjectives in the following sentences, then circle the noun they modify.

1. <u>Sa</u> [tante] est très chic.

2. Leurs enfants sont pénibles.

3. Quel âge a ton frère?

4. Votre fils est super gentil.

5. C'est une photo de ma grand-mère.

6. Il n'a pas son cahier.

C Fill in the blanks with the appropriate possessive adjectives.

Madeleine Comment s'appelle _____**ton**_____ demi-frère?

Étienne _____ demi-frère s'appelle André. Il est sympa mais

_____ amis sont pénibles.

Madeleine Et _____ parents, ils sont comment?

Étienne _____ parents s'appellent Lucie et Georges. Ils sont

marrants. Ils ont deux petits chiens. _____ chiens

s'appellent Plif et Plouf. Et toi, tu as un chien, n'est-ce pas?

Madeleine Oui. _____ chien s'appelle Puce.

D What are the possible meanings of the phrases below? In your own words, explain how the use of third person possessive adjectives in French is different from English.

son frère   **sa sœur**   **ses cousins**

_____

_____

_____

_____

_____

_____

Contractions with de

> **In English** You learned in Chapter 2 about contractions. You may remember that a contraction is a shortened form of a group of words. A contraction contains an apostrophe to show where letters have been left out.
>
> I **do not** know the answer.   I **don't** know the answer.
>
> In English, the spelling of a contraction can be irregular.
>
> They **will not** leave before noon.   They **won't** leave before noon.
>
> You may also recall that in English, contractions are optional, and in some situations, they may be considered too informal.

A What contractions could be used in the sentences below?

1. He does not know her. _____ **doesn't** _____

2. We can not believe what happened. _____

3. I am going to write him a letter. _____

4. They are coming tomorrow. _____

5. Mary is in the living room. _____

6. He did not do his homework. _____

> **In French** When the prepostion **de** is placed in front of the definite article **le** or **les**, the contractions **du** and **des** are used. These contractions are required.
>
> **de + le → du**   Le bureau **du** professeur est marron.
>
> **de + les → des**   Comment est le père **des** sœurs Lebrun?
>
> When the preposition **de** appears before the articles **la** or **l'**, there is no contraction.
>
> **de + la → de la**   Comment s'appellent les frères **de la** copine de Guy?
>
> **de + l' → de l'**   Elle est comment, la mère **de l'**ami de Charles?

B How many contractions with **de** are in the following sentences? Write the contraction with **de** on the line. If there is no contraction, leave the line blank.

1. Le livre du professeur est vieux. _____ **du** _____

2. Michel est l'ami des frères Picard. _____

3. C'est le mari de la mère de mes cousins. _____

4. Elle est comment, la sœur du garçon roux? _____

5. C'est la voiture du grand-père d'Anton. _____

6. Comment s'appelle la sœur de l'ami de Luc? _____

7. J'aime bien la maison des parents de Zoë. _____

CONTRACTIONS WITH DE

C Check the correct box to tell which preposition completes each sentence.

	du	de la	de l'	des
1. C'est l'ami _____ oncle d'Édouard.			✓	
2. C'est la sœur _____ frères Bocuse.				
3. C'est le frère _____ père de Marc.				
4. C'est la nièce _____ ami de Renée.				
5. C'est la femme _____ cousin d'Yves.				
6. C'est le neveu _____ parents de Marie.				
7. C'est la tante _____ fille blonde.				
8. C'est le fils _____ professeur d'Alfred.				

D Complete the following conversation with **du, de la, de l'**, or **des**.

Arnaud   Qui c'est, ça?

Laetitia   C'est le père _____ mari de ma tante. Il est sympa.

Arnaud   Et la fille brune?

Laetitia   C'est la nièce _____ cousine de mon demi-frère.

Arnaud   Qui c'est le garçon roux?

Laetitia   C'est le fils unique _____ cousin de ma mère. Il s'appelle
Amaury.

Arnaud   Et la madame rousse? C'est la tante d'Amaury?

Laetitia   Non, non. C'est la femme _____ oncle de ma tante Sylvie.

Arnaud   Et le monsieur mince? C'est qui?

Laetitia   Thierry? C'est le frère _____ mari _____ demi-
sœur de ma mère.

Arnaud   Oh là là! C'est une grande famille!

C'est versus il/elle est

In English To identify or describe people, you can use a variety of personal pronouns *(he, she, it)* and demonstrative pronouns *(this, that, those)*.

> Who's that? It's Christopher.
>
> That's my father. He's an architect.
>
> This is my friend Julie. She is Canadian.

A Fill in the blanks with a pronoun from the box.

Those	He	That	These
She	This	It	

1. _____These_____ are my parents, Henry and Lucille.

2. Edith? _____ is a very nice girl.

3. _____ is my French teacher, Mme Duquenne.

4. _____ are my cousins who live in Québec.

5. Let me introduce to you my brother. _____ is a college student.

6. Who's the blond girl? _____ is Josette, a good friend of mine.

7. _____ is Vincent, the new student.

In French To identify or describe a person, you can use the phrases c'est and il/elle est. These phrases are not interchangeable, however.

Use c'est...
- with a person's name   C'est Norbert.
- with an article/possessive adjective + a noun   C'est une élève.

                                                C'est mon père.

- with an article + a noun + an adjective   C'est un homme intelligent.

Use il/elle est...
- with an adjective by itself   Il est intelligent.

                                                Elle est blonde.

C'EST VERSUS IL/ELLE EST

B Find c'est and il/elle est in the following sentences. Underline the noun or noun phrase that follows c'est, and circle the adjective(s) that follows il/elle est.

1. C'est <u>mon oncle</u>.

2. Ça, c'est Roger. Il est génial.

3. Elle est créative, à mon avis.

4. Il est assez jeune et il a les yeux marron.

5. Éléonore? C'est une copine.

6. Elle n'est ni petite ni grande.

7. C'est un garçon pénible.

C Check the correct box to tell which phrase completes each sentence.

	C'est	Il est	Elle est
1. _____ ma tante Virginie.	✓		
2. _____ le fils de M. Lagaffe.			
3. _____ rousse.			
4. _____ un gros chat.			
5. _____ très paresseux.			
6. _____ vieux et méchant.			
7. _____ un monsieur fort.			
8. _____ le beau-père d'Arnaud.			

D How would you translate the following sentences into French? Explain why you chose the phrase c'est or elle est.

She's an athletic girl.   **She's athletic.**

_____

_____

_____

_____

_____

_____

Le with days of the week

In English To say that you regularly do something on a certain day of the week, you make the day plural *(Sundays)* or you can use an adjective, such as *every (every Sunday)*.

> Louise has piano lessons on **Saturdays**.
> We see a movie **every Friday**.

If you are talking about something that is going to happen on one specific day, you use the singular *(Sunday)* or an adjective like *this* or *next*.

> Louise has a piano lesson **Sunday/this Sunday/next Sunday**.

A Check the appropriate column to indicate whether the following sentences refer to events that happen regularly or that will happen on one specific day.

	Regularly	One Specific Day
1. They leave for Hawaii this Wednesday.		✓
2. I do homework every Sunday.		
3. Marla does yoga on Mondays.		
4. On Friday I have a dentist appointment.		
5. You ride the bus on Thursdays.		
6. Her birthday party is on Saturday.		
7. I'll see you on Thursday.		
8. Sam works at the mall on Fridays.		

In French To say you do something regularly on a certain day of the week, you add the article **le** in front of the day and leave it singular.

> Nous avons anglais **le** vendredi. *(We have English class on Fridays.)*
> Je chante **le** mardi et **le** jeudi. *(I sing every Tuesday and Thursday.)*

To say that you are doing something on one specific day of the week, do not use the article in front of the day of the week.

> J'ai un examen **jeudi**. *(I have an exam on Thursday.)*

LE WITH DAYS OF THE WEEK

B Check the appropriate column to indicate whether the following sentences refer to events that happen regularly or that will happen on one specific day.

	Regularly	One Specific Day
1. Samedi, je joue au hockey.		✓
2. Elle dessine le mardi.		
3. Je rends visite à mon oncle dimanche.		
4. Le mardi et le jeudi, on a chimie.		
5. Louise voyage lundi matin.		
6. Zacharie surfe sur Internet le vendredi.		
7. Nous mangeons au café le mercredi.		

C Write four sentences telling what Serge does regularly throughout the week.

lundi	mardi	mercredi	jeudi	vendredi	samedi
jouer au base-ball	nager à la piscine	jouer au base-ball	étudier à la bibliothèque	cours de musique	rendre visite à sa grand-mère

1. **Serge joue au base-ball le lundi et le mercredi.**

2. _____

3. _____

4. _____

5. _____

D Compare the following two sentences. Besides the differences pointed out on page 29, what other difference do you notice about the days of the week in English and in French?

We're going to the movies Saturday. **Nous allons au cinéma samedi.**

_____

_____

_____

Adjectives as nouns

> **In English** To avoid repeating a noun, you can use an adjective as a noun by placing **the** before the adjective and **one** or **ones** after the adjective. Notice in the following sentences how **one(s)** stands for the noun *(car, boots)*, which you don't repeat.
>
> Do you like the red car or **the blue one**?
> I don't like small televisions. I prefer **the big ones.**

A Circle the phrase **the + adjective + one(s)** in the each sentence and underline the noun it refers to.

1. I cannot see the brick <u>building</u>, but I can see the glass one.

2. This backpack isn't mine; give me the black one.

3. The gold necklace is more expensive than the silver one.

4. We don't have to do all the exercises, only the important ones.

5. I'd rather go to the good, affordable university than the overpriced one.

6. Tanasha is wearing her corduroy pants today, not the cotton ones.

7. Do you like this small dog or the big one?

> **In French** To avoid repeating a noun, you can use an **article** followed by an **adjective**. The **article + adjective** phrase acts as a noun and agrees in gender and number with the noun.
>
> Est-ce que tu aimes la voiture rouge ou **la bleue**?
> Je n'aime pas la petite télé. Je préfère **la grande.**

B Circle the phrase **article + adjective** in the each sentence and underline the noun to which it refers.

1. Tu préfères le <u>sac à dos</u> vert ou le bleu?

2. Avez-vous les cahiers bleus ou les rouges?

3. Je n'aime pas le tee-shirt jaune, mais j'aime bien l'orange.

4. Est-ce que j'achète les baskets blanches ou les noires?

5. C'est qui, ton amie, la fille rousse ou la blonde?

6. Est-ce que vous aimez le portable noir ou le gris?

7. Yves aime les shorts bleus, mais Xavier préfère les verts.

8. Est-ce que Marguerite achète le sweat-shirt rose ou le violet?

ADJECTIVES AS NOUNS   **CHAPITRE 4**

C Circle the correct phrase in the following sentences.

1. Est-ce que Pierre vend le vieil ordinateur ou (la nouvelle / le nouvel)?

2. Prenez-vous les stylos bleus ou (le rouge / les rouges)?

3. Le tee-shirt blanc, ça va, mais je préfère (le noir / les noirs).

4. Qu'est-ce que j'achète? Le grand dictionnaire ou (la petite / le petit)?

5. Qui est la sœur de Jean Baptiste? La fille brune ou (la blonde / le blond)?

6. J'aime la voiture rouge, mais je préfère (le blanc / la blanche).

D Answer the following questions negatively. Use the adjectives in parentheses as nouns.

1. Est-ce que vous aimez les stylos noirs? (bleu)

    Non, j'aime les bleus.

2. Est-ce que tu aimes les nouvelles radios? (vieux)

_____

3. Est-ce qu'il préfère le tee-shirt vert? (blanc)

_____

4. Est-ce que tu achètes la grande voiture? (petit)

_____

5. Est-ce qu'elle n'aime pas les matières difficiles? (ennuyeux)

_____

6. Est-ce que les baskets rouges sont belles? (gris)

_____

E Compare the following sentences. English uses one to refer to the absent noun. What does French do? Why is agreement of gender and number important?

I like the black car, but I love the green one.
J'aime bien la voiture noire, mais j'adore la verte.

_____

_____

_____

_____

_____

Holt French 1   **32**   Grammar Tutor

The verb faire

In English To talk about sports and other activities, you can use a variety of verbs, such as **to play, to do, to make,** and **to go.**

> Steven **plays** many sports.
> We don't know what we **are doing** tonight.
> I plan on **making** an amateur film.
> My cousins like **to go** fishing.

A Complete the following sentences with an appropriate verb.

1. What do you _____**do**_____ for fun?

2. Tara _____ most of her clothes.

3. When are we _____ swimming?

4. What sports do you _____?

5. I like to _____ jogging every evening.

6. My friends _____ community theater.

7. What are you _____ this weekend?

8. Can Sam _____ a cake for tomorrow?

In French The verb **faire** can mean *to do, to make, to play*, or it can be used in certain expressions as an action verb. Compare the meaning of the following sentences:

Nous **faisons** de l'aérobic.	We *do* aerobics.
Tu **fais** une pizza.	You're *making* pizza.
Ils **font** du sport.	They *play* sports.
Je **fais** du vélo.	I *bike*.

The verb **faire** is an irregular verb so its forms need to be memorized.

faire *(to do, to make)*

je	**fais**	nous	**faisons**
tu	**fais**	vous	**faites**
il, elle, on	**fait**	ils, elles	**font**

Qu'est-ce que vous **faites** dimanche?
Françoise **fait** du jogging.

THE VERB FAIRE   **CHAPITRE 5**

B Write an action verb in English that best corresponds to the underlined phrase with **faire**.

1. Je préfère <u>faire du ski</u>.   **to ski**_____

2. Nous <u>faisons du vélo</u>. _____

3. Est-ce que tu <u>fais du jogging</u>? _____

4. Jeanne <u>fait du patin à glace</u>. _____

5. Ignace adore <u>faire du surf</u>. _____

6. Est-ce que vous <u>faites du skate</u>? _____

C Complete each sentence so the verb matches the subject.

_____ 1. Qu'est-ce que Mathieu…

_____ 2. Est-ce que vous…

_____ 3. Lundi soir, je…

_____ 4. Denise…

_____ 5. Quand est-ce que nous…

_____ 6. Mes cousines…

a. fais du patin à glace.
b. fait du vélo.
c. fait demain?
d. faisons du ski?
e. faites du théâtre?
f. font de la vidéo amateur.

D Complete the following paragraph with the correct forms of the verb **faire**.

Tu **(1)** _____ beaucoup de sport? Moi, j'adore

(2) _____ du sport. Je **(3)** _____

régulièrement du patin et de l'athlétisme. En hiver, mes amis et moi, nous

(4) _____ du ski. Mes cousins Stéphane et Marc n'aiment

pas le sport. Ils **(5)** _____ de la vidéo et de la photo. Et mon

frère, il **(6)** _____ du théâtre. Je ne comprends pas!

E Compare the answers to the question below. What conclusion might you draw about questions containing the verb **faire**?

Qu'est-ce que tu fais?   **Je fais du jogging.**

                              Je parle au téléphone.

                              J'écoute de la musique.

_____

_____

Question words

In English When you ask for specific information, you use **question words**. The question word usually comes at the beginning of the sentence.

Where is he going?
Why is the sky blue?
Who is at the door?
What are you doing?
When do you play tennis?
How are you feeling?

A Circle the correct question word to complete each sentence.

1. (Where / Who) do you live?

2. (What / When) does summer vacation begin?

3. (How / What) time is it?

4. (What / Where) do you like to do after school?

5. (How / Who) did you do that?

6. (What / Where) are you from?

7. (Why / How) doesn't she call me back?

8. (Who / When) is the science teacher?

In French To ask for information, question words are also used. The question word is followed by **est-ce que** plus a subject and a verb.

(Where)	**Où est-ce qu'**il nage?
(Why)	**Pourquoi est-ce qu'**il n'aime pas le football?
(With whom)	**Avec qui est-ce que** tu joues au tennis?
(What)	**Qu'est-ce qu'**il fait en automne?
(When)	**Quand est-ce qu'**il fait du théâtre?
(How)	**Comment est-ce qu'**on fait du ski?

You don't use **est-ce que** with the question word **qui** *(who)* or with question words when they are followed by the verb **être**.

Qui fait du patin à glace?
Où est ton frère?
Comment sont tes parents?

Question words can be placed at the end of a sentence in less formal speech.
On va au stade **quand**?

QUESTION WORDS

B Circle the correct question word to complete each sentence.

1. (Quand / Qui) est-ce qu'on va à la bibliothèque?

2. (Qu' / Quand) est-ce que tu fais demain?

3. (Comment / Pourquoi) est ton amie?

4. (Qui / Avec qui) est-ce que tu vas au cinéma?

5. (Pourquoi / Où) est-ce qu'elle n'aime pas la télé?

6. (Où / Qu') est-ce que vous faites en été?

7. (Qui / Où) est-ce que tu nages?

8. (Quand / Qui) est la fille blonde?

C Complete the following conversation with appropriate question words.

Camille	_____ Qu' _____ est-ce que tu fais ce week-end?
Enzo	Je ne fais rien.
Camille	On va au théâtre ce week-end.
Enzo	_____?
Camille	Samedi soir.
Enzo	_____?
Camille	Au théâtre Molière.
Enzo	_____?
Camille	Avec Hugo et Irène.

D Write an appropriate question for each answer.

1. — **Quand est-ce que tu vas faire du surf?**

   — Dimanche matin.

2. — _____

   — C'est le professeur d'allemand.

3. — _____

   — Il s'appelle Benjamin Gichard.

4. — _____

   — À l'école Bénédicte.

5. — _____

   — Avec Nathan et Isabelle.

Adverbs

In English An **adverb** is a word or phrase that tells *when, where, how, how much, to what extent,* or *how often.* Adverbs modify verbs, adjectives, or other adverbs.

> We <u>play</u> hockey **well**. (The adverb *well* modifies the verb *play*.)
>
> She goes to work **very** <u>early</u>. (The adverb *very* modifies the adverb *early*.)
>
> The movie was **too** <u>long</u>. (The adverb *too* modifies the adjective *long*.)

Many adverbs that tell how an action is done are formed by adding **-ly** to the end of an adjective. If the adjective ends in **-y,** the **-y** changes to **-i** before **-ly.**

> quick → **quickly**   peaceful → **peacefully**   happy → **happily**

In English, the placement of adverbs is generally variable.

> **Quietly,** he opened the door.
>
> He opened the door **quietly.**
>
> He **quietly** opened the door.

A Circle the adverb in each sentence. Then underline the word it modifies.

1. She quietly tiptoed up the stairs.

2. I will buy new shoes tomorrow.

3. He was really surprised about the party.

4. You can truly imagine what life was like in the 1800s.

5. I always read the newspaper.

6. The thief answered the questions nervously.

7. The alarm clock rang softly.

In French **Adverbs** are also used to modify verbs, adjectives, or other adverbs. Many adverbs that tell how an action is done are formed by adding **–ment** to the feminine form of the adjective.

> sérieux → **sérieuse** → **sérieusement**
>
> timide → **timide** → **timidement**

The adjectives **bon** and **mauvais** have irregular adverbs.

> **bon** → **bien** *(well)*
>
> **mauvais** → **mal** *(badly)*

In French, adverbs are usually placed after the verb.

> Les élèves <u>travaillent</u> **sérieusement**.
>
> Ma cousine <u>joue</u> **bien** au hockey.
>
> Je <u>perds</u> **rarement** mes devoirs.

B Circle the adverb in each sentence. Then underline the word it modifies.

1. Tu joues régulièrement au football?

2. Pourquoi est-ce qu'il va rarement au cinéma?

3. Nous faisons nos devoirs facilement.

4. Elle joue mal au basket.

5. Les élèves mangent rapidement.

6. Tu chantes bien!

C Complete the following sentences with adverbs formed from the adjectives in parentheses.

1. Le garçon sportif nage _____ rapidement _____. (rapide)

2. _____, c'est le week-end. (heureux)

3. Est-ce que tu joues _____ à des jeux vidéo? (régulier)

4. Mon frère parle _____ au téléphone. (rare)

5. Francis joue _____ de la guitare. (bon)

6. Jade prête _____ ses fournitures scolaires. (généreux)

7. J'entends _____ la musique. (mauvais)

8. Madeleine et Jean dansent _____. (facile)

D Compare the following sentences and then answer the questions.

He raises his hand quickly.   **Il lève rapidement sa main.**
I rarely watch TV.   **Je regarde rarement la télé.**
The new student is friendly.   **La nouvelle élève est sympathique.**

1. Some English words that end in **-ly** are not adverbs. How do the French translations help you know which **-ly** words are adverbs?

_____

_____

2. How is adverb placement different in French than in English?

_____

_____

_____

Aller and the near future

> **In English** You can use the present progressive form of the verb **to go** with an infinitive of another verb to talk about the **near future**.
>
> We **are going to eat** some ice cream.
>
> I **am going to buy** some clothes.
>
> In these sentences, the verb phrases **are going** and **am going** place the action of the sentence in the future. The action verbs **to eat** and **to buy**, in their infinitive forms, tell what someone *is going to do*.
>
> Of course, you can also use the verb **to go** to tell where you are going. In such sentences, the verb is followed by a place rather than an infinitive of another verb.
>
> She **is going** <u>to town</u> on Wednesday.
>
> As usual, they **are going** <u>to the mall</u>.

A Check the appropriate column to indicate whether the sentence implies near future or simply tells where someone is going.

	Near Future	Where
1. We're going to take a test on Friday.	✓	
2. Chris is going to take the train.		
3. They are going to the movies.		
4. My mother is going to the gym.		
5. Amy is going to sing in the choir.		
6. I'm going to leave in three weeks.		
7. We're going to a new campground.		

> **In French** You can use the verb **aller** with a place to tell where someone is going.
>
> Nous **allons** au parc.
>
> Je **vais** à l'école.
>
> You can also use **aller** with an infinitive to tell what someone is going to do or what is going to happen in the near future.
>
> Vous **allez étudier** la géo?
>
> Lisette **va jouer** au volley.
>
> The verb **aller** is irregular:
>
> | | | | |
> |---|---|---|---|
> | je | **vais** | nous | **allons** |
> | tu | **vas** | vous | **allez** |
> | il/elle/on | **va** | ils/elles | **vont** |

ALLER AND THE NEAR FUTURE   CHAPITRE **5**

B Check the appropriate column to indicate whether the sentence implies near future or simply tells where someone is going.

	Near Future	Where
1. Nous allons à la piscine.		✓
2. Mathilde va au musée.		
3. Ils vont faire du ski.		
4. Vous allez jouer au football.		
5. Mes parents vont faire un pique-nique.		
6. Est-ce que tu vas au stade?		
7. Les filles vont à la patinoire.		

C Complete the following sentences with the correct form of **aller**.

1. Michèle ne _____va_____ pas aller au lac.

2. Tu _____ avoir beaucoup de devoirs.

3. Vendredi, ils _____ aller au musée.

4. Vous _____ faire les magasins dimanche?

5. Nous _____ regarder un film samedi.

6. Je ne _____ pas jouer au tennis.

7. Guillaume ne _____ pas manger avec nous.

D Complete the following sentences logically, telling what the people are going to do in these places.

1. Je _____ vais nager _____ à la plage.

2. Mes amis et moi, nous _____ à la bibliothèque.

3. Marc et Brigitte _____ au café.

4. Claude _____ au cybercafé.

5. Vous _____ à la montagne.

6. Je _____ à la Maison des jeunes et de la culture.

7. Tu _____ au parc.

8. Mes parents _____ à la campagne.

The partitive

In English There are two types of nouns in English: count nouns and mass nouns. A count noun is something you can count, such as an apple or some books. When you use count nouns, you can refer to the whole item or to more than one of the item using the indefinite articles **a**, **an**, or the word **some**.

> I would like **a** ham sandwich.
> She borrowed **some** DVDs.

A mass noun is something you wouldn't usually count, such as water, tea, or sugar, so you don't use **a** or **an** with it. Instead, you can refer to a part of or some of the item using the words **some**, **some of**, or **any**.

> May I have **some** milk?
> Do you have **any** flour?

In some cases, you don't need to use an article in English.

> He's buying cookies, flour, and tomatoes.

A Circle the nouns in the following sentences. Then check the appropriate column to indicate whether they are count nouns or mass nouns.

	Count	Mass
1. Bring us some water, please.		✓
2. Does Casey have a car?		
3. We don't have any milk.		
4. She ate a large sandwich.		
5. Marie brought some cheese.		

In French There are count nouns and mass nouns. You've already learned to refer to count nouns using the indefinite articles **un**, **une**, and **des**.

> Je veux **un** croissant.
> Vous voulez **des** œufs?

To say that you want *part of* or *some of* an item, use a **partitive article**. Partitive articles match the gender of the object. Use **du** with masculine singular nouns and **de la** with feminine singular nouns. If a noun begins with a vowel, use **de l'** whether it is feminine or masculine. With plural nouns, use **des**.

> Tu veux **du** beurre? *(beurre* is masculine and singular)
> Je veux **de la** confiture. *(confiture* is feminine and singular)
> Elle veut **de l'**eau. *(eau* is a singular noun beginning with a vowel)
> J'aimerais **des** céréales. *(céréales* is plural)

Unlike in English, in French you can't leave out the article.

> Il prend **de la** tarte.   *He's having pie.*

THE PARTITIVE

B Circle the nouns, then underline the articles in the following sentences. Then check the appropriate column to indicate whether they are partitive articles or indefinite articles.

	Partitive	Indefinite
	✓	

1. Je veux du pain, s'il vous plaît.

2. Vous avez des pommes?

3. J'aimerais un croissant.

4. Tu veux du poivre?

5. Vous voulez de la glace?

6. Je mange des céréales.

7. Nous avons de la tarte.

C Complete each sentence with **du, de la, de l', un, une,** or **des**.

1. J'achète _____ des _____ bananes.

2. Est-ce qu'il y a _____ jus de pomme?

3. Elle prend _____ tartine avec _____ confiture.

4. Vous prenez _____ beurre?

5. Tu veux _____ omelette?

6. J'aimerais _____ chocolat chaud.

7. Elle prend _____ toast ou _____ céréales.

8. Dans le jus, il y a _____ oranges _____ bananes.

9. J'aime manger _____ œufs et _____ bacon.

D Compare the following two sentences. What is the difference in meaning?

Il mange une tarte.
Il mange de la tarte.

_____

_____

_____

The imperative

CHAPITRE **6**

> **In English** An **imperative** is a command, request, or strong suggestion to do (or not do) something. The imperative is formed by using the infinitive form of the verb without the word *to*. Notice that no subject is stated in imperatives.
>
> **Brush** your teeth and **go** to bed.
> **Do** the dishes, please.
> Here, **take** one!
> Please, **don't wake** her up!

A Decide whether each item is a statement (**S**) or an imperative (**I**).

1. Don't eat that! __I___

2. This is my little brother. _____

3. Have some pie. _____

4. Don't forget the milk! _____

5. Please pass the potatoes. _____

6. He is watching television again. _____

7. We don't need to wake up early. _____

8. Read this newspaper article. _____

> **In French** The imperative is formed using the **tu, nous,** or **vous** form of the present tense of the verb, without the subject. With **-er** verbs, you drop the **-s** at the end of the **tu** form.
>
> **Tu regardes** la télévision. ⟶ **Regarde** la télévision!
> **Tu vas** au café. ⟶ **Va** au café.
> **Nous écoutons** Paul. ⟶ **Écoutons** Paul.
> **Vous mangez** de la glace. ⟶ **Mangez** de la glace!
>
> If the verb isn't a regular **-er** verb, the spelling of the **tu** form doesn't change.
>
> **Tu fais** tes devoirs. ⟶ **Fais** tes devoirs!
> **Vous finissez** votre dîner. ⟶ **Finissez** votre dîner!
> **Nous attendons** le bus. ⟶ **Attendons** le bus.
>
> To make a command negative, put **ne** before the verb and **pas** after it.
>
> **Regarde** la télé! ⟶ **Ne regarde pas** la télé!

THE IMPERATIVE

B Decide whether each sentence is a statement or an imperative. Add a period to statements and an exclamation point to imperatives.

1. Écoute ce CD___!__

2. Prenez une pizza_____

3. On va au café_____

4. Ne choisis pas le porc_____

5. Nous faisons du ski_____

6. Allons au cinéma ce soir_____

7. J'ai envie de manger des légumes_____

C Complete each command with the correct form of the verb in parentheses.

1. Vous avez faim? _____Mangez_____! (manger)

2. Tu veux t'amuser? _____ du vélo! (faire)

3. Allons au parc et _____ au volley! (jouer)

4. Tu aimes faire les magasins? _____ au centre commercial! (aller)

5. Vous voulez maigrir? _____du sport! (faire)

6. Vous avez de la limonade? _____-moi un verre, s'il vous plaît. (donner)

D Use the imperative to give your friend's little sister some advice based on her comments.

1. J'ai faim.

    Prends un sandwich! _____

2. J'aime la musique.

    _____

3. Je voudrais faire du sport.

    _____

4. J'ai soif.

    _____

5. Je n'ai pas envie d'étudier.

    _____

Demonstrative adjectives

> **In English** Demonstrative adjectives point out people and things. They must agree in number with the nouns they describe. We use this and these for things that are nearby, and that and those for things that are farther away.
>
> | SINGULAR | PLURAL |
> |---|---|
> | I like this scarf. | Do you like these sandals? |
> | I need that book. | She wants those boots. |

A Underline the demonstrative adjectives in the sentences below. Check the appropriate column to indicate whether they are singular or plural.

	Singular	Plural
1. This backpack is not mine.	✓	
2. Did you make that pie?		
3. How much are those socks?		
4. These toys belong to Katie.		
5. I bought that little red hat.		
6. Did you write these stories?		
7. This black shirt is very stylish.		

> **In French** Demonstrative adjectives also point out people and things. They must agree in number and gender with the nouns they describe. The singular demonstrative adjectives are ce, cette, and cet. All three of these words can mean *this* or *that*. Use cette with feminine singular nouns. Use ce with masculine singular nouns that begin with a consonant, and cet with masculine singular nouns that begin with a vowel or vowel sound.
>
> Tu préfères ce manteau ou cet anorak?
> Je vais acheter cette chemise.
>
> Use ces with plural nouns whether they are masculine or feminine and whether they begin with a consonant or vowel sound. Ces can mean either *these* or *those*.
>
> J'adore ces chaussures.
>
> To distinguish *this* from *that* and *these* from *those,* add -ci or -là to the end of the noun. Use -ci for things that are nearby and -là for things that are farther away.
> J'aime bien ces bottes-ci, mais je n'aime pas ces bottes-là

DEMONSTRATIVE ADJECTIVES

B Underline the demonstrative adjectives in the sentences below. Check the appropriate columns to indicate whether they are singular or plural, and masculine or feminine.

	S	P	M	F
1. Elle aime bien ce stylo rouge.	✓		✓	
2. Tu n'aimes pas cette chemise?				
3. Nous préférons ces tee-shirts bleus.				
4. Pauline adore ce manteau-là.				
5. Il n'achète pas ce short gris.				
6. Vous aimez ces lunettes de soleil?				
7. Je préfère cet anorak-ci.				

C Complete each sentence with the appropriate demonstrative adjective.

1. Élodie préfère _____ ce _____ jean.

2. Tu n'aimes pas _____ costume?

3. Mon père achète _____ CD de Céline Dion.

4. Je voudrais _____ chaussettes-là.

5. Lisette n'aime pas _____ écharpe horrible.

6. Marc adore _____ ordinateur!

7. Je n'aime pas _____ cravate violette.

8. C'est combien, _____ bottes-là?

D Combine elements from each box to write four sentences telling what everyone will buy at the store.

Je	cette	anorak
Tu	cet	jupe
Hélène	ce	baskets
Hortense et Joseph	ces	lunettes
Nous		pantalon

1. Je vais acheter ces baskets.

2. _____

3. _____

4. _____

5. _____

Interrogative adjectives

In English The interrogative adjectives are **which** and **what**. They are both used to ask questions about nouns.

Which play did they see?

What person told you that?

Sometimes the verb *to be* is used between the word **what** and the noun it modifies. In this case, **what** is an interrogative pronoun.

What is the name of the store where she works?

The word **what** can also be used in exclamations followed by a noun phrase.

What a pretty sweater!

A Underline the interrogative adjective or pronoun in each sentence.

1. What fell off the shelf?

2. What is the problem, sir?

3. What ugly shoes!

4. Which course is Lola taking?

5. Which scarf do you like best?

In French The interrogative adjective is **quel**. Like any other adjective, it agrees in number and gender with the noun it modifies. Even though they have different spellings, all four forms are pronounced the same way.

	Singular	**Plural**
Masculine	Quel chemisier?	Quels chemisiers?
Feminine	Quelle jupe?	Quelles jupes?

The forms of **quel** are always followed by a noun or by a form of the verb **être** and then the noun.

Quelle cravate est-ce que tu vas acheter?

Quelles sont tes cravates préférées?

A form of **quel** can also be used as an exclamation, as in *What . . . !* or *What a . . . !*

Quel beau pull!

B Underline the interrogative adjective in each sentence.

1. Quel est le numéro de téléphone de Sophie?

2. Quelle couleur!

3. Quel jean est-ce que tu prends?

4. Quels sont tes magasins préférés?

5. Quelle pointure faites-vous?

6. Quel beau manteau!

INTERROGATIVE ADJECTIVES CHAPITRE **7**

C Complete the following sentences with the correct form of **quel**.

1. _____Quels_____ magasins est-ce que tu préfères?

2. _____ pizza est-ce que tu prends?

3. _____ sont ses couleurs préférées?

4. _____ chemisier est-ce que Florence porte ce soir?

5. _____ jolie jupe!

6. _____ chat méchant!

7. _____ chaussures est-ce que tu achètes?

8. _____ est ton pantalon préféré?

Compare In French, **qu'est-ce que** also means *what*, but it is used differently than **quel**. **Qu'est-ce que** is not an interrogative adjective so it is not followed directly by a noun or by the words **est** or **sont**. Compare the following sentences.

Qu'est-ce que tu aimes porter?   *What do you like to wear?*

Quelle <u>taille</u> est-ce que tu fais?   *What size do you wear?*

Quelles <u>sont</u> tes couleurs préférées?   *What are your favorite colors?*

D Complete the following interview with either **qu'est-ce que** or a form of **quel**.

M. Roux _____Quel_____ est votre nom, mademoiselle?

Sabine Sabine Nicoud.

M. Roux _____ vous faites?

Sabine Je fais les magasins.

M. Roux _____ vous aimez acheter?

Sabine Des vêtements.

M. Roux _____ vêtements est-ce que vous cherchez?

Sabine Une jupe en jean et un chemisier.

M. Roux _____ est votre magasin préféré?

Sabine J'aime bien Maryse.

M. Roux Merci beaucoup.

Sabine Pas tu tout.

M. Roux Eh… _____ vous pensez de ma cravate?

Sabine Franchement, elle est un peu tape-à-l'œil.

M. Roux _____ vous dites *(saying)*? Elle est très chic!

The passé composé of -er verbs   CHAPITRE 7

> **In English** There are several ways to talk about what happened in the past. Compare the following sentences.
>
> We **washed** the car.
>
> We **have washed** the car.
>
> We **did wash** the car.
>
> For regular verbs, the simple past tense is formed by adding –ed to the verb.
>
> walk → **walked**   look → **looked**
>
> To say what didn't happen, you add **not** after the helping verb. For the simple past, you use the verb phrase **did + not (didn't)** + verb.
>
> We **haven't** washed the car.   We **did not** wash the car.

A Underline the past tense verbs or verb phrases in the following sentences.

1. Rita <u>ordered</u> soup and salad.

2. Marion worked at the ice cream stand.

3. Edwin talked to Susanne all afternoon.

4. Marianne hasn't cleaned her room.

5. I didn't finish the book last night.

6. Gabriel lived in Senegal for ten years.

> **In French** To talk about what happened in the past, you can use the **passé composé**. The **passé composé** is made up of a helping verb and a past participle. The helping verb in most cases is a form of the verb **avoir**. The past participle of most **-er** verbs is formed by replacing the **-er** with **-é**. While the forms of **avoir** change to match the subject, the past participle remains the same.
>
> | | | | |
> |---|---|---|---|
> | j' | **ai mangé** | nous | **avons mangé** |
> | tu | **as mangé** | vous | **avez mangé** |
> | il/elle/on | **a mangé** | ils/elles | **ont mangé** |
>
> To say what didn't happen, place **ne... pas** around the helping verb.
>
> Je **n'ai pas** trouvé de chemise à ma taille.

B Underline the past participles and circle the helping verbs.

1. Qu'est-ce que tu [as] <u>acheté</u> ce week-end?

2. Nous avons trouvé ces jeans.

3. J'ai mangé de la pizza.

4. Claire a étudié à la bibiothèque.

5. Les élèves n'ont pas visité le musée.

THE PASSÉ COMPOSÉ OF –ER VERBS

C Complete the following sentences with the **passé composé** of the verbs in parentheses.

1. Philippine _____ a essayé _____ trois jeans. (essayer)

2. Nous _____ un cerf-volant. (acheter)

3. Est-ce que tu _____ au téléphone avec Emmanuelle? (parler)

4. Dominique _____ de canne à pêche. (ne pas trouver)

5. Je _____ la nouvelle chanson. (ne pas écouter)

6. Jérôme et Isaac _____ ce matin. (nager)

7. Vous _____ ? (ne pas décider)

D Paul asks Lorraine about several activities, and she tells him that they were done yesterday. Fill in Lorraine's answers.

Paul	Tu vas étudier aujourd'hui?
Lorraine	Non, j'ai étudié hier. _____
Paul	Tes parents achètent une voiture?
Lorraine	_____
Paul	Toi et tes amis, vous allez jouer au tennis cet après-midi?
Lorraine	_____
Paul	Tu vas téléphoner à Éric?
Lorraine	_____
Paul	Tes frères regardent le film maintenant?
Lorraine	_____
Paul	Tu vas surfer sur Internet aujourd'hui?
Lorraine	_____

The passé composé of irregular verbs   CHAPITRE **7**

In English Some verbs have irregular past tense forms. Here are a few.

INFINITIVE	SIMPLE PAST	PAST PARTICIPLE
to do	did	(has/have) done
to go	went	(has/have) gone
to see	saw	(has/have) seen
to swim	swam	(has/have) swum
to bring	brought	(has/have) brought

A Underline the verb or verb phrase in each sentence. Then write its infinitive form.

1. My uncle <u>fought</u> in the war. _____ **to fight** _____

2. Her older brother drove to school. _____

3. I ate the whole pizza. _____

4. My aunt came to visit. _____

5. We haven't caught any fish. _____

6. The kitten hid inside the sack. _____

7. She has told us everything. _____

8. Joseph sat patiently for hours. _____

In French Some verbs also have irregular past participles. You need to memorize their forms in order to form the **passé composé**.

avoir → **eu**	J'ai **eu** un problème avec mon nouveau tuba.
boire → **bu**	Il **a bu** une limonade au café.
être → **été**	Nous **avons été** au magasin.
faire → **fait**	Qu'est-ce que tu **as fait**?
lire → **lu**	Elles **ont lu** les romans de Proust.
mettre → **mis**	J'ai **mis** une veste.
pleuvoir → **plu**	Il **a plu** hier.
prendre → **pris**	Vous **avez pris** un sandwich au jambon?
voir → **vu**	J'ai **vu** un super cerf-volant au magasin.
vouloir → **voulu**	Elle n'**a** pas **voulu** acheter un VTT.

The **passé composé** of **il y a** *(there is)* is **il y a eu** *(there was)*.
   Il y a eu un accident devant le magasin de vêtements.

THE PASSÉ COMPOSÉ OF IRREGULAR VERBS   CHAPITRE **7**

B Underline the **passé composé** in each sentence. Then write its infinitive form.

1. Ils <u>ont voulu</u> manger au café. _____ **vouloir** _____

2. Vous avez lu un bon livre? _____

3. J'ai fait du ski en hiver. _____

4. Pourquoi tu n'as pas voulu aller? _____

5. J'ai été à la bibliothèque. _____

6. Est-ce qu'il a plu hier? _____

7. Elle a mis son maillot de bain. _____

8. Nous avons eu un accident. _____

C The sentences below tell what's going to happen in the near future. Rewrite them to say that each of the events occurred in the past.

1. Vous allez voir un film super.

   Vous avez vu un film super. _____

2. Séverine va prendre le déjeuner.

   _____

3. Tu vas lire un magazine en français.

   _____

4. Ils vont faire un pique-nique au parc.

   _____

5. Je vais mettre des chaussures de randonnée.

   _____

6. Nous n'allons pas boire de café.

   _____

D Complete the following sentences logically using the **passé composé**.

1. J'_____ **ai vu** _____ un film au cinéma.

2. Il _____ un croque-monsieur.

3. Mes amis _____ un pique-nique au parc.

4. Tu _____ un manteau?

5. Nous _____ les bandes dessinées.

Negative expressions

In English Several different expressions can be used to make negative sentences, such as **not**, **never**, **not ever**, **nobody**, **nothing**, **no one**, **not yet**, **no longer**, **none**.

> I **never** wake up late.
> I have **nothing** to wear for the party.
> We are **no longer** going to buy it.

Certain negative words can be used as subjects.
> **No one** goes to school on Saturdays.
> **Nothing** is more important to me than music.

Two negative words cannot be combined to form a negation in English.

> INCORRECT: I didn't see nobody.   CORRECT: I didn't see anybody.

A Underline the negative expressions in the following sentences.

1. I <u>never</u> go swimming in the evenings.

2. I have not seen anybody around today.

3. I am hungry because I ate nothing this morning.

4. Nobody goes there anymore.

5. There is none left.

6. I am not going to watch any movies tonight.

7. We no longer eat red meat.

In French Several different expressions can also be used to make negative sentences. Negative expressions are formed by **ne** and negative words. You've already used

ne... pas *(not)*, **ne... ni... ni** *(neither, nor)*, and **ne... jamais** *(never)*. Here are some other ones.

ne... pas encore	*not yet*	**ne... personne**	*no one*
ne... plus	*no longer*	**ne... rien**	*nothing*

The words **personne** *(no one)* and **rien** *(nothing)* can also be used as subjects. When they act as subjects, they come before **ne** and the verb.

> **Personne** n'a joué avec moi au parc.

> **Rien** n'est facile.

When used as objects, **rien** goes immediately after the conjugated verb, but **personne** goes after the whole verb phrase.

> Je n'<u>ai</u> **rien** fait au parc.
> Je n'<u>ai vu</u> **personne** au parc.

NEGATIVE EXPRESSIONS

B Underline the negative expressions in the following sentences.

1. Étienne <u>ne</u> va <u>jamais</u> à la plage.

2. Il n'a plus d'amis.

3. Personne ne joue au football.

4. Il ne fait rien le week-end.

5. Nous n'avons pas encore parlé avec ses parents.

6. Rien n'est intéressant.

7. Il n'aime ni le cinéma ni les jeux vidéo.

C Complete the following conversation with the negative expressions from the box.

ne (n')… pas encore	Personne ne (n')	ne… pas	Rien ne (n')	ne (n')… plus

Honoré   Je _____ ne _____ peux ____ pas _____ sortir? Et pourquoi?

Maman   Tu _____ as _____ fait des corvées.

Honoré   Mais si. J'ai débarrassé la table.

Maman   Et la vaisselle? _____ a fait la vaisselle.

Honoré   La lave-vaisselle peut faire la vaisselle.

Maman   Désolée, mais on _____ a _____ de lave-vaisselle.

Honoré   Ah, maman. C'est pénible, faire la vaisselle!

Maman   _____ est facile, Honoré.

D Rewrite the following sentences to make them negative. Replace the underlined word with a negative expression.

1. Nous déjeunons <u>toujours</u> au café.

    Nous ne déjeunons jamais au café.

2. <u>Tout le monde</u> a fait du patin à glace. _____

    _____

3. J'ai <u>beaucoup</u> étudié au cybercafé.

    _____

4. Tu as <u>encore</u> faim?

    _____

5. Vous nagez <u>toujours</u> au lac?

    _____

54

The passé composé with être

In English You can talk about the past using the **present perfect**. The present perfect includes a helping verb and the past participle of the main verb. In an English present perfect, the helping verb is always a form of the verb *to have*.

> Connie **has gone** to the store.
> They **have remodeled** their apartment.

A Underline the complete verb in each sentence. Then circle the helping verb.

1. Carl has written a letter to his congressman.
2. I have seen this movie before.
3. Cheryl hasn't received her invitation yet.
4. He has come to fix the dishwasher.
5. My cousins have lived in that house for many years.
6. You have read *The Little Prince*, right?

In French You can talk about the past using the **passé composé**, which is made up of a helping verb and a past participle. The helping verb is usually a form of the verb **avoir**. In some instances, mainly with verbs of motion, the helping verb is a form of the verb **être**. The helping verb **être** is used with the following verbs:

> **aller   arriver   descendre   devenir   entrer   monter**
>
> **mourir   naître   partir   rester   retourner   tomber   venir**

Since the helping verb is **être**, the past participle matches the gender (masculine or feminine) and number (singular or plural) of the subject.

je	**suis allé(e)**	nous	**sommes allé(e)s**
tu	**es allé(e)**	vous	**êtes allé(e)(s)**
il	**est allé**	ils	**sont allés**
elle	**est allée**	elles	**sont allées**

> Sylvie **est allée** au cinéma et moi, son frère, je **suis allé** au cybercafé.
> Alors les filles, vous **êtes arrivées**?

When the subject is the pronoun **on,** then the participle agrees with the understood subject that **on** stands for.

> Eh bien petite, **on est tombée**? *(Well little girl, did you fall down?)*

The following verbs have irregular past participles.

> mourir → **mort**   Mes grands-parents **sont morts**.
> naître → **né**   Ma sœur **est née** ici.
> venir/devenir → **venu/devenu**   Les filles **sont devenues** professeurs.

THE PASSÉ COMPOSÉ WITH ÊTRE

B Underline the complete verb in each sentence. Then circle the helping verb.

1. Francine est née à Avignon.

2. Nanette est tombée dans l'escalier.

3. Les Granger sont partis en vacances.

4. Nous sommes restés chez Tante Huguette.

5. Est-ce que tu es sorti avec ma sœur?

6. Je suis arrivé hier soir.

C Complete each sentence with the **passé composé** of the verb in parentheses.

1. Monsieur, quand est-ce que vous _____ êtes arrivé _____ ?
   (arriver)

2. Louise _____ en Afrique. (aller)

3. Le petit garçon _____ du balcon!
   (tomber)

4. Laurent et moi, nous _____ le même
   jour. (naître)

5. Marie-Thérèse, tu _____ professeur?
   (devenir)

6. Mes sœurs _____ chez mamie. (rester)

D Write complete sentences using the **passé composé** and the cues given.

1. les filles / descendre / à la salle à manger
   Les filles sont descendues à la salle à manger.

2. Geneviève / sortir / à huit heures

   _____

3. Le nouveau tapis / arriver / ce matin

   _____

4. est-ce que / Jules et Olivier / retourner / ?

   _____

5. mes grands-parents / mourir / l'année dernière

   _____

6. Marc et moi / ne... pas / aller / à la MJC

   _____

Inversion

In English Yes-or-no questions with the verb *to be* require the subject to go after the verb. In other words, there is subject-verb **inversion.**

> <u>Anne</u> **is** French. → **Is** <u>Anne</u> French?
> <u>They</u> **are** lost. → **Are** <u>they</u> lost?

Inversion only happens with the verb *to be* or a helping verb, and it does not matter whether the question is formal or informal.

> <u>He</u> **has** finished. → **Has** <u>he</u> finished?

A Determine whether the following sentences are questions or statements. Write a question mark for questions and a period for statements.

 1. Is Henry absent today __?__

 2. He has gone to the party _____

 3. Is Cafe Paris on this street _____

 4. Have you found the map _____

 5. There are too many questions _____

 6. Am I dressed appropriately _____

 7. Are your parents home _____

 8. You are very smart _____

In French Formal questions are formed with **inversion.** The pronoun subject and verb are reversed and a hyphen is added between them.

> <u>Tu</u> **vas** à la banque?   → **Vas-tu** à la banque?
> <u>Vous</u> **faites** du ski?   → **Faites-vous** du ski?

If the pronoun **il, elle,** or **on** is the subject, and the verb ends in a vowel, a **-t-** is added between them. This is to make the pronunciation easier.

> Il a deux sœurs?   → **A-t-il** deux sœurs?
> On travaille beaucoup? → **Travaille-t-on** beaucoup?

If the subject is a noun, the corresponding subject pronoun is added for inversion.

> Janine vient avec nous?   → Janine **vient-elle** avec nous?
> Pourquoi est-ce que les élèves parlent? → Pourquoi les élèves **parlent-ils?**

In the **passé composé,** reverse the subject pronoun and the helping verb.

> Tu as trouvé un plan de la ville? → **As-tu** trouvé un plan de la ville?
> Vous avez compris?   → **Avez-vous** compris?

INVERSION

B Determine whether the following sentences are questions or statements. Write a question mark for formal questions and a period for statements.

    1. Fait-il chaud__?__

    2. Marie habite chez sa tante_____

    3. Comment allez-vous_____

    4. Pierre est tombé du deuxième étage_____

    5. Tes parents ont-ils téléphoné_____

    6. Pascal n'a-t-il pas parlé_____

    7. Vous allez écouter la radio_____

    8. Ont-elles lu toute la soirée_____

C Rewrite the following questions with inversion.

    1. Est-ce que vous êtes allé en métro?

    Êtes-vous allé en métro?

    2. Est-ce que le taxi est déjà parti?

    _____

    3. Où est-ce que tu habites?

    _____

    4. Tes parents veulent que tu rentres tôt?

    _____

    5. Tu as pris le bus pour aller au centre-ville?

    _____

    6. Sabine, est-ce qu'elle a acheté des timbres?

    _____

D Translate the following English questions into French using inversion. How are they similar to the English construction? How are they different?

    Is he your brother? Did he go to school today?

_____

_____

_____

_____

Prepositions with countries and cities CHAPITRE 10

In English To say where you are, where you are going, or where you are coming from, you can use the prepositions **in**, **to**, or **from** with the name of a country or city.

I live **in** Philadelphia.
We're going **to** Canada.
Nicole is **from** Switzerland.

A Complete each sentence with **in**, **to**, or **from**.

1. Does he often go _____ to _____ Montreal?

2. Why don't we move _____ Texas?

3. I'll call you when I'm _____ Saint Louis.

4. This cheese came _____ France.

5. How often do you go _____ Ireland?

6. Her cousins live _____ Belgium.

7. Our new classmate is _____ Dakar.

8. Is his family originally _____ New York?

In French When you say you're **in**, going **to**, or coming **from** a country or city, the prepositions you use vary according to the kind of location you're referring to. Use the preposition **à** before the names of most cities. Notice that **à** can mean either **to** or **in**, depending on its context.

Nous allons **à** Nice.
Il est **à** Marseille.

To say **from** most cities, use the preposition **de**.
J'arrive **de** Chicago à quatorze heures.

To say you're **in** or going **to** a country, you generally use **au** before masculine countries and **en** before feminine countries and countries that begin with a vowel. If the name of the country is plural, such as the United States, use the preposition **aux**.

Elle va **au** Japon.
Nous allons **en** Suisse.
Allez-vous **aux** États-Unis?

To say **from** a country, use **du**, **de**, **d'**, or **des** if the country is plural.
Brigitte arrive **du** Canada.
Marc et Georges arrivent **de** France.
Ils arrivent **des** États-Unis.

B Underline the prepositions before names of countries or cities in the following sentences. Then, indicate their meaning by circling **to**, **in**, or **from**.

1. Stéphane voudrait aller <u>au</u> Canada.   to   in   from

2. Tu as un frère qui habite <u>à</u> Londres?   to   in   from

3. Mes amis ont passé un week-end en Italie.   to   in   from

4. Je suis allé à la Martinique.   to   in   from

5. Moulay vient du Maroc.   to   in   from

6. Nous prenons le train pour aller en Espagne.   to   in   from

7. Elle va aller au Japon.   to   in   from

8. Son oncle vient des États-Unis.   to   in   from

> **In French** As with other nouns, names of countries are either masculine or feminine.
>
> | | | |
> |---|---|---|
> | la Chine | les États-Unis (m.) | l'Espagne (f.) |
> | la Russie | l'Angleterre (f.) | l'Italie (f.) |
> | le Canada | les Pays-Bas (m.) | la Tunisie |
> | le Japon | l'Allemagne (f.) | le Mexique |
> | le Maroc | le Brésil | la Suisse |

C What do most feminine countries have in common? Which country is the exception?

_____

_____

_____

D Complete each sentence with **à**, **en**, **au**, **aux**, **de**, or **de la**.

1. Charlotte est maintenant ___**aux**___ États-Unis.

2. Les élèves vont _____ Russie.

3. Qu'est-ce qu'on peut acheter _____ Maroc?

4. Lourdes habite _____ Guadalajara, _____ Mexique.

5. Nous allons passer une semaine _____ New York.

6. Daniel vient _____ Tunisie.

7. Je vais visiter les villages _____ Allemagne et _____ Italie.

8. Est-ce qu'il pleut souvent _____ Brésil?

9. Mes amis sont partis _____ Seattle et ils vont _____ San Francisco.

Level 2
Grammar Tutor Activities

The adjectives beau, nouveau, vieux CHAPITRE **1**

In English The adjectives **beautiful**, **new**, and **old** are like other English adjectives. They are placed before the noun they describe, and their spelling does not change when describing masculine and feminine nouns, or singular and plural nouns.

Do you think Julie is a **beautiful** <u>actress</u>?
Mr. Moore is our **new** <u>teacher</u>.
My **old** <u>neighbors</u> now live in a boathouse.

A Circle the adjective in each sentence and underline the noun it describes.

1. I want to visit Paris, because everyone says it is a beautiful city.

2. The students loved listening to old records.

3. It is a beautiful house but the plumbing doesn't work.

4. Henry came to school riding his new bicycle.

5. The old part of the city has streets made of bricks.

6. The magician amazed everyone with his new trick.

In French The adjectives **beau**, **nouveau**, and **vieux** are irregular adjectives. Unlike most French adjectives, they are placed **before** the noun they describe.

Mon amie a une **belle** <u>maison</u>.
M. Michaud est notre **nouveau** <u>professeur</u>.
Le **vieux** <u>chat</u> dort beaucoup.

The feminine forms are **belle**, **nouvelle**, and **vieille**. The plural is formed by adding **-s.**

Paris est une **vieille** ville.
Où sont les **nouvelles** voitures?

There are two masculine forms. Before a masculine noun that begins with a vowel sound, the forms are **bel**, **nouvel**, and **vieil**. Before a masculine noun that begins with a consonant, the forms are **beau**, **nouveau**, and **vieux**. The plural of the masculine forms are **beaux**, **nouveaux**, and **vieux**.

Farid est un **nouvel** élève.
Il a un **vieux** chien et deux chats.
Ses chats sont **beaux**.

THE ADJECTIVES BEAU, NOUVEAU, VIEUX   CHAPITRE **1**

B Circle the adjective in each sentence and underline the noun it describes.

1. Ma tante habite dans une belle ville.

2. Nous avons une vieille voiture.

3. Ce chapeau est très vieux.

4. Derrière la maison il y a un beau jardin.

5. Tu aimes bien ce bel anorak?

6. Mes parents m'ont offert une nouvelle bicyclette.

C Complete each sentence by circling the correct adjective.

1. Ce sont de (belles / beaux) animaux.

2. On a visité les (vieilles / vieux) églises de la ville.

3. Dans un magasin très chic, j'ai acheté cette (belle / belles) jupe.

4. J'ai besoin d'une (nouvelle / nouveau) valise pour le voyage.

5. Nous sommes restés dans un (vieil / vieux) hôtel.

6. Est-ce que vous habitez dans le (nouvelle / nouvel) appartement?

7. Mes amis adorent les (vieilles / vieux) films français.

8. Tu connais le (nouvel / nouveau) élève, n'est-ce pas?

D Rewrite the following sentences, replacing the underlined words with the words in parentheses. Make any necessary changes.

1. <u>Mon oncle</u> est très vieux. (Ma tante)

   Ma tante est très vieille.

2. Connaissez-vous notre vieille <u>école</u>? (hôpital)

   _____

3. C'est une belle <u>chanson</u>. (film)

   _____

4. Mes <u>copines</u> sont belles. (copains)

   _____

5. Nous avons acheté une nouvelle <u>voiture</u>. (ordinateur)

   _____

6. Tu aimes mes nouvelles <u>lunettes</u>? (pantalons)

   _____

Direct objects

> **In English** A **direct object** is the person or thing in a sentence that directly receives the action of the verb. It answers the question *whom?* or *what?*
>
> I gave him **the book**. (*the book* answers the question, *What did I give him?*)
> I introduced **Peter** to Mary. (*Peter* answers the question, *Whom did I introduce?*)
>
> Direct objects usually come after the verb. Adjectives, adverbs, and articles may come between a verb and its direct object.
>
> The library <u>has</u> interesting **books**.
> The car company <u>will introduce</u> a new **truck** this month.
>
> Compare the following sentences. In the second sentence, the preposition **to** comes between the verb **walks** and the direct object **school**, so **to school** is a prepositional phrase and *not* a direct object.
>
> Scott walks the **dog**.　　　Scott walks <u>to school</u>.

A Underline the direct object in each sentence.

1. The library also lends <u>DVDs</u>.

2. Her parents drive an antique car.

3. We need candles for the birthday cake.

4. I'm meeting George at the park.

5. I take the bus to school on occasion.

6. The dog always obeys his master.

7. She doesn't understand the chemistry lesson.

8. Did you take pictures of the fireworks?

> **In French** A **direct object** is also a noun that receives the verb's action. It follows the verb and is not directly preceded by a preposition.
>
> Sophie <u>cherche</u> une **robe**.
> Michel <u>écoute</u> le **professeur**.
> Elle va à l'école. (*l'école* follows *à* and is not a direct object)
>
> Like English, adjectives, adverbs, and articles may come between a verb and its direct objéct.
> Patrice et Roland <u>aiment</u> bien **le sport**.
> Lisette <u>porte</u> votre **casquette**.

DIRECT OBJECTS CHAPITRE **2**

B Underline the direct object in each sentence.

1. Tu as ton <u>sac</u>?

2. Monique cherche le livre de maths.

3. Je ne vois pas Jean.

4. J'aime ce chemisier blanc.

5. Delphine veut acheter ce cadeau.

6. Est-ce que tu as invité Magali à la fête?

7. Elle trouve ce bouquet de fleurs très beau.

8. Nous prenons un sandwich au café.

C Complete each of the following sentences logically. Then circle the direct object in each sentence.

1. J'aime bien _____ les céréales pour le petit-déjeuner_____.

2. Nous avons trouvé _____

   _____.

3. Avez-vous vu _____

   _____?

4. Au magasin, j'ai choisi _____

   _____.

5. Tu as invité _____

   _____?

6. Mes amis et moi, nous attendons _____

D Which of the following sentences has a direct object? Explain your choice.

   J'aime l'école.   **Je vais à l'école.**

   _____

   _____

   _____

   _____

66

Direct object pronouns

> **In English** Direct object pronouns refer to someone or something that receives the action of the verb. They replace direct object nouns to avoid repetition. Direct object pronouns are placed after the verb.
>
> English object pronouns that replace things are it and them. Object pronouns that can refer to people are him, her, you, me, us, and them.
>
> I saw that <u>film</u> and I enjoyed it immensely.
> Mom took <u>Peter</u> to school. She picked him up later.
> They were not using their mountain <u>bikes</u> so they sold them.

A Circle the direct object pronoun and underline the noun it refers to.

1. Finish your <u>homework</u> now and hand it in tomorrow

2. I bought an apple for later, but I ate it immediately.

3. If you don't know Russell, let me introduce him to you!

4. I heard a lot about your brothers, but I never met them.

5. I wanted to see two movies, but my friend had already seen them.

6. Did you phone Grandmother or did you email her?

7. Do you like these flowers? I bought them for my mom.

8. I sent you my first novel. You never read it, did you?

> **In French** Direct object pronouns can also be used to avoid repeating direct object nouns that have already been mentioned.
> —Tu aimes <u>le sirop de menthe</u>?
> —Pas du tout. Je **le** déteste.
>
> The direct object pronouns are as follows:
>
> **me** *(me)*   **nous** *(us)*
> **te** *(you)*   **vous** *(you)*
> **le/la** *(him/her, it)*   **les** *(them)*
>
> In the present tense, direct object pronouns go before the conjugated verb. If there is an infinitive, they go before the infinitive. Note that before a verb beginning with a vowel sound, **me, te, le,** and **la** change to **m', t',** and **l'**.
> Je **vous** invite tous chez moi.
> Le film est bon et ils veulent **le** regarder.
> Ma grand-mère **m'**aime beaucoup.
> Je **l'**ai cherché, mais je ne **l'**ai pas trouvé.

DIRECT OBJECT PRONOUNS

B Circle the direct object pronoun and underline the noun it refers to.

1. Elle essaye les <u>robes</u> et |les| achète.

2. La jupe est horrible. Elle ne la prend pas.

3. Est-ce que vous montez les lits ou les descendez?

4. Marcel, je te souhaite bon anniversaire!

5. Monsieur et Madame Langlois, je vous invite chez moi.

6. J'adore les feux d'artifice et je vais les voir cette année.

7. Cette carte est belle. Tu veux l'envoyer?

C Write answers to the following questions. Use an appropriate pronoun to avoid repeating the underlined words in each answer.

1. Tu aimes <u>les tartes aux pommes</u>?

   Non, je ne les aime pas. _____

2. Tu prends <u>le bus</u> pour aller à l'école?

   _____

3. Est-ce que tu invites <u>tes professeurs</u> à tes fêtes?

   _____

4. Achètes-tu souvent <u>ces magazines</u>?

   _____

5. Tu attends <u>ta copine</u>?

   _____

6. Qui fait <u>la vaisselle</u> chez toi?

   _____

D Compare the following sentences In your own words, explain the placement of ne... pas in sentences that contain direct object pronouns.

Je ne le prends pas.   Je ne vais pas le prendre.

_____
_____
_____
_____
_____

Indirect objects

In English An **indirect object** is the person *to whom* or *for whom* something is done. The indirect object noun can either go before or after the direct object. However, when it follows the direct object, the preposition **to** must be used.

My parents gave **my cousin** a gift.
My parents gave a gift **to my cousin**.

You can ask yourself *to whom* or *for whom* the action occurs in order to determine what the indirect object is. Verbs such as **to send, to show,** and **to give** often have indirect objects.

I sent **my uncle** a thank you note.
(*To whom* did I send a thank you note? *To* **my uncle**.)

A Circle the indirect objects in the following sentences.

1. I wrote my best friend many e-mails while I was away.

2. Who sent that package to you?

3. I brought my grandmother a bouquet of daisies.

4. My parents bought my brother and me a new computer!

5. Let's write our congresswoman a letter.

6. We gave the dog a big, juicy bone.

In French An **indirect object** is also the person who benefits from the action of the verb. It is almost always preceded by the preposition **à.** Indirect objects are often used with verbs of giving and receiving (**donner, offrir, envoyer**) and of communicating (**parler, téléphoner, dire**).

Je vais envoyer une invitation **à ton cousin.**
J'écris **à Agnès.**
Les élèves parlent **au professeur.**

B Circle the indirect objects in the following sentences.

1. Tu peux offrir un CD à Sophie.

2. Je dois téléphoner à mes parents.

3. Est-ce que vous pouvez donner ce livre à Jean-Luc?

4. Le prof d'histoire va rendre les devoirs aux élèves.

5. Nous pouvons parler à Mylène et à François à la fête.

6. Ma tante offre toujours des chocolats aux enfants.

INDIRECT OBJECTS

C Rewrite the following scrambled sentences so the words are in the correct order. Then circle the indirect object in each sentence.

1. Nous / des cadeaux / à / donnons / nos amis

    Nous donnons des cadeaux à nos amis.
    _____

2. J' / une carte de vœux / écris / à / mes grands-parents

    _____

    _____

3. Les Hébert / aux / leur maison / parents de Martin / vendent

    _____

    _____

4. Notre chien / le journal / apporte / aux filles

    _____

    _____

5. Je / mon père / vais / de l'argent / à / demander

    _____

    _____

6. J'offre / à / mon / un ballon / petit ami

    _____

    _____

7. Tu / une invitation / sœurs d'Alice / n'envoies / pas / aux

    _____

    _____

D Compare the following sentences. What can you conclude about English and French verbs that take direct and indirect objects?

Il **répond** à la lettre.	He **answers** the letter.
Il **téléphone** à Alice.	He **phones** Alice.
Elle **demande** toujours à Marc.	She always **asks** Marc.

_____

_____

_____

_____

Indirect object pronouns

CHAPITRE **2**

In English An indirect object noun can be replaced by an **indirect object pronoun**. In English, these are me, you, him, her, us, you *(plural)*, and them.

    My grandmother told me that story years ago.

    I gave your books to them.

When both direct and indirect objects are expressed as pronouns in the same sentence, the indirect object pronoun goes after **to** or **for**.

    Rachel sent **it** to **her**.

    He's preparing **it** for **you**.

A Underline the indirect object pronoun in each sentence.

    1. Who gave <u>me</u> this present?

    2. He did not know her, but offered it to her anyway.

    3. Why did you give him a small tip?

    4. Who writes you so many letters?

    5. Frank gave it to us last week.

    6. She explained everything to me.

    7. Could you leave the lights on for them?

In French **Indirect object pronouns** are also used to avoid repeating the noun. They are placed before the conjugated verb or before an infinitive.

me (m') *(to/for me)*	**nous** *(to/for us)*
te (t') *(to/for you)*	**vous** *(to/for you,* formal, plural*)*
lui *(to/for him/her)*	**leur** *(to/for them)*

    Alors, je **vous** envoie une invitation à ma fête.

    Il va **lui** offrir des fleurs.

If you have a sentence with both direct and indirect object pronouns, place the pronouns in the following order.

me		le		
te	*before*	la	*before*	lui
nous		l'		leur
vous		les		

    J'envoie **cette carte** à mon ami. ⟶ Je **la** lui envoie.

    Je te donne **son numéro de téléphone.** ⟶ Je te **le** donne.

INDIRECT OBJECT PRONOUNS

B Underline the indirect object pronoun in each sentence.

1. Nous allons <u>te</u> l'acheter.

2. Je ne lui prête pas mes choses.

3. Il vous a dit tout, n'est-ce pas?

4. Son père va la lui prêter.

5. Est-ce que vous allez nous le vendre?

6. Gilles ne veut pas me le montrer.

7. Tu vas la leur envoyer?

C Complete the following sentences with the correct indirect object pronouns.

1. —Qu'est-ce que je dois faire pour M. Pelletier?

   —Tu dois _____ lui _____ écrire une lettre.

2. —Tu poses souvent des questions aux professeurs?

   —Non, je _____ pose rarement des questions.

3. —Quand est-ce que tu vas nous montrer les photos?

   —Je vais _____ les montrer demain.

4. —Vas-tu acheter un CD à Simone?

   —Oui, je vais _____ acheter celui-ci.

D Write the answer to each question using a direct and an indirect object pronoun.

1. Qui nous envoie cette lettre? (Grégoire)

   Grégoire nous l'envoie. _____

2. Qui m'écrit les e-mails? (Lorraine)

   _____

3. Qui nous rend les livres? (Sylvie et Maude)

   _____

4. Qui va t'acheter la voiture? (mon grand-père)

   _____

5. Qui donne ce cadeau à Bruno? (sa tante)

   _____

6. Qui va prêter les bicyclettes aux garçons? (M. Dupuy)

   _____

The pronoun y

> **In English** To avoid repeating a place name, you can say **there** instead.
>
> —Are you going <u>to Quebec</u>?
> —Yes, I'm going **there**.
>
> In English, as long as your meaning is clear, you don't have to include the word **there**.
>
> —Is he at the doctor's office?
> —No, he's not.

A Underline the words that could be replaced with **there**.

1. Mom's <u>at the store</u>.
2. I can't wait to go to Montreal.
3. John and Julie are in the library.
4. Her best friend is moving to Seattle.
5. The State Fair takes place in Dallas.
6. They go to France often.
7. Are you going to the art museum?

> **In French** To avoid repeating places and locations, you can use the pronoun y. Y can replace names of places that start with a preposition of location such as **à, dans, en, sur,** and **chez.**
>
> —Tu peux aller <u>au supermarché</u>?
> —Bien sûr. J'y vais tout de suite.
>
> —Est-ce que le sucre est <u>sur la table</u>?
> —Oui, il y est.
>
> The pronoun y follows the same rules of placement as direct and indirect object pronouns. It goes before the conjugated verb, or if there is an infinitive, directly before the infinitive.
>
> —Tu aimes aller au café?
> —Je n'y vais pas souvent, mais de temps en temps, j'aime bien y aller.

B Underline the words that could be replaced by the pronoun y.

1. Maman va <u>au supermarché</u> le lundi.

2. Est-ce qu'on peut aller à la piscine cet après-midi?

3. Laure fait de l'athlétisme au stade.

4. Didier et Thomas vont chez ses parents.

5. Cécile est allée à Berlin l'été dernier.

6. Le poivre est sur la table.

7. Nous prenons le bus pour aller au centre commercial.

C Write affirmative answers to the following questions, using the pronoun y.

1. Est-ce que Mylène habite à Bordeaux?

    Oui, Mylène y habite. _____

2. Va-t-elle chez ses grands-parents?

    _____

3. Vous prenez un sandwich au café?

4. Est-ce que tes copains étudient à la bibliothèque?

    _____

5. Tu vas aller en Chine?

    _____

6. Les filles parlent au coin de la rue?

    _____

7. Est-ce qu'elle va aller aux États-Unis demain?

    _____

8. Tu manges dans ta voiture?

    _____

D Give examples of sentences in the present and near future to illustrate how the placement of the pronoun y is similar to the placement of other object pronouns.

_____

_____

_____

The pronoun en

> **In English** When talking about quantities, you can use the words **some, any, of it/them**, a number, or an expression of quantity like **a lot**, to avoid repeating a noun.
>
> I've got some almonds. Do you want **some**?
> I need sugar. Do you have **any**?
> I love green tea. I drink **a lot of it**.
> Do you have seedless watermelons? I would like two **of them**.

A Circle the words **some, any, of it/of them**, or an expression of quantity in the following sentences. Then underline the noun to which it refers.

1. I love chocolate so I eat a lot of it.
2. Juice? No, I don't want any.
3. I haven't read my e-mails because there are too many of them.
4. I made homemade ice cream. Do you want some?
5. I would like to buy your CDs, but not all of them.
6. Yes, this is my popcorn and you can grab some.
7. I bought a box of candy but I don't have any left.
8. I love horror movies, so I watch all of them.

> **In French** *Some* and *any* can sometimes be translated as **en**. The pronoun **en** replaces an **indefinite** or **partitive article + noun.**
>
> —Tu veux du yaourt? *(Would you like some yogurt?)*
> —Non, merci, je n'**en** veux pas. *(No, thanks, I don't want any.)*
>
> —Est-ce qu'il y a des ordinateurs ici? *(Are there any computers here?)*
> —Oui, il y **en** a. *(Yes, there are some.)*
>
> **En** also replaces nouns that follow numbers or expressions of quantity. In this case, you normally still use the number or the expression of quantity in the sentence with **en**.
>
> —Tu manges beaucoup de sandwiches?
> —Oui, j'**en** mange **beaucoup.** J'**en** prends souvent **un** à midi.
> —Moi, j'**en** prends souvent **deux**!
> —Et moi, je n'**en** prends pas.
>
> Like object pronouns, **en** is placed before the conjugated verb or before the infinitive if there is one.
>
> De la glace? Je n'**en** veux pas. Mais demain, je vais **en** manger.

THE PRONOUN EN

B Circle the pronoun en in the following sentences. Then underline the noun it refers to.

1. —Avez-vous un <u>frère</u>? —Oui, j'en ai un.

2. —Est-ce que tu as de l'argent? —Non, je n'en ai pas.

3. —Veux-tu de la soupe? —Oui, j'en veux.

4. —As-tu beaucoup de temps? —Non, je n'en ai pas beaucoup.

5. —Combien d'œufs est-ce qu'il y a? —Il y en a plusieurs.

6. —Est-ce que vous connaissez des professeurs ici? —Oui, j'en connais deux.

7. —As-tu assez de café? —Oui, j'en ai assez.

8. —Il n'a pas d'amis? —Mais si, il en a beaucoup.

C Respond to each sentence with the numbers in parentheses and the pronoun en.

1. Il y a trente élèves dans cette classe, n'est-ce pas? (26)

   Non, il y en a vingt-six.

2. Karine a dix-huit ans, n'est-ce pas? (17)

   _____

3. Les élèves ont cinq pages à lire, n'est-ce pas? (50)

   _____

4. Il y a beaucoup de pêches, n'est-ce pas? (2)

   _____

5. Tu vas acheter dix bananes, n'est-ce pas? (8)

   _____

6. Nous avons vingt bougies, n'est-ce pas? (12)

   _____

7. Ignace parle deux langues, n'est-ce pas? (3)

   _____

8. Cette maison a trois salles de bains, n'est-ce pas? (4)

   _____

Placement of object pronouns CHAPITRE **3**

> **In English** A sentence can have more than one object. When both a direct and an indirect object pronoun are in the same sentence and the direct object pronoun comes first, the indirect object pronoun goes after the preposition *to* or *for*.
>
> Robert gives **the roses** *to Alice*. ⎫ Robert gives **them** *to her*.
> Robert gives *Alice* **the roses**. ⎭
>
> I'm making **a salad** *for Henry*. ⎫ I'm making **it** *for him*.
> I'm making *Henry* **a salad**. ⎭

A Rewrite the following sentences with direct and indirect object pronouns.

1. Anne always offers her friends advice.

   Anne always offers it to them. _____

2. Why did you lend your computer to Joseph?

   _____

3. I plan to give you my posters.

   _____

4. Olivia is baking a cake for her sister.

   _____

5. Victor bought his parents a picture frame.

   _____

6. We haven't told Eric the password.

   _____

> **In French** You can also have more than one object pronoun in the same sentence. Place the pronouns in the order presented below. Notice the position of the pronoun **y** and **en** with the other pronouns.
>
> | me | | le | | | | | | |
> |------|--------|-----|--------|------|--------|---|--------|----|
> | te | *before* | la | *before* | lui | *before* | y | *before* | en |
> | nous | | l' | | leur | | | | |
> | vous | | les | | | | | | |
>
> Just like single object pronouns, double object pronouns go before the conjugated verb or in front of the infinitive.
>
> Marc va acheter du lait à la crémerie? Oui, Marc va **y en** acheter.
> Tu peux me donner des fraises? Bien sûr. Je **t'en** donne.

PLACEMENT OF OBJECT PRONOUNS

B Unscramble each sentence and rewrite it in the correct order.

1. Il / la / jamais / ne / me / prête

   Il ne me la prête jamais. _____

2. Tu / les / donner / vas / leur

   _____

3. Nous / envoyer / en / pouvons / leur

   _____

4. Tu / y / peux / les / trouver

   _____

5. Vous / en / souvent / achetez / y

   _____

6. Je / en / offre / t' / beaucoup

   _____

7. Maurice / les / voit / y / ne / pas

   _____

C Rewrite the following sentences with double object pronouns.

1. J'achète des croissants à la boulangerie.

   J'y en achète. _____

2. Je donne la boîte à l'employée.

   _____

3. Marie-France va nous prêter ses notes d'histoire.

   _____

4. Les parents doivent lire des livres à leurs enfants.

   _____

5. Tu n'envoies jamais de cartes postales à tes amis.

   _____

6. Nous allons acheter des fraises au marché.

   _____

7. Je ne veux pas te donner mon gâteau.

   _____

78

Object pronouns with the passé composé CHAPITRE 4

In English Direct and indirect object pronouns go after the verb. If the verb is composed of a **helping verb + past participle**, the object pronoun goes after the past participle.

I haven't seen them.
We have told you the truth.
Mike had written it before leaving.

A Unscramble each sentence and rewrite it in the correct order.

1. I / it / yet / bought / have / not / .

   I have not bought it yet. _____

2. Have / my / shown / I / collection / you / ?

   _____

3. We / finished / will / them / have / .

   _____

4. I / her / this / bought / shirt / had / for / .

   _____

5. Has / him / she / phoned / ?

   _____

6. My / it / me / have / friends / given / to / .

   _____

In French Direct and indirect object pronouns usually go before the conjugated verb. In the **passé composé,** the direct and indirect object pronouns go before the helping verb avoir or être.

Je l'ai visité ce matin.
Nous lui avons parlé.
Mes copains m'ont téléphoné.

The past participle of the **passé composé** with **avoir** agrees in gender and number with the direct object if the direct object comes before the verb.

Nous avons gagné la compétition. *(No agreement needed.)*
La compétition? Nous l'avons gagnée. *(There is agreement here because the direct object precedes the verb.)*

The past participle does not agree with a preceding indirect object.
Virginie? Je lui ai parlé ce matin.

OBJECT PRONOUNS WITH THE PASSÉ COMPOSÉ   CHAPITRE **4**

B Unscramble each sentence and rewrite it in the correct order.

1. Je / ai / à / poubelle / jetées / la / les /.

   Je les ai jetées à la poubelle. _____

2. Est-ce que / tu / les / ne / as / pas / trouvés / ?

   _____

3. Je / un / préparé / sandwich / lui / ai /.

   _____

4. Il / nous / ne / pas / donné / a / l'adresse /.

   _____

5. Nous / au / achetés / marché / avons / les /.

   _____

C Complete the following sentences with the **passé composé** of the verb in parentheses and an appropriate object pronoun.

1. Corinne n'a pas écrit à ses parents, mais elle _____**leur a téléphoné**_____. (téléphoner)

2. Tu n'as pas encore envoyé la lettre, mais tu _____. (écrire)

3. Eugénie n'offre jamais de cadeaux à ses sœurs, mais elle _____ ses choses. (prêter)

4. Je n'ai pas vu Serge, mais je _____ au téléphone. (parler)

5. Frédéric n'aime pas sa cousine, mais il _____ pour son équipe de volley. (choisir)

6. Nous n'avons pas fini nos devoirs, mais nous _____ au professeur. (rendre)

D Why do these past participles agree or not agree with the objects?

1. Je les ai invités à ma boum.

   _____

2. J'ai vu ma sœur hier.

   _____

3. Ma cousine? Je lui ai parlé ce matin.

   _____

Quelqu'un, quelque chose

In English To refer to people whose identity is not known or not being revealed, you can use the indefinite pronoun **someone**. To refer to a thing, you can use the pronoun **something**.

> We just saw **someone** walk through the door.
> I have **something** important to tell you.

The negative equivalents of **someone** and **something** are **no one** and **nothing**.

> **No one** walked through the door.
> I have **nothing** to say.

In questions and negative sentences, you use **anyone** and **anything**.

> Do you know **anyone** who speaks Flemish?
> I can't tell you **anything** about it.

A Circle the correct word to complete each sentence.

1. I didn't see (anyone / nobody) at the park.

2. Are you doing (anything / nothing) Friday night?

3. (Anyone / Someone) is calling your name.

4. There is (anything / nothing) to eat.

5. She says she doesn't have (anything / nothing) to wear.

6. There must be (anyone / someone) here.

7. (Anything / Nothing) interesting has happened.

In French To say *someone* or *something,* use the indefinite pronouns **quelqu'un** (to refer to a person) or **quelque chose** (to refer to a thing). These pronouns are used in both affirmative and interrogative sentences.

> **Quelqu'un** a téléphoné.
> Tu veux manger **quelque chose**?

The negative equivalents of **quelqu'un** and **quelque chose** are **ne... personne** *(no one)* and **ne... rien** *(nothing)*. As you have learned, **ne** is placed in front of the verb and **personne/rien** after it. In the **passé composé,** **ne** goes in front of the form of **avoir** or **être. Rien** goes in front of the past participle, but **personne** goes after the past participle.

> Je **n'ai rien** vu.
> Je **n'ai** vu **personne**.

If **personne** or **rien** are the subjects, they are placed in the subject position and **ne** is placed before the verb.

> **Personne n'est** venu.
> **Rien n'est** tombé.

QUELQU'UN, QUELQUE CHOSE   CHAPITRE **4**

B Circle the correct expression to complete each sentence.

1. Je n'ai (quelque chose / [rien]) mangé.

2. (Quelqu'un / Personne) n'est sorti hier soir.

3. J'ai acheté (quelque chose / rien) pour toi.

4. Est-ce que tu connais (quelqu'un / personne) d'intelligent?

5. Je ne vois (quelqu'un / personne) ici.

6. Il n'y a (quelque chose / rien) de nouveau.

7. Est-ce qu'il y a (quelqu'un / quelque chose) qui parle allemand?

C Rewrite the following sentences to make them negative.

1. Il y a quelqu'un dans le laboratoire.

   Il n'y a personne dans le laboratoire. _____

2. Quelqu'un veut parler avec vous.

   _____

3. Quelque chose est arrivé.

   _____

4. Je voudrais boire quelque chose.

   _____

5. Nous avons invité quelqu'un d'important.

   _____

6. Guy a acheté quelque chose de bon.

   _____

7. Quelqu'un a gagné la compétition.

   _____

D What two French expressions can be translated as *anything*? Give two sentences in English, then give their French equivalents to support your answer.

English: _____

French: _____

English: _____

French: _____

Reflexive verbs

> **In English** Sometimes the action of a verb is directed (or reflected) back on the subject. When this happens, the verb may be followed by a **reflexive pronoun**, such as **myself, yourself, himself, herself, itself, themselves, ourselves,** and **yourselves.** Study how the reflexive pronouns are used in the following sentences to show that the subject acts upon itself.
>
> I looked at **myself** in the mirror.
> He made **himself** some dinner.
> The children dress **themselves** for school.

A Check the appropriate column to indicate whether the action in the sentence is reflexive or non-reflexive.

	Reflexive	Non-reflexive
1. He washed the car.		✓
2. The dog scratched itself behind the ear.		
3. Do you ever talk to yourself?		
4. The speech was made by the President.		
5. We enjoyed ourselves at the party.		
6. She asked Anne where she left her keys.		
7. He bought himself a CD at the store.		

> **In French** **Reflexive verbs** are used when the same person performs and receives the action of the verb. The pronoun **se** used before the infinitive identifies the verb as reflexive (**se laver, se réveiller**).
>
> Maryse va **se brosser** les cheveux. *(reflexive verb)*
> Maryse va **brosser** le chat. *(non-reflexive verb)*
>
> Unlike English, French reflexive pronouns are placed before the verb.
>
> Je **me lève.**   Nous **nous levons.**
> Tu **te lèves.**   Vous **vous levez.**
> Il/Elle/On **se lève.**   Ils/Elles **se lèvent.**
>
> In negative sentences, place **ne… pas** around the reflexive pronoun and verb.
> Je **ne** **me peigne** **pas,** je me brosse les cheveux.

REFLEXIVE VERBS

B Check the appropriate column to indicate whether the verb in the sentence is reflexive or non-reflexive.

	Reflexive	Non-reflexive
1. Il se réveille à 7h20.	✓	
2. Je vais à la piscine tous les jours.		
3. Elle s'habille avant le petit-déjeuner.		
4. Mes frères se lèvent de bonne heure.		
5. Henri prend son dîner au restaurant.		
6. On prend une douche tous les matins.		
7. Il faut se brosser les dents après le repas.		

C Complete the following sentences with the correct form of the reflexive verb in parentheses.

1. Ma cousine _____ se lève _____ à 6h. (se lever)

2. Tu ne _____ pas? (se dépêcher)

3. Nous _____ tôt. (se réveiller)

4. Jeanne et Claire ne _____ pas avant midi. (s'habiller)

5. On _____ tous les jours. (se baigner)

6. Vous _____ avant de prendre une douche? (se raser)

7. Je _____ les mains avant de manger. (se laver)

8. Combien de fois par jour est-ce qu'il _____ les dents? (se brosser)

D Compare the following French and English sentences. What differences do you see and how could you explain them?

Je me brosse les cheveux. *I brush my hair.*

Elle se lave les mains. *She washes her hands.*

_____

_____

_____

_____

_____

_____

Reflexive verbs in the passé composé and in commands

In English The past tense of verbs that take a reflexive pronoun is similar to the past tense of other verbs.

> He **fixed himself** a sandwich.

Like other English verbs, the helping verb is a form of **have**.

> We **have enjoyed ourselves** here.

In **affirmative** and **negative commands,** the reflexive pronoun goes after the verb.

> Behave **yourselves**!
> Don't cut **yourself** with the knife.

A Circle the correct reflexive pronoun in each sentence. Underline the noun to which the reflexive pronoun refers.

1. Children, enjoy (yourself / yourselves) at the amusement park.

2. We have often asked (ourselves / themselves) that question.

3. Frank heard (yourself / himself) on the radio.

4. They treated ourselves / themselves) to a banana split.

5. I have already helped (myself / himself) to some salad.

6. Patricia has never burnt (herself / yourself) ironing.

7. Have you ever made (yourself / themselves) a foot-long sandwich?

In French The helping verb of reflexive verbs in the **passé composé** is always **être**. In the **passé composé,** the past participle agrees in gender and number with the reflexive pronoun if it is a direct object.

Je	me suis lavé(e).	Nous	nous sommes lavé(e)s.
Tu	t'es lavé(e).	Vous	vous êtes lavé(e)(s).
Il	s'est lavé.	Ils	se sont lavés.
Elle	s'est lavée.	Elles	se sont lavées.
On	s'est lavé(e)(s).		

When a direct object follows a reflexive verb (**se laver les cheveux**), the reflexive pronoun is an indirect object and the past participle does not agree with the reflexive pronoun.

> Iris s'est lavée. *(se is the direct object; there is agreement)*
> Iris s'est lavé les cheveux. *(se is the indirect object; no agreement is needed)*

In **affirmative commands,** the reflexive pronoun is attached to the end of the verb with a hyphen. **Te** changes to **toi** in this situation.

> Lève-toi!   Couchez-vous!   Dépêchons-nous!

In **negative commands,** the reflexive pronoun is placed immediately before the verb.

> Ne **te** lève pas!   Ne **vous** couchez pas!   Ne **nous** dépêchons pas!

REFLEXIVE VERBS IN THE PASSÉ COMPOSÉ AND IN COMMANDS   CHAPITRE **5**

B Circle the correct reflexive verb in each sentence.

1. Adèle, tu (t'es lavé / s'est lavé) la figure?

2. Pierre et Henri, ne (couchez-vous / vous couchez) pas tard!

3. Chantal, (dépêche-toi / te dépêche)!

4. Est-ce que les enfants (s'est habillé / se sont habillés)?

5. Élise (s'est réveillé / s'est réveillée) de bonne heure.

6. Moi, je (me suis séché / t'es séché) les cheveux.

7. Alfred, (coiffe-toi / coiffe-nous)!

C Complete each sentence with the **passé composé** of the verb in parentheses.

1. Olivier et moi, nous _____ **nous sommes réveillés** _____ tôt. (se réveiller)

2. Constance _____ la figure. (se laver)

3. Monique et Corinne _____. (se maquiller)

4. Tous les copains _____ rapidement. (se préparer)

5. Tu _____ les cheveux. (se sécher)

6. Odile et Claude, vous _____ trop tard. (se coucher)

D Write an affirmative or negative command telling the people indicated what to do or not do.

1. Emmanuelle: se lever

   Lève-toi! _____

2. les enfants: se déshabiller

   _____

3. Monsieur Lecler: ne pas se dépêcher

   _____

4. Françoise: se réveiller

   _____

5. toi et moi: se brosser les dents

   _____

6. Paul: ne pas se raser

   _____

The imparfait

> **In English** To say what used to happen habitually in the past, you use either the simple past tense or the words **used to** or **would** + **a verb.**
>
> I **drank** milk all the time when I was a kid.
>
> My brother and I **used to** play marbles when we were little.
>
> During the week, she **would** get up at 7:00.

A Check the appropriate column to indicate whether the sentence refers to an action in the past or in the present.

	Past	Present
1. We always walk to school together.		✓
2. We used to spend every summer at the lake.		
3. We would stay in a cabin in the woods.		
4. I love looking at the stars in the sky.		
5. My parents used to have a lot of fun.		
6. Sometimes I just swim in the stream.		
7. There was a river where we would fish.		

> **In French** To tell what things were like or what used to happen repeatedly in the past, you use the **imparfait.** To form the **imparfait,** drop the **-ons** ending from the present-tense **nous** form and add the following endings.
>
> | | **parler** | **finir** | **vendre** |
> |---|---|---|---|
> | je | parlais | finissais | vendais |
> | tu | parlais | finissais | vendais |
> | il/elle/on | parlait | finissait | vendait |
> | nous | parlions | finissions | vendions |
> | vous | parliez | finissiez | vendiez |
> | ils/elles | parlaient | finissaient | vendaient |
>
> Verbs like **manger** and **commencer** that have a spelling change in the present-tense **nous** form have the same spelling change before **imparfait** endings that begin with **-a.**
>
> nous mang**e**ons → je mang**e**ais, BUT nous **mangions, vous** mang**iez**
>
> nous commen**ç**ons → tu commen**ç**ais, BUT nous **commencions, vous commenciez**
>
> All verbs are regular in the **imparfait** except **être,** which uses **ét-** as the imperfect stem.
>
> j'**étais,** tu **étais,** il/elle/on **était,** nous **étions,** vous **étiez,** ils/elles **étaient**

THE IMPARFAIT

B Check the appropriate column to indicate whether the sentence refers to an action in the past or in the present.

	Past	Present
1. Je travaillais le samedi.	✓	
2. Nous faisions souvent du ski en hiver.		
3. Tu promènes ton chien tous les jours?		
4. Caroline avait soif.		
5. Il fait froid.		
6. Vous étiez très fatigués.		
7. On allait au cinéma le vendredi.		

C Complete each sentence with the correct imparfait verb ending.

1. Je lis__ais____ des bandes dessinées.

2. Nous all_____ au supermarché le dimanche.

3. Bruno et Sylvie habit_____ à la campagne.

4. Tu promen_____ ton chien après l'école?

5. Quand j'ét_____ petit, je mange_____ des escargots.

6. Ma sœur sort_____ la poubelle le vendredi.

7. Mes frères et moi, nous voul_____ toujours nager dans le lac.

D Complete the following paragraph with the imparfait of the verbs in parentheses.

Quand j'_____ (avoir) six ans, ma famille et moi, nous

_____ (habiter) à la campagne. Nous

n'_____ (avoir) pas beaucoup d'argent mais nous

_____ (être) heureux. J'_____ (aimer)

grimper aux arbres et ma petite sœur _____ (jouer) toujours

avec les animaux. Mes parents _____ (travailler) au marché

le samedi. Ils _____ (vendre) des légumes et des œufs.

E Compare the verbs in the sentences below. Explain why their stems are different.

Je commençais à parler.   **Nous commencions à parler.**

_____

_____

_____

The passé composé and the imparfait CHAPITRE 6

> **In English** There are several ways to talk about the past in English. The following verb forms are usually used to describe completed events that occurred in the past.
>
> We **played** tennis.   We **did play** tennis.   We **have played** tennis.
>
> To describe actions that were ongoing in the past or to tell what used to happen, you can use **was** or **were** along with the **-ing** form of a verb, or you can use the helping verb **used to**.
>
> We **were playing** tennis.   We **used to play** tennis.

A Check the appropriate column to indicate whether the sentence describes a completed event in the past or something that was an ongoing activity or condition in the past.

	Completed event	Ongoing event or condition
1. Brian went to the store, didn't he?	✓	
2. We used to have so much fun!		
3. Did you hear the phone ring?		
4. Joanie was watching TV last night.		
5. It was cold and rainy.		
6. I finally made my decision.		
7. It used to rain every afternoon.		

> **In French** To talk about the past, you can use the **passé composé** and the **imparfait**. Use the **passé composé** to describe completed events in the past or tell what someone did in a set period of time.
>
> Une fois, j'**ai fait** un château de sable incroyable!
>
> Nous **avons pris** le petit-déjeuner à 7h.
>
> Use the **imparfait** to tell how things were or what used to happen repeatedly.
>
> Quand j'**étais** jeune, nous **allions** à la plage chaque été.
>
> Ils **jouaient** aux billes tous les jours.
>
> You can also use the **imparfait** to describe people and things in the past.
>
> Il **faisait** très beau. Il y **avait** beaucoup de fleurs.
>
> Anaïs **était** toujours heureuse.

THE PASSÉ COMPOSÉ AND THE IMPARFAIT   CHAPITRE **6**

B Check the appropriate column to indicate whether the sentence describes a completed event in the past or something that was an ongoing activity or condition in the past.

	Completed event	Ongoing event or condition
1. Il faisait toujours beau le matin.		✓
2. Jean était jeune et sportif.		
3. J'allais au café avec mes copains.		
4. Je n'ai pas fait la vaisselle hier soir.		
5. David a pris le bus.		
6. Odile a eu une bonne note en maths.		
7. Elles étaient occupées cette semaine.		

C Complete the following sentences with the imparfait or the passé composé of the verbs in parentheses.

1. Ce matin, il _____**est allé**_____ chez ses grands-parents. (aller)

2. Normalement, elle _____ de bonnes idées. (avoir)

3. Il _____ toujours chaud en été. (faire)

4. D'abord, nous _____ le train. (prendre)

5. De temps en temps, Patricia _____ en retard. (arriver)

6. Vous _____ souvent au cirque? (aller)

7. Nous jouions aux dames quand tu _____. (téléphoner)

8. Quand Henri _____ jeune, il
_____ jouer au train électrique. (être, aimer)

D Depending on the context, the English past tense can be equivalent to the French imparfait or passé composé. Tell which tense you would use to translate these sentences. Explain your choice.

1. I wrote letters to my cousins yesterday.

_____

_____

2. When I was young, I wrote letters to my cousins every month.

_____

_____

_____

The comparative with adjectives and nouns   CHAPITRE **6**

In English To say that an object or person has more, less, or the same amount of a characteristic as another object or person, you use the **comparative**. To make comparisons with adjectives, you can use the expressions **more... than, less... than,** and **as... as.**

My book is **more** interesting **than** yours.
Timmy is **less** impatient **than** Jeremy.
Our class is **as** difficult **as** theirs.

When the adjective has only one or two syllables, instead of using **more,** you add the suffix **-er.**

Frances is **taller than** Jim.

To make comparisons with nouns, you can use **more... than, fewer... than, less... than, as much... as,** or **as many... as.**

I have **more** books **than** you.
Timmy has **fewer** games **than** Jeremy.
Our class has **as much** homework **as** theirs.

A Underline the comparative phrases in the following sentences. Then indicate whether the sentences are using adjectives or nouns to make a comparison.

1. My suitcase is <u>heavier than</u> yours.	adjectives	nouns
2. This poster is as colorful as that one.	adjectives	nouns
3. John ate as much pizza as Rachid.	adjectives	nouns
4. A boulevard is wider than a street.	adjectives	nouns
5. There are fewer houses than here.	adjectives	nouns
6. Are movies less interesting than books?	adjectives	nouns

In French To make comparisons with adjectives, you can use **plus... que, moins... que,** or **aussi... que.** Remember to make the adjective agree with the noun in number and gender. With **c'est,** there is no agreement.

La ville est **plus** bruyant<u>e</u> **que** la campagne.
Les cochons sont **moins** grand<u>s</u> **que** les vaches.
La ville? C'est **aussi** intéressant **que** la campagne.

To make comparisons with nouns, use **plus de... que, moins de... que,** or **autant de... que.**

Il y a **plus** d'arbres **que** dans la ville.
Nous avons **moins** de vaches **que** vous.
J'ai **autant** d'amis **que** Marcelle.

THE COMPARATIVE WITH ADJECTIVES AND NOUNS   CHAPITRE **6**

B Underline the comparative phrases in the following sentences. Then indicate whether the sentences are using adjectives or nouns to make a comparison.

1. Julie est <u>moins courageuse que</u> Chloé. | adjectives | nouns

2. Il y a plus d'animaux qu'en ville.   adjectives   nouns

3. L'histoire, c'est plus intéressant que les maths.   adjectives   nouns

4. J'ai autant de livres que Michèle.   adjectives   nouns

5. Les rues sont plus propres qu'à New York.   adjectives   nouns

6. Ma vie est aussi stressante qu'à Paris.   adjectives   nouns

C Write comparative sentences using the given clues.

1. la prairie / = beau / la montagne

   La prairie est aussi belle que la montagne.

2. le village / + tranquille / la ville

   _____

3. les chèvres / – gros / les chevaux

   _____

4. l'eau ici / = propre / à la campagne

   _____

5. les cochons / + sale / les canards

   _____

6. les bicyclettes / = dangereux / les patins

   _____

D Complete the following comparatives according to your own experiences and opinions.

1. Les poules sont _____ mignonnes _____ les lapins.

2. À la ferme, il y a _____ moutons _____ d'ânes.

3. On a _____ théâtres _____ de cinémas.

4. Le musée d'art reçoit _____ visiteurs _____ le musée d'histoire.

5. Les chats sont _____ marrants _____ les chiens.

6. J'ai _____ CD _____ mes amis.

7. Faire un pique-nique, c'est _____ ennuyeux _____ faire les magasins.

Holt French 2   92   Grammar Tutor

The superlative with adjectives CHAPITRE 6

In English Superlatives are used to single out something as *the most* or *the least*. To form the superlatives of most adjectives of one or two syllables, use the definite article the before the adjective and the suffix -est at the end of the adjective. For longer adjectives, use the formula the most + *adjective*. The formula the least + *adjective* is used for all adjectives to indicate the least of a quality.

> That's the greatest story I've ever heard.
> This is the most entertaining show!
> This chair is the least comfortable of them all.

A Underline the superlative phrases in the following sentences.

1. Frieda is <u>the kindest</u> person I know.

2. It is Paul who writes the most beautiful letters.

3. Of all my friends, Jack is the most talkative.

4. Barbara is the least timid among all of us.

5. Rowena is the smartest girl in the class.

6. The snake is the least appealing animal I can imagine.

In French Superlatives serve the same purpose as in English. If an adjective usually precedes the noun, use the following formula. Notice that both articles and adjectives agree in gender and number with the noun.

> le/la/l'/les + plus/moins + *adjective* + de...

> Paris est <u>la plus grande</u> ville de France.

If an adjective usually follows the noun, use two definite articles: one before the noun and another before plus or moins.

> C'est <u>la</u> ville <u>la</u> plus intéressante de la région.

B Underline the superlative phrases in the following sentences.

1. François est <u>le plus grand de</u> mes amis.

2. Amélie est la fille la plus créative de notre famille.

3. Dorothée est l'élève la moins préparée de la classe.

4. Les Salines est la plus belle plage du monde.

5. Chez Yves est le magasin le plus élégant du pays.

6. Où se trouve le restaurant le plus cher du quartier?

THE SUPERLATIVE WITH ADJECTIVES

C Unscramble the following words to form superlative sentences.

1. Le TGV / de / plus / train / le / France / rapide / est / le

   Le TGV est le train le plus rapide de France.

2. La chimie / moins / facile / la / du / est / classe / la / lycée

   _____

3. C'est / moins / du / ville / la / la / intéressante / pays

   _____

4. Vous / la / plus / avez / jolie / de / la / maison / rue

   _____

5. C'est / plus / de / église / vieille / la / ville / la

   _____

6. J'ai / moins / acheté / magasin / cher / le / du / anorak / l'

   _____

D Rewrite the following sentences to single out the students at school as the most or the least.

1. Louise est très généreuse.

   Louise est l'élève la plus généreuse de l'école.

2. Lise est très intelligente.

   _____

3. Jérôme n'est pas obéissant.

   _____

4. Jacques est très fort.

   _____

5. Anne-Marie est très gentille.

   _____

6. Olivia n'est pas sérieuse.

   _____

7. Jean-Paul n'est pas sportif.

   _____

The passé composé and the imparfait   CHAPITRE 7

> **In English** The **simple past** is used to describe actions or states that began, ended, or were going on in the past, for a sequence of events, or for reactions.
>
> | | |
> |---|---|
> | I **saw** that movie and I **liked** it. | *(end of action, reaction)* |
> | I **got up**, **ate** breakfast, and **went** to school. | *(sequence of events)* |
> | Back then things **cost** less, so we **were** happier. | *(ongoing states)* |
>
> To describe actions that were ongoing at a certain time, you can use the **past progressive**. The simple past can then be used to interrupt the ongoing action. To say what you did habitually in the past, you can use the formula: **used to + infinitive**
>
> | | |
> |---|---|
> | At 7 P.M., I **was studying**. | *(ongoing action)* |
> | We **were jogging** when it suddenly **hailed**. | *(ongoing action, interruption)* |
> | I **used to watch** cartoons every Saturday. | *(habitual action)* |

A Circle the verb(s) in each sentence. Then write what each verb is expressing.

1. Travis used to climb trees as a kid.   ____habitual action____

2. I read that book and it made me cry.   _____

3. We played soccer, talked, and went home.   _____

4. Ian used to climb a different hill every month.   _____

5. You were sleeping when the fire alarm rang.   _____

6. Samantha had a big dog when she was a kid.   _____

7. We ignored Frankie so he got angry.   _____

> **In French** When talking about these aspects of the past, use the **imparfait**:
>
> | | |
> |---|---|
> | 1. to give background information | C'était l'hiver et il faisait froid. |
> | 2. to say what was going on | Michel dormait quand nous sommes arrivés. |
> | 3. for habitual actions in the past, often after expressions like souvent, tous les jours, d'habitude | Je jouais souvent avec mes poupées. |
>
> Use the **passé composé**:
>
> | | |
> |---|---|
> | 1. to say what happened on a specific occasion | Je suis allé au marché à 11h. |
> | 2. to show a sequence of events, often with expressions like d'abord and ensuite. | D'abord, il a pris une douche et ensuite, il s'est habillé. |
> | 3. to talk about a change or a reaction to something, often with expressions like soudain, à ce moment-là, au moment où | Nous jouions au tennis au moment où il a commencé à neiger. |

THE PASSÉ COMPOSÉ AND THE IMPARFAIT CHAPITRE **7**

B Circle the verb(s) in each sentence. Then write whether each verb is in the **passé composé** (PC) or the **imparfait** (I).

1. J'ai lu ce livre et j'ai pleuré. _____PC, PC_____

2. Louise avait dix ans et elle habitait à Paris. _____

3. On a couru, on s'est baigné et on a dîné. _____

4. D'habitude, nous allions à la plage. _____

5. Je dormais quand soudain je suis tombé. _____

6. Il faisait beau. Les oiseaux chantaient. _____

7. Nous sommes rentrés chez nous à minuit. _____

C Complete the following paragraph with the **passé composé** or the **imparfait** of the verbs in parentheses.

Je/J'_____ (passer) un très bon week-end! Dimanche,

c'_____ (être) mon anniversaire. Quand

je/j'_____ (être) petite, on _____

(aller) toujours au parc zoologique pour mon anniversaire. Pas cette année.

Dimanche matin, mes parents _____ (préparer) un petit-

déjeuner délicieux. Ensuite, nous _____ (partir) en voiture

pour la montagne. Il _____ (faire) beau. Nous

_____ (faire) du ski toute la journée. Quand nous

_____ (rentrer), nous _____ (être)

fatigués mais heureux. Plus tard, pendant que je _____

(se mettre) en pyjama, je/j' _____ (entendre) quelqu'un à la

porte. C'_____ (être) ma meilleure amie. Elle

_____ (apporter) un gros gâteau d'anniversaire!

D Translate the following sentences. Circle the words that affected your choice of **passé composé** or **imparfait**.

1. First, we went fishing.

_____

2. We usually went fishing.

_____

Verbs with être or avoir in the passé composé CHAPITRE 7

> **In English** You've learned that a **direct object** is a person or thing that receives the action of the verb. In the following sentence, *the tent* is the direct object because it answers the question, *what* have we pitched?
>
> We have just pitched <u>the tent</u>.
>
> In English, having a direct object doesn't affect the verb. In the present perfect, for instance, the helping verb is always a form of **to have** and the past participle stays the same, whether there is a direct object or not.
>
> Pete **has left** <u>the house</u>.
> Pete **has left** and won't come back.

A Circle the verbs and underline the direct objects.

1. Of course we have finished our homework!
2. Who has brought in the milk?
3. Doreen hasn't taken her driving test.
4. We have forgotten our canteens!
5. Which movies have you seen lately?
6. Scott hasn't published his poems.
7. I haven't entered the data yet.
8. The bellhop has taken our luggage to the room.

> **In French** Some verbs like **sortir, passer, monter,** and **descendre** are usually conjugated with **être** in the **passé composé.** When this is the case, the past participle agrees with the subject.
>
> Elle **est sortie** de la maison. Ensuite, ils **sont montés** dans la voiture.
>
> However, when these verbs have a **direct object,** they use **avoir** as the helping verb in the **passé composé.** When the helping verb is a form of **avoir,** the past participle does not agree with the direct object unless the direct object comes before the verb.
>
> —Elle **a sorti** <u>la tente</u> de son sac?
> —Oui, elle **l'a sortie.**
> —Elles **ont sorti** <u>les lanternes</u> de la voiture?
> —Oui, elles <u>les</u> **ont sorties.**

VERBS WITH ÊTRE OR AVOIR IN THE PASSÉ COMPOSÉ CHAPITRE **7**

B Circle the verbs and underline the direct objects.

1. Ils ont passé une année en France.

2. Vous avez monté nos bagages?

3. Nous les avons descendus ce matin.

4. J'ai sorti mes lunettes de mon sac.

5. Est-ce qu'elle te l'a passée?

6. Nous avons descendu les tentes de la voiture.

7. Bien sûr, je les ai déjà montés.

C Write the correct endings of the past participles in the sentences below. If no change is needed, write an X in the space provided.

1. Thérèse est sorti__e___ de sa maison.

2. Michel et moi, nous sommes monté_____ au troisième étage.

3. Ils ont monté_____ les tentes près du lac.

4. Mme Kléber, vous êtes descendu_____ par l'escalier?

5. Les allumettes? Elle nous les a passé_____.

6. Elles ont monté_____ les journaux.

7. Ma cousine a descendu_____ sa valise.

D Complete the following paragraph with the **passé composé** of the verbs in parentheses.

Mme Vallée _____ (sortir) sa voiture du garage de bonne

heure. Ensuite, elle _____ (descendre) la rue Marbeuf.

Comme d'habitude, elle _____ (passer) chez Mme Allard.

À 8 heures du matin, Mme Vallée et Mme Allard _____

(descendre) l'escalier de l'immeuble. Elles _____ (sortir)

par la porte d'entrée et elles _____ (monter) dans la voiture.

Vingt minutes plus tard, elles _____ (arriver) au lac.

Ensuite, les deux amies _____ (sortir) deux fauteuils pliants.

Et la crème solaire? Elles l'_____ (sortir) aussi.

The future

In English The **future tense** is used to talk about actions or events that are yet to take place. The future tense is formed by placing the helping word **will** before the base form of the verb.

My children **will drive** electric cars.
The people of the future **will** only **use** solar energy.

To make a sentence in the future tense negative, you add **not** after **will**. **Will not** can combine to form the contraction **won't**.

She **will not forget** what happened.
She **won't forget** what happened.

A In each of the following sentences, circle the helping verbs and underline the main verbs.

1. We |will| <u>do</u> the dishes after the movie.

2. Dad will be pleased with your grades.

3. We won't stay here past Saturday.

4. The couple will have a baby this fall.

5. Martin won't hesitate to help us.

6. Our team will win the game.

In French As in English, the **future tense** is used to talk about what will happen in the future. The future tense is usually formed by adding the following endings to an infinitive: **-ai, -as, -a, -ons, -ez, -ont.** In the case of **-re** verbs, the final **-e** is dropped before adding the future tense endings.

	parler	**finir**	**vendre**
je	parlerai	finirai	vendrai
tu	parleras	finiras	vendras
il/elle/on	parlera	finira	vendra
nous	parlerons	finirons	vendrons
vous	parlerez	finirez	vendrez
ils/elles	parleront	finiront	vendront

Many of the irregular present-tense verbs are regular in the future.

boire	Je **boirai** dès que possible.
connaître	Ce soir, tu **connaîtras** mes parents.
dire	Jacques nous **dira** quelque chose.
mettre	Nous la **mettrons** sur la table.
ouvrir	À quelle heure est-ce que vous **ouvrirez** le magasin?
suivre	Elles **suivront** le flamant rose.

THE FUTURE   CHAPITRE **7**

B In each of the following sentences, underline the stems of the verbs and circle the future endings.

1. Les amis se baigneront après le petit-déjeuner.

2. Quand nous arriverons au café, nous boirons.

3. Christine attrapera un grand poisson.

4. Je voyagerai beaucoup l'été prochain.

5. La prochaine fois, tu emporteras une lampe de poche.

6. Vous camperez en Bretagne.

C The sentences below tell what's going to happen using **aller** and an infinitive. Rewrite them to tell what will happen using the future tense.

1. Je ne vais pas travailler aujourd'hui.

   Je ne travaillerai pas aujourd'hui. _____

2. Nous allons choisir une université.

   _____

3. Tu vas écrire une lettre à une école technique.

   _____

4. Vous allez vivre dans une ferme.

   _____

5. Tes enfants vont grimper aux arbres.

   _____

6. Tout le monde va se coucher de bonne heure.

   _____

D Fill in the left chart with the forms of **avoir** in the present tense. Fill in the right chart with the endings of the future tense. Compare the two charts. How might the similarities and differences help you remember how to talk about the future?

AVOIR		LE FUTUR	
j'_____	nous _____	je jouer_____	nous jouer_____
tu _____	vous _____	tu jouer_____	vous jouer_____
il _____	ils _____	il jouer_____	ils jouer_____

_____

_____

_____

The future (irregular verbs)

In English Some verb forms are **irregular** in the past tense, such as *make/made*, *catch/caught*, *find/found*, *sit/sat*. Since the future tense is formed by adding **will** before the base form of the verb, there are no irregular verbs in the future tense.

This morning we made pancakes and tomorrow we **will make** french toast.

We **will** never **catch** as large a fish as the one we caught today.

A Write the future tense of the verbs that are underlined.

1. We <u>had</u> many friends all over the world.   will have

2. You <u>saw</u> the pyramids in Egypt.

3. My friends <u>had</u> fun in the cruise ship.

4. Who <u>gave</u> me a snow globe?

5. I <u>bought</u> many souvenirs.

6. We <u>drove</u> all around the island.

7. My brother <u>took</u> many digital pictures.

8. We <u>were</u> amazed by the sights.

In French Some verbs are **irregular** in the future tense. Their endings are regular (**-ai**, **-as**, **-a**, **-ons**, **-ez**, **-ont**) but they have an irregular stem.

aller:	**ir-**	J'**irai** à Paris l'été prochain.
avoir:	**aur-**	Tu **auras** une nouvelle voiture.
devoir:	**devr-**	Elle **devra** étudier.
être:	**ser-**	Il **sera** très heureux.
faire:	**fer-**	Nous **ferons** du ski tout l'hiver.
pouvoir:	**pourr-**	Vous **pourrez** nager au lac.
venir:	**viendr-**	Mes cousins **viendront** samedi.
voir:	**verr-**	Tu **verras** des arbres et des animaux.
vouloir:	**voudr-**	Je **voudrai** voyager.

Verbs with spelling changes in the present tense, such as **appeler** and **acheter**, change in all forms of the future tense.

J'**achèterai** une carte téléphonique.

Nous t'**appellerons** tous les jours.

THE FUTURE (IRREGULAR VERBS)

B Write the infinitive forms of the verbs that are underlined.

1. Nous <u>verrons</u> nos grands-parents. _____ **voir** _____

2. Thomas <u>fera</u> un long voyage. _____

3. Vous <u>devrez</u> aller à la campagne. _____

4. Tu <u>seras</u> très content là-bas. _____

5. Je <u>viendrai</u> vous voir souvent. _____

6. Elles n'<u>iront</u> pas à la rivière. _____

7. Nous <u>pourrons</u> prendre le bus. _____

C Complete the following sentences with the future tense of the verbs in parentheses.

1. La semaine prochaine, nous _____ **irons** _____ à la campagne. (aller)

2. Nous _____ beaucoup d'oiseaux. (voir)

3. J'_____ à la pêche. (aller)

4. Il _____ beau, je pense. (faire)

5. Mon frère _____ grimper aux arbes. (vouloir)

6. Mes parents _____ que c'est trop dangereux. (dire)

7. Tu _____ voir les photos quand nous
_____. (pouvoir, revenir)

D Answer each question saying the person will do it tomorrow.

1. Lucie ne revient pas aujourd'hui?

   Non, elle reviendra demain. _____

2. Tu ne vas pas au lycée aujourd'hui?

   _____

3. Madame, vous ne faites pas les magasins aujourd'hui?

   _____

4. Ton ami ne veut pas jouer avec toi aujourd'hui?

   _____

5. Les élèves ne voient pas le film aujourd'hui?

   _____

6. Je ne dois pas l'acheter aujourd'hui?

   _____

The subjunctive

In English Verbs may be in one of three moods: **indicative, imperative,** or **subjunctive.** Most verbs are in the **indicative mood** which is used to make statements of fact. The **imperative mood** is used to make commands.

> *Indicative:* Dorothy **eats** like a bird.
> *Imperative:* **Eat** your vegetables!

The **subjunctive mood** is not often used in English. It is sometimes used in formal situations, as in subordinate clauses following an expression of necessity.

> It is important that he **read** this book. *(You can tell from the form **he read** that the verb is not in the indicative mood, which would be **he reads**.)*

A Check the appropriate column to indicate whether the mood of the underlined verb is in the indicative or subjunctive mood.

	Indicative	Subjunctive
1. La Paz <u>is</u> the world's highest capital city.	✓	
2. It is necessary that he <u>rehearse</u> now.		
3. It is important that your sister <u>listen</u>.		
4. I think your brother <u>wants</u> to come with us.		
5. It is important that he <u>see</u> a doctor.		
6. Daisy <u>speaks</u> three languages.		

In French Verbs may also be in the indicative, imperative, or subjunctive mood. Unlike in English, the **subjunctive mood** is frequently used in French. One of its uses is to express necessity, following phrases such as **il faut que** and **il est important que.**

> **Il faut que** vous **achetiez** des médicaments.

To form the subjunctive of most verbs, drop the **-ent** ending from the present-tense **ils** form and add these endings: **-e, -es, -e, -ions, -iez, -ent.**

	parl~~ent~~	finiss~~ent~~	vend~~ent~~
que je	parle	finisse	vende
que tu	parles	finisses	vendes
qu'il/elle/on	parle	finisse	vende
que nous	parlions	finissions	vendions
que vous	parliez	finissez	vendiez
qu'ils/elles	parlent	finissent	vendent

Verbs, such as **boire, devoir, prendre, venir,** and **voir,** that have stem changes in the present indicative have the same changes in the subjunctive.

Indicative: ils **boivent,** nous **buvons**   *Subjunctive:* que je **boive,** que nous **buvions**
Indicative: ils **prennent,** vous **prenez**   *Subjunctive:* qu'il **prenne,** que vous **preniez**
Indicative: ils **voient,** vous **voyez**   *Subjunctive:* que tu **voies,** que vous **voyiez**

THE SUBJUNCTIVE

B Check the appropriate column to indicate whether the mood of the underlined verb is in the indicative or subjunctive.

	Indicative	Subjunctive
1. Il faut que tu <u>sortes</u> le chien.		✓
2. Au petit-déjeuner, je <u>prends</u> des céréales.		
3. Il faut qu'elle <u>vienne</u> tout de suite.		
4. Il est important que je <u>parle</u> avec toi.		
5. Nous <u>devons</u> faire nos devoirs.		
6. Il faut que tu <u>dormes</u> beaucoup.		

In French The forms of the following verbs are irregular in the subjunctive.

	aller	**être**	**avoir**	**faire**
que je/j'	aille	sois	aie	fasse
que tu	ailles	sois	aies	fasses
qu'il/elle/on	aille	soit	ait	fasse
que nous	allions	soyons	ayons	fassions
que vous	alliez	soyez	ayez	fassiez
qu'ils/elles	aillent	soient	aient	fassent

Il faut que j'aille chez le docteur.

C Complete each of the following sentences with the correct subjunctive form of the verb in parentheses.

1. Il faut que nous _____**nous levions**_____ de bonne heure. (se lever)

2. Il est important qu'on _____ le petit-déjeuner tous les jours. (prendre)

3. Marc, il faut que tu _____ chez le docteur. (aller)

4. Il faut que j' _____ ce soir. (étudier)

5. Il est nécessaire que tu _____ en forme. (être)

6. Il est important qu'ils _____ les médicaments. (acheter)

7. Simone et Sophie, il faut que vous _____ une trousse de premiers soins. (avoir)

8. Il est important que nous _____ de la crème solaire. (mettre)

9. Il faut que Mamie _____ patiente. (être)

10. Allez les enfants, il faut que vous _____ du lait. (boire)

Uses of the subjunctive

CHAPITRE **8**

> **In English** Whereas the indicative mood is used to express facts, the **subjunctive mood** is used to express more subjective feelings. It sometimes follows expressions of hope, necessity, and importance.
>
>   His parents <u>prefer that</u> he **stay** home.
>   I <u>recommend that</u> she **exercise** more.
>   The teacher <u>demands that</u> he **study** more.

A Underline the verb or expression of hope, necessity, or importance and circle the verb that is in the subjunctive mood.

1. I <u>wish</u> that your friend [were] nicer to me.

2. It is important that you be on time.

3. Lauren wishes that she were taller.

4. I recommend that he bring a compass.

5. They prefer that Jack work the late shift.

6. Can the doctor demand that her patient undergo surgery?

> **In French** The **subjunctive mood** is also used to express subjective feelings. It commonly follows expressions of necessity, requests or wishes, and certain emotions.
>
>   <u>Il faut que</u> je **fasse** mes devoirs.
>   <u>Il est important que</u> nous **ayons** un régime équilibré.
>   <u>Il est nécessaire que</u> tu m'**aides**.
>   <u>Je veux qu</u>'ils **viennent** à ma boum.
>   <u>Nous sommes contentes que</u> tu **sois** en bonne santé.
>   <u>Tu es triste que</u> je **parte**?
>   <u>Il est bon</u> que vous **parliez** plusieurs langues.

B Underline the expression of necessity, the wish, or the emotion and circle the verb that is in the subjunctive mood

1. <u>Il est bon que</u> nous [mangions] beaucoup de légumes.

2. Je suis contente que tu aimes ce livre.

3. Il est nécessaire que vous lui disiez la vérité.

4. Mes parents veulent que j'aille à l'université.

5. Il faut que nous rentrions à la maison.

6. Je suis triste que tu sois malade.

USES OF THE SUBJUNCTIVE

C Complete each sentence with an appropriate expression from the box.

Il est bon que	Je veux que	Il faut que
Je suis triste que	Je ne veux pas que	

1. _____Je veux que_____ nous invitions les frères Pépin.

2. Il n'y a pas de boissons. _____ tu en achètes.

3. _____ Claire ne vienne pas. C'est dommage!

4. _____ tes cousins viennent. Ils sont pénibles!

5. Nous serons beaucoup ce soir. _____ nous ayons un gros gâteau.

D Complete the following paragraph with the correct forms of the verbs in parentheses. Choose between the **subjunctive** or the **indicative**.

Chère Corinne,

Mes parents et moi, nous _____ (être) en bonne santé. Je suis triste que tu ne _____ (venir) pas nous voir pendant les vacances. Je sais que tu _____ (être) toujours occupée mais je veux que tu _____ (changer) d'avis. Il faut que nous nous _____ (voir)! Dis que tu viendras!

Ton amie,
Laetitia

E Complete each opinion or request logically.

1. Madame, vous êtes fatiguée. Il est important que

_____

_____

2. Mes amis regardent la télé tout le temps. Je veux que

_____

_____

3. Tu as mal aux dents? Il faut que tu

_____

_____

4. Je me suis coupé le doigt. Il est nécessaire que

_____

_____

The conditional

> **In English** The **conditional** is used to express what would happen or what someone would do if certain conditions existed. The conditional is formed by adding **would** before the base form of the verb.
>
> In that situation, I **would take** public transportation.
> We **would** really **like** to go to Africa.

A Underline the verbs that are in the conditional.

1. She <u>would help</u> you if you asked her.
2. Joe would buy this bike if it were less expensive.
3. Would you turn in your own girlfriend to the principal?
4. In that situation, I would ask my family's advice.
5. I would love to meet your friends.
6. He would never go on a safari.
7. You would look handsome in that suit.

> **In French** The **conditional** is used to express what would happen. The conditional is formed by adding the imperfect endings to the stem of the future tense. As you might recall, most future stems are the infinitive forms of the verb. For **-re** verbs, the final **-e** is dropped before adding the endings.
>
> | | **parler** | **finir** | **vendre** |
> |---|---|---|---|
> | je | parlerais | finirais | vendrais |
> | tu | parlerais | finirais | vendrais |
> | il/elle/on | parlerait | finirait | vendrait |
> | nous | parlerions | finirions | vendrions |
> | vous | parleriez | finiriez | vendriez |
> | ils/elles | parleraient | finiraient | vendraient |
>
> Since the conditional shares the same stems as the future, the same spelling changes that appear in the future appear in the conditional.
>
> | | | |
> |---|---|---|
> | aller: **ir-** | être: **ser-** | venir: **viendr-** |
> | avoir: **aur-** | faire: **fer-** | voir: **verr-** |
> | devoir: **devr-** | pouvoir: **pourr-** | vouloir: **voudr-** |
>
> Tu **devrais** bien manger. Tu **pourrais** aussi prendre des vitamines.

B Underline the verbs that are in the conditional.

1. S'il faisait beau, je <u>jouerais</u> au tennis.

2. Tu pourrais me passer du sel?

3. J'aimerais être dentiste.

4. Ça serait super si tu venais cet été.

5. Est-ce que vous voudriez visiter le musée d'art?

6. Qu'est-ce que tu ferais à ma place?

7. Tu devrais faire du yoga tous les jours.

C Use the elements given to write complete conditional sentences, saying what would happen if you were school president.

1. je / écouter / les élèves et les professeurs

    J'écouterais les élèves et les professeurs.

2. je / vouloir organiser / un bal

    _____

3. tous les élèves / avoir / un ordinateur

    _____

4. je / parler / avec le directeur

    _____

5. nous / pouvoir sortir / plus tôt

    _____

6. la classe de français / faire / un voyage en France

    _____

7. je / être / un bon président

    _____

D Imagine you won a million dollars. Write three sentences in French saying what you would do. Circle any verbs with an irregular stem.

    _____

    _____

    _____

    _____

Si clauses

> **In English** To say what someone would do if things were different, you use an **if** clause that expresses a contrary-to-fact situation, such as **if I were, if we had, if they could,** followed by a **result** clause. The **if** clause contains a verb in the past subjunctive, and the **result** clause is in the conditional. Either clause can come first.
>
> If you *wanted* to be in good health, you **would exercise.**
> I **would buy** vegetables if I *were* you.

A In the following sentences, underline the verbs that are in the conditional. Circle any verbs in the past.

1. If I had the money, I would buy the latest mobile phone.

2. I would help you if I had the time.

3. If Gisela spoke French, she would live in France.

4. If you wanted to lose weight, you would exercise more.

5. If I were you, I would call your parents.

6. Peter would know more about current events if he read the newspaper.

> **In French** A sentence can also can have an **if** clause and a **result** clause. The **if** clause begins with **si** and is in the **imparfait**. The **result** clause is in the **conditional**. As in English, either clause can come first.
>
> Si tu *voulais* être en bonne santé, tu **ferais** de l'exercice.
> J'**achèterais** des légumes si j'*étais* à ta place.
>
> You can also use **si + on + imparfait** to invite someone to do something.
> Si on faisait de l'exercice?   *(How about exercising?)*

B In the following sentences, underline the verbs that are in the conditional. Circle any verbs in the imperfect.

1. Mes cousins viendraient plus souvent si on avait une grande maison.

2. Si tu voulais, tu pourrais jouer aux cartes avec nous.

3. Ça serait magnifique si nous gagnions.

4. J'aimerais bien l'inviter si je savais danser.

5. Si Henri pouvait, il irait à Dakar.

6. Si vous aviez un long week-end, vous auriez le temps de camper.

C Circle the verbs that correctly complete the following sentences.

1. Si j'(habitais / habiterais) au Mexique, je parlais / parlerais) espagnol.

2. Nous (cherchions / chercherions) un emploi si nous (voulions / voudrions) de l'argent.

3. Si mes parents (gagnaient / gagneraient) plus d'argent, nous (voyagions / voyagerions).

4. S'ils (avaient / auraient) un enfant, ils (avaient / auraient) beaucoup de responsabilités.

5. Je/J' (étais / serais) dans un groupe de rock si je (jouais / jouerais) de la guitare.

6. Si elle (allait / irait) voir le médecin, elle (arrêtait / arrêterait) de tousser.

7. Vous me (téléphoniez / téléphoneriez) si vous (vouliez / voudriez) me parler.

8. Si tu (comprenais / comprendrais) l'anglais, tu (pourrais / pouvais) lire cette lettre.

D Write five complete sentences, combining phrases from each column.

Si clause	Result clause
je / se sentir malade	faire un régime
tu / avoir mal à la tête	prendre des médicaments
nous / vouloir maigrir	devoir arrêter
je / être stressé(e)	être fort(s)
vous / fumer	aller chez le médecin
mes amis / faire de la musculation	écouter de la musique

1. Si je me sentais malade, j'irais chez le médecin. _____

2. _____

3. _____

4. _____

5. _____

6. _____

The relative pronouns qui, que, dont CHAPITRE **9**

In English Relative pronouns are words like *that, which, who,* or *whom* that are used to refer to something or someone that has been already mentioned.

He's the new student **who** joined the hockey team.

You can use relative pronouns to avoid two short, choppy sentences. A relative pronoun can join two pieces of information about a single topic into one sentence.

They liked the song. I sang the song. ⟶ They liked the song **that** I sang.

Relative pronouns can be the subject of a clause or a direct object within a clause. **Who** and **whom** refer to people.

Joe is the tennis player **who** won the match. (***who** is the subject of the clause*)
Sylvia is someone **whom** I admire. (***whom** is a direct object*)

That and **which** usually refer to things.

They played in the snow, **which** had begun to melt.
This is the book **that** I read.

In English, you can sometimes leave out the relative pronoun.

This is the book I read.

A Underline each relative pronoun. Indicate whether it is a subject or direct object, and whether it represents a person or thing.

	Subject	Object	Person	Thing
		✓	✓	

1. Linda is a friend <u>whom</u> I trust.
2. Billy read from a book that he wrote.
3. They gave me a toy that glows in the dark.
4. The bulb which was flickering burned out.
5. We visited Mrs. Franklin who is sick.

In French Relative pronouns also begin a clause and refer to someone or something previously mentioned. The relative pronouns **qui, que,** and **dont** are used for both people and things. **Qui** *(that, which, who)* is the subject of its clause and is followed by a verb.

C'est un film **qui** <u>est</u> basé sur une histoire vraie.

Que or **qu'** *(that, which, whom)* stands for the direct object of the clause. It is followed by a subject and a verb.

C'est un film **qu'**<u>on</u> <u>joue</u> au cinéma Rex.

Dont *(that, whom, whose)* replaces a prepositional phrase starting with **de**. It immediately follows the noun it represents.

C'est un film. Tout le monde parle **de ce film.**
C'est un film **dont** tout le monde parle.

THE RELATIVE PRONOUNS QUI, QUE, DONT   CHAPITRE 9

B Underline each relative pronoun. Indicate whether it is a subject or an object, and whether it represents a person or thing.

	Subject	Object	Person	Thing
		✓		✓
1. C'est un film que je n'aime pas.				
2. Louise est une amie qui est sincère.				
3. Elle est la dame que j'ai connue à Paris.				
4. C'est l'histoire d'une fille qui est pilote.				
5. C'est un auteur dont j'ai lu tous ses livres.				
6. Voici l'arbre qui est tombé sur sa maison.				
7. Je veux voir le film dont je t'ai parlé.				

C Complete the following sentences with **qui, que, qu'**, or **dont**.

1. La chanson _____qu'_____ il a chantée est très belle.

2. C'est une histoire _____ finit bien.

3. Le musée _____ je t'ai parlé est très intéressant.

4. Chris et Cécile sont les copains _____ j'ai rencontrés au cinéma.

5. Ça parle de deux jeunes filles _____ vont à Québec.

6. Le film _____ nous avons envie de voir passe au cinéma Max.

7. Maman parle à un monsieur _____ a fait le tour du monde.

8. Juliette Binoche est l'actrice _____ mon père préfère.

9. Le chien _____ ma sœur adore habite juste à côté.

10. Nous aimons les films _____ ont beaucoup de suspense.

D Read the sentence below. Why does the past participle **lues** end in **–es**?

Les bandes dessinées que j'ai lues ce matin sont drôles.

_____

_____

_____

Interrogative pronouns

In English The interrogative phrases **which one** and **which ones** are used in questions to refer to something that has been previously mentioned. In the following sentences, **which one** refers to <u>that car</u> and **which ones** refers to <u>my posters</u>.

—I like <u>that car</u>. —**Which one**?
—I'm giving away <u>my posters</u>. —**Which ones** do you want?

A In the following conversation, circle the interrogative phrases **which one** and **which ones**. Then underline the noun to which each phrase refers.

Nina	Hi, Paul. Do you want to catch a <u>movie</u>?
Paul	Which one? The new horror movie?
Nina	No, the one with those two comedians.
Paul	Two comedians? Which ones?
Nina	Those two guys that appear in a commercial together.
Paul	A commercial? Which one?
Nina	You know, the one with the new computer.
Paul	Oh, yeah. They're real funny. Where is the movie showing?
Nina	At the Plaza Theater and at the Gothic Theater. Which one do you prefer?
Paul	Let's go to the Plaza Theater!

In French **Interrogative pronouns** are pronouns that are used to ask questions that refer back to someone or something previously named. The interrogative pronoun **lequel** is used to ask *which one(s)*. The forms of this pronoun agree in gender and number with the nouns to which they refer .

	Masculine	**Feminine**
Singular	lequel	laquelle
Plural	lesquels	lesquelles

—J'aime <u>cette série</u>. —Laquelle?
—Il y a <u>un jeu</u> et <u>un soap</u> à la télé. Lequel préfères-tu regarder?

INTERROGATIVE PRONOUNS CHAPITRE **9**

B In the following conversation, circle the interrogative pronouns and underline the nouns to which they refer.

Maya Tu veux regarder un <u>film</u>?

Pierrot Lequel?

Maya Le nouveau film de guerre avec ton actrice préférée.

Pierrot Mon actrice préférée? Laquelle? Catherine Deneuve?

Maya Non. On la voit à la télé, tu sais, dans les émissions de télé.

Pierrot Lesquelles?

Maya Je ne sais pas! Mais alors, tu veux voir le film? Ça passe au deux cinémas près d'ici.

Pierrot Lesquels?

Maya Tu es impossible, Pierrot!

C Ask your friend which one(s) he's exactly talking about using a correct form of the interrogative pronoun **lequel**.

1. Le film m'intéresse. _____ **Lequel?** _____

2. Tu n'aimes pas l'actrice? _____

3. Tu as lu le roman? _____

4. Je veux écouter tes CD. _____

5. Mes amies viendront. _____

6. Tu as suivi la série? _____

7. As-tu vu le documentaire? _____

8. Je cherche mes bottes. _____

D Respond to the following statement with an interrogative pronoun. Then, explain in your own words how you knew which form of the pronoun to use. What words told you the number or gender of the noun to which the pronoun refers?

—Il est mignon, ce petit chat.

_____

_____

_____

_____

_____

Demonstrative pronouns

In English The **demonstrative** phrases *this one, that one, these,* and *those* are used in statements to refer to something that has been previously mentioned.

    —Which shoes are yours?

    —These.

We use *this one/that one* to refer to singular nouns and *these/those* to refer to plural nouns. *This one* and *these* are used to talk about things that are nearby, and *that one* and *those* for things that are farther away.

    —Which book do you recommend reading?

    —**This one** is more intriguing than **that one.**

A Underline the demonstrative phrases in the sentences below. Check the appropriate column to indicate whether they are singular or plural.

	Singular	Plural
1. <u>This one</u> is my favorite sitcom.	✓	
2. I really prefer that one.		
3. These are his favorite actors.		
4. Mary raved about that one.		
5. I thought those were great.		
6. Did you already listen to these?		
7. I never miss this one.		

In French **Demonstrative pronouns** are used to say *this one, that one, these,* or *those.* The forms agree in gender and number with the nouns they stand for.

    Tu aimes les feuilletons? **Celui** qu'on passe ce soir est super!

	Masculine	**Feminine**
Singular	celui	celle
Plural	ceux	celles

To distinguish *this one* from *that one,* and *these* from *those,* add **-ci** and **-là** to the pronoun. Use **-ci** for things that are nearby and **-là** for things that are farther away.

    Regarde les jeux qu'on passe à la télé. **Celui-ci** est bon, mais **celui-là** est ennuyeux.

DEMONSTRATIVE PRONOUNS

B Underline the demonstrative pronouns in the sentences below. Check the appropriate columns to indicate whether they are singular (S) or plural (P), and masculine (M) or feminine (F).

	S	P	M	F
1. Je prends <u>celui-là</u>.	✓		✓	
2. Tu n'aimes pas celles-là?				
3. Nous préférons celui qui passe à 20h.				
4. Pauline déteste ceux-là.				
5. Je ne regarde jamais ceux qui sont déprimants.				
6. Vous aimez celle-ci?				
7. Ceux-là sont très drôles!				

C Complete each sentence with the appropriate demonstrative pronoun.

1. Mes films préférés sont _____ceux_____ qui me font rire.

2. Ton jeu favori est _____ qui passe sur TF1?

3. La présentatrice dont je parle est _____ qui a les yeux verts.

4. Les bons documentaires sont _____ qui nous intéressent.

5. Ma chaîne préférée est _____ qui a les informations.

6. Les actrices que j'aime sont _____ qui font du théâtre.

7. Les reportages que je regarde sont _____ qui valent le coup.

D Respond to each question negatively, using an appropriate demonstrative pronoun with either -ci or -là.

1. Voulez-vous cette boîte de conserve-ci?

   Non, pas celle-ci. _____

2. Vous aimez ces décorations-là?

   _____

3. Vous avez suivi ce jeu-ci?

   _____

4. Vous voulez ces médicaments-ci?

   _____

5. Aimez-vous cette vedette-là?

   _____

Review of the subjunctive

In English The **subjunctive** mood is mostly used in formal English when we wish to express necessity or the importance of something.

>   It is important that we **find** our passports.

The subjunctive looks like the infinitive form of the verb. Notice that even for the third singular person, there is no final **-s**.

>   It is vital that he **arrive** on time.

The subjunctive form of the verb *to be* is **be** for all persons.

>   It is necessary that you **be** patient.

A Circle the correct form of the verb to complete each sentence.

   1. I recommend that he (visit / visits) Paris.

   2. I think that Paris (be / is) a beautiful city.

   3. It is important that your friend (make / makes) a hotel reservation.

   4. It's not necessary that you (be / are) with the tour group.

   5. It is obvious that the guide (know / knows) a lot about history.

   6. I've read that the museum (have / has) a great gift shop.

   7. It is especially important that everyone (have / has) a passport.

In French The **subjunctive** mood is used frequently. One of the most important uses of the subjunctive is to express necessity and obligation.

>   Il ne faut pas que tu **partes** à l'étranger sans passeport.
>   Il est nécessaire que tu **prennes** le métro.

The **nous** and **vous** subjunctive forms look the same as the **imparfait**.

>   Il faut pas que nous **partions** et que vous **restiez** ici.

All other forms are based on the present-tense **ils** form. Drop the **-ent** ending and add **-e** for **je**, **-es** for **tu**, **-e** for **il/elle/on**, and **-ent** for **ils/elles**.

>   ils viennent → que je **vienne**, que tu **viennes**, qu'on **vienne**, qu'elles **viennent**

Aller, **être**, **avoir**, and **faire** have irregular forms in the subjunctive.

>   avoir: **aille, ailles, aille, allions, alliez, aillent**
>   être: **sois, sois, soit, soyons, soyez, soient**
>   avoir: **aie, aies, ait, ayons, ayez, aient**
>   faire: **fasse, fasses, fasse, fassions, fassiez, fassent**

B Circle the correct form of the verb to complete each sentence.

1. Il faut que nous (allions / allons) au centre commercial.

2. Le magasin Passeport (ait / a) des valises à bon prix.

3. Il faut que j' (achète / achèterais) deux valises.

4. Il n'est pas nécessaire que les valises (soient / sont) grandes.

5. Je trouve que le prix (soit / est) plus important que la couleur.

6. Il n'est pas nécessaire que mes parents y (alliez / aillent) avec nous.

7. Il faut que tu m' (emmenais / emmènes) au centre commercial.

C Complete each sentence with the subjunctive of the verb in parentheses.

1. Il faut que tu m'_____ écrives _____ des cartes postales. (écrire)

2. Il est nécessaire que ton chien _____ avec quelqu'un gentil pendant les vacances. (être)

3. Il faut absolument qu'il se _____ vacciner. (faire)

4. Il n'est pas nécessaire que nous _____ à la plage. (aller)

5. Il ne faut pas que tu _____ le plan. (oublier)

6. Est-ce qu'il est nécessaire que j' _____ une trousse de toilette? (avoir)

D Say what everyone has to do in Paris. Use the expression **il faut que** and the elements given.

1. nous / visiter le Louvre

   Il faut que nous visitions le Louvre. _____

2. vous / aller à l'Arc de Triomphe

   _____

3. je / prendre beaucoup de photos

   _____

4. tu / monter à Montmartre

   _____

5. Hélène / ne oublier pas son permis de conduire

   _____

6. tes amis / visiter les Tuileries

   _____

Level 3
Grammar Tutor Activities

Verbs followed by the infinitive CHAPITRE 1

> **In English** The **infinitive** consists of the word **to** plus the base form of a verb, such as *to learn.* There are many verbs that are followed by the infinitive.
>
> They **want to study** Italian.
> We **intended to leave** early.
> I **hope to attend** college
>
> The infinitive can also follow the **-ing** form of the verb **to go** to talk about the near future.
>
> My brothers **are going to cook** tonight.

A Circle the infinitive in each sentence and underline the verb it follows.

1. He <u>agreed</u> to study with us.

2. Our class is going to visit the art museum.

3. Amy finally decided to study chemistry.

4. I wanted to be the captain of the ski team.

5. We are going to meet at the library at 4 o'clock.

6. The students tried to understand the lesson.

7. I intend to finish the book even though it's 700 pages long.

> **In French** The infinitive is the basic, unconjugated form of the verb with an *er, -ir,* or *-re* ending. As in English, there are many verbs that are followed directly by an infinitive. Three such verbs are **vouloir, devoir,** and **pouvoir.**
>
> Marc **veut jouer** au tennis avec nous.
> Je **dois finir** mes devoirs.
> Nous **pouvons sortir** ce soir.
>
> You can also use an infinitive after the present-tense form of **aller** to tell what you're going to do or what's going to happen.
>
> Je **vais étudier** les arts plastiques cette année.
>
> The verb **venir** conjugated in the present followed by **de** + an infinitive is used to express the recent past, what has just happened.
>
> Caroline **vient de partir** en vacances.

VERBS FOLLOWED BY THE INFINITIVE   CHAPITRE 1

B Circle the infinitive in each sentence and underline the verb it follows.

1. Je <u>vais</u> [faire] du skate au parc.

2. On peut aller au cinéma si vous voulez.

3. Mathilde veut monter à cheval.

4. Nous venons de jouer au basket.

5. Où est-ce que vous allez voir un film d'horreur?

6. On doit prendre le bus ou le métro.

C Complete each sentence with the present-tense form of the verb in parentheses.

1. Je _____viens_____ de faire les magasins. (venir)

2. Est-ce que tu _____ aller au cinéma vendredi? (vouloir)

3. Je ne _____ pas jouer aux échecs avec vous. (pouvoir)

4. Nous _____ de regarder un film super! (venir)

5. Vous _____ faire de la vidéo amateur? (vouloir)

6. Hélène _____ jouer de la guitare. (pouvoir)

7. Mes amis _____ étudier pour leur examen. (devoir)

8. Je _____ parler avec le conseiller d'éducation. (aller)

D Imagine it is 11:00 in the morning. Based on the following schedule, write five sentences saying what Luc has just done and what he is going to do.

	samedi
8h00	nager à la piscine
10h00	ranger ma chambre
12h00	manger chez mes grands-parents
3h00	faire mes devoirs
5h00	emprunter des DVD

1. _____

2. _____

3. _____

4. _____

5. _____

Feminine form of nouns

In English The nouns of most professions denote both males and females.

My aunt is a chemical **engineer** and my uncle is a civil **engineer.**

Rosie wants to be a **nurse** just like her brother, who is an intensive care **nurse.**

In some instances, the nouns have distinct male and female forms.

Lola wants to be a **comedienne** just like her brother, a stand-up **comedian.**

Many of the nouns with distinct female forms are formed by either adding the syllable **–ess** to the end of the masculine form or changing the ending to **-ess**.

She dreamt of being a **countess** married to a rich **count.**

My aunt is a **waitress** and my uncle is a **waiter.**

A Match the masculine forms of the nouns in the left column with the feminine forms in the right column.

___d__ 1. comedian

_____ 2. actor

_____ 3. host

_____ 4. businessman

_____ 5. prince

_____ 6. shepherd

a. princess
b. sheperdess
c. actress
d. comedienne
e. hostess
f. businesswoman

In French Many feminine nouns are formed by adding **-e** to the masculine form.

un avocat → une avocate   un marchand → une marchande

In some instances, the masculine ending changes to a feminine ending.

un musicien → une musicienne

un serveur → une serveuse

un acteur → une actrice

un boulanger → une boulangère

un fermier → une fermière

Adding the suffix **-esse** forms the feminine forms of a few nouns.

un prince → une princesse   un maître → une maîtresse

Many nouns have the same forms for both females and males. The article indicates the gender of the person.

un dentiste → une dentiste   un architecte → une architecte

Some nouns of professions which were historically held by men are masculine whether they refer to a man or a woman.

un auteur   un juge   un professeur   un pilote

FEMININE FORM OF NOUNS

B Match the masculine forms of the nouns in the left column with the feminine forms in the right column.

_____c___ 1. médecin

_____ 2. vendeur

_____ 3. boucher

_____ 4. ingénieur

_____ 5. prince

_____ 6. mécanicien

> a. bouchère
> b. ingénieur
> c. médecin
> d. princesse
> e. mécanicienne
> f. vendeuse

C Complete each sentence with the feminine form of the word in parentheses.

1. Clara est devenue _____ **architecte** _____. (architecte)

2. La _____ et son mari sont très gentils. (maître)

3. Ma cousine est une _____ formidable. (artiste)

4. Leur fille est _____. (informaticien)

5. Tu connais l'_____? Elle est allemande. (avocat)

6. Ma sœur aimerait être _____. (pâtissier)

7. Emma va devenir _____ parce qu'elle adore les animaux. (vétérinaire)

D Write complete sentences saying that the person in parentheses also has the same profession.

1. Antoine est architecte. (Sarah)

   Sarah est architecte aussi. _____

2. Mme Tessier est coiffeuse. (son mari)

   _____

3. Romain est auteur. (Amélie)

   _____

4. Valentin est couturier. (sa femme)

   _____

5. Louis est agriculteur. (sa sœur)

   _____

The future perfect

In English The **future perfect** tense expresses an action completed in the future before another action in the future. For example:

> The bus leaves at 8:00. You will arrive at the stop at 8:15. When you arrive, the bus **will have left**.

The future perfect is formed with **will** + **have** + **past participle.**

> I **will have finished** my homework by dinnertime.
> Next March, we'll **have been** in this house for ten years.

A In the following sentences, underline the verbs that are in the future perfect tense.

1. By the time you get back, I <u>will have cleaned</u> my room.

2. By this time next year, I will have graduated.

3. My cousin will have visited every state by the time she's forty.

4. By the time we get there, everybody will have left.

5. If he keeps it up, he will have changed jobs four times in one year.

6. In June, my parents will have been married 25 years.

7. We will have driven more than 500 miles by the time we get to Montreal.

8. They will have moved in before the month of August.

In French The **future perfect** is also used to talk about something that will have happened before another future action or by a certain time in the future.

> J'**aurai fini** avant midi.
> *I will have finished before noon.*

In French, the future perfect is used after the conjunction **quand** when the main verb is in the future. Notice that in English you would use the past perfect.

> Quand j'**aurai fini** mes études, je travaillerai avec ma mère.
> *When I have finished my studies, I will work with my mother.*

The future perfect is formed with the future tense of **être** or **avoir** plus the past participle.

> Tu **seras arrivée** avant nous.
> Quand elle **aura acheté** le cadeau pour Laure, elle te le montrera.
> Nous ne **nous serons** pas encore **réveillés** quand tu partiras.

THE FUTURE PERFECT CHAPITRE **2**

B In the following sentences, underline the verbs that are in the future perfect tense.

1. Je te téléphonerai quand j'<u>aurai trouvé</u> un travail.

2. Vous sortirez quand vous aurez terminé vos devoirs.

3. Que feras-tu quand tu auras dépensé tout ton argent?

4. Nous nous lèverons quand le président aura fini son discours.

5. Je vous répondrai quand j'aurai reçu votre lettre.

6. Dans quinze jours, tu seras déjà arrivé en Afrique.

7. Elle construira notre maison quand elle sera devenue architecte.

8. Quand ils auront dîné, ils partiront tout de suite.

C Complete each sentence with the future perfect of the verb in parentheses.

1. Tu arriveras quand je _____ **serai sorti(e)** _____. (sortir)

2. Elle apportera les boissons quand nous

_____ de manger. (finir)

3. Il vous téléphonera quand vous _____.
(se coucher)

4. Nous arriverons sûrement quand ils

_____ le restaurant. (fermer)

5. Vous prendrez le métro quand nous

_____ vous emprunter votre voiture.
(venir)

D Using the following chain of events in Julien's future, write three more
sentences, each one telling what will have happened before another future action.

étudier à l'étranger → devenir professeur → connaître un pilote
→ voyager partout → écrire un roman

1. **Quand Julien aura étudié à l'étranger, il deviendra professeur.** _____

2. _____

3. _____

4. _____

5. _____

Present participles

In English The **present participle** is formed by adding **-ing** to the verb. When participles are adjectives, they are often used in front of nouns.

> Alice has a **talking** parrot.
> Do you know the story of **Sleeping** Beauty?

The present participle can also be used with the verb **to be** to form the progressive tense.

> Thomas is **working** at the hospital.

A Underline the present participle in each sentence. Then indicate whether it is used as an adjective or a verb.

1. Tamasha told me a depressing story.   adjective   verb

2. Mr. Brown was looking for a job.   adjective   verb

3. Nobody was hiring at the time.   adjective   verb

4. He was very cold during the freezing winter.   adjective   verb

5. The smell of burning tires was unpleasant.   adjective   verb

6. The family is now living in Happy Canyon.   adjective   verb

---

In French The **present participle** of most verbs is formed by removing the **-ons** from the present-tense **nous** form of the verb and adding **-ant**.

> nous écout~~ons~~ ⟶ **écoutant**   nous pren~~ons~~ ⟶ **prenant**
> nous finiss~~ons~~ ⟶ **finissant**   nous fais~~ons~~ ⟶ **faisant**

Être, avoir, and **savoir** have irregular present participles.

> être ⟶ **étant**   avoir ⟶ **ayant**   savoir ⟶ **sachant**

When used as an adjective, the present participle agrees with the noun being described.

> C'est une histoire **passionnante**.

When the present participle is used as a verb, it often follows **en**. Use **en** + **present participle** to say that someone is doing something while doing something else.

> Ils sont partis de chez nous **en chantant**.

En + **present participle** may also express how or why something is done.

> **En étudiant**, tu réussiras.

The present participle can be used without **en**.

> **Étant** étudiante en architecture, je voudrais faire un stage dans votre cabinet.

The present participle may also be used instead of a relative clause. This construction is typical of formal speech and writing.

> En Chine, les personnes **parlant** français sont rares. *(parlant = qui parlent)*

PRESENT PARTICIPLES CHAPITRE **2**

B Underline the present participle in each sentence. Then indicate whether it is used as an adjective or a verb.

1. En <u>partant</u> à 7 heures, tu arriveras à l'heure.   adjective | verb |

2. Son travail est vraiment déprimant.   adjective   verb

3. Il gagne beaucoup d'argent en faisant des heures
   supplémentaires.   adjective   verb

4. On parle des employés étant licenciés.   adjective   verb

5. En lisant, j'ai beaucoup appris.   adjective   verb

6. Il m'a raconté une histoire intéressante.   adjective   verb

C Complete each sentence with the present participle of the verb in parentheses.

1. En _____ **sortant** _____ du lycée, j'ai vu mon cousin Olivier. (sortir)

2. Nous avons discuté en _____ au café. (aller)

3. _____ passionné d'art, Olivier étudie l'histoire de l'art
   moderne. (être)

4. Il apprend beaucoup en _____ les musées. (visiter)

5. Moi, je trouve les musées d'art peu _____. (intéresser)

6. À mon avis, cette comédie est plus _____. (amuser)

7. _____ ma passion, je deviendrai acteur ou chanteur.
   (savoir)

D Rewrite each sentence changing the si clause to en + present participle.

1. Si tu suis des cours de langues, tu seras interprète.
   En suivant des cours de langues, tu seras interprète. _____

2. Si tu fais un séjour au Mexique, tu apprendras l'espagnol plus vite.

3. Tu réussiras ton examen oral si tu écoutes des émissions en espagnol.

   _____

4. Tu pourras travailler à Barcelone si tu parles bien espagnol.

   _____

5. Si tu es interprète, tu rencontreras des personnes intéressantes.

   _____

Relative pronouns with ce

In English The relative pronoun **what** can be used to link a main clause and a subordinate clause. Sometimes **what** replaces an unnamed antecedent.

> I don't know **what** I can do about it.
> Tell **what** happened.

Sometimes **what** stands for *something that.*

> **What** *(Something that)* I really like is bread pudding.
> Bread pudding is **what** *(something that)* I really like.

What can be either the subject or the object of a clause.

> I know **what** happened next. (subject)
> I know **what** Max got you for your birthday. (object)

A Underline the relative pronoun in each sentence. Check the appropriate column to indicate whether it is a subject or object.

	Subject	Object
		✓

1. I don't know <u>what</u> you're talking about.
2. They liked what they saw in Rome.
3. What's interesting is the color of this house.
4. They don't know what's best for them.
5. I'll tell you what the princess likes.
6. No one knows what will happen next.

In French The relative pronouns **ce qui** and **ce que** both mean *what* and are used to refer to a general idea or to something that hasn't been mentioned.

Ce qui is the subject of the clause it introduces. It is usually followed by a verb.

> **Ce qui** est incroyable, c'est la fin de la fable.
> Je ne sais pas **ce qui** est arrivé au palais.

Ce que (or **ce qu'**) is the object of the clause it introduces. It is usually followed by a subject and verb.

> **Ce que** j'aime, c'est les fables.
> Le génie a accordé au prince **ce qu'**il souhaitait.

Ce dont is used when the verb of the clause requires **de,** such as *parler de, avoir peur de,* or *avoir besoin de.*

> Le roi ne savait pas **ce dont** la reine parlait.
> La princesse n'a pas trouvé **ce dont** elle avait besoin.

B Underline the relative pronoun in each sentence. Check the appropriate column to indicate whether it is a subject or object.

	Subject	Object
1.		✓
2.		
3.		
4.		
5.		
6.		

1. <u>Ce que</u> je lis, c'est une légende.

2. Je ne sais pas ce qu'on met dans la potion.

3. Ce qui m'intéresse, c'est le Moyen-Orient.

4. Ce qu'on raconte n'est pas vrai.

5. Dis-moi vite ce qui est arrivé!

6. Le géant mangea tout ce qu'il trouva.

C Complete the following sentences with **ce qui, ce que, ce qu'**, or **ce dont**.

1. Tu ne nous as pas dit _____ce que_____ tu as lu hier soir.

2. _____ ne me plaît pas dans cette maison, c'est les fantômes.

3. Tu veux faire disparaître _____ tu as peur?

4. Tu sais _____ est arrivé à l'héroïne?

5. _____ elle n'aime pas du tout, c'est les monstres.

6. Avec sa baguette magique, le magicien faisait apparaître _____ il avait besoin.

7. La marraine ne savait pas _____ la fille avait souhaité.

8. _____ prend beaucoup de temps, c'est de préparer une potion magique.

9. _____ j'ai envie, c'est un tapis volant!

10. Le prince n'a pas accepté _____ le sorcier lui avait offert.

D Explain the use of the relative pronouns in the following sentences. Tell why one sentence uses **qui** and the other **ce qui**.

C'est l'histoire d'une fille qui tue l'ogre.
Je ne sais pas ce qui est arrivé à la fin.

_____

_____

_____

_____

_____

Adjective placement and meaning   CHAPITRE **3**

> **In English** Adjectives in English are almost always placed before the nouns they modify, no matter what meaning they have.
>
> The story is about a **poor** <u>family</u>. *(not rich)*
> The **poor** <u>girl</u> was lost in the woods. *(unfortunate)*

A Circle the adjectives in the following sentences and underline the nouns they modify.

1. It is an [ancient] <u>legend</u> from Africa.

2. People say that it is a true story.

3. There was a great king whom everyone respected.

4. He had a daughter who loved expensive jewelry.

5. One day, a poor farmer finds a necklace.

6. It is the only necklace in the world that sings.

> **In French** Some adjectives have a different meaning depending whether they are placed before a noun or after a noun.
>
> | | |
> |---|---|
> | un **ancien** professeur | *a former professor* |
> | une légende **ancienne** | *an ancient (old) legend* |
> | un **vrai** cauchemar | *a real nightmare* |
> | une histoire **vraie** | *a true story* |
> | un **grand** homme | *a great man* |
> | un homme **grand** | *a tall man* |
> | dans **certains** pays | *in certain (some) countries* |
> | un succès **certain** | *a sure success* |
> | un **cher** ami | *a dear friend* |
> | une montre **chère** | *an expensive watch* |
> | le **dernier** étage | *the last floor* |
> | le mois **dernier** | *the previous month* |
> | un **pauvre** homme | *a poor (unfortunate) man* |
> | un homme **pauvre** | *a poor (destitute) man* |
> | sa **propre** chambre | *his/her own room* |
> | une chambre **propre** | *a clean room* |
> | un **sale** caractère | *a nasty temper* |
> | des mains **sales** | *dirty hands* |
> | son **seul** enfant | *her only child* |
> | un enfant **seul** | *a lonely child* |

IRREGULAR ADJECTIVES CHAPITRE **3**

B Circle the adjectives in the following sentences and underline the nouns they modify.

1. C'est une <u>légende</u> ancienne d'Afrique.

2. On dit que c'est une histoire vraie.

3. Il y avait un grand roi que tout le monde respectait.

4. Il avait une fille qui aimait les bijoux chers.

5. Un jour, un fermier pauvre trouva un collier.

6. C'était le seul collier du monde qui chantait.

C Complete each response by writing the correct adjective from the box either before or after the noun. Some adjectives will be used more than once.

cher	grand	pauvre	propre

1. —Tu ne partages plus ta chambre avec ton frère?

   —Non. J'ai ma _____ propre _____ chambre
   _____ maintenant.

2. —Ton nouvel ordinateur a coûté beaucoup d'argent?

   —Oui, c'est un _____ ordinateur _____.

3. —Henri est un bon ami, n'est-ce pas?

   —Oui, c'est un _____ ami _____.

4. —Véronique nettoie toujours sa chambre?

   —Oui, c'est une _____ chambre _____.

5. —Combien mesure ton père?

   —C'est un _____ homme _____
   qui mesure 2 mètres.

6. —Est-ce que les Archambault sont riches?

   —Pas du tout! C'est une _____ famille
   _____.

D Translate the following sentence into French. How would the meaning change if you positioned the adjective differently?

   Nicole was the only student in the classroom.

   _____

   _____

   _____

The plus-que-parfait

In English The **past perfect** is used to refer to an action that was completed before another past action. The past perfect is made up of the past tense of the verb *to have* and the past participle of the action verb.

> She **had** already **arrived** when I got there.
> We called Scott and Doreen, but they **had** already **left**.

Sometimes the previous action is implied rather than stated.

> I **had seen** the movie before.

A Underline the verbs in the past perfect in the following sentences.

1. She <u>had</u> always <u>considered</u> Lois a close friend.

2. They had not forgotten us after all.

3. When we drove up to the farm, we saw that everybody had left.

4. We had just started to eat when the phone rang.

5. They had drunk some water before starting the race.

6. Charlene had never been to a circus before.

7. In truth, I barely recognized it, since it had changed so much.

In French The **plus-que-parfait** (past perfect) is also used to tell what happened in the past before something else that is either mentioned in the same sentence or implied.

> J'**avais allumé** la télé quand le téléphone a sonné.
> Ahmed **était** déjà **allé** en France.

The **plus-que-parfait** is made up of the imperfect form of the helping verbs **avoir** or **être** and the past participle of the action verb.

	dire	**rentrer**
j'	avais dit	étais rentré(e)
tu	avais dit	étais rentré(e)
il/elle/on	avait dit	était rentré(e)(s)
nous	avions dit	étions rentré(e)s
vous	aviez dit	étiez rentré(e)(s)
ils/elles	avaient dit	étaient rentré(e)s

The rules for agreement of past participles in the **plus-que-parfait** are the same as those for the **passé composé.**

> Elle **était partie** quand le festival a commencé.

THE PLUS-QUE-PARFAIT

B Underline the verbs that make up the plus-que-parfait in the following sentences.

1. Nous <u>avions déménagé</u> l'année d'avant.

2. Ils avaient voyagé en France.

3. Je n'y suis pas allé parce que j'avais oublié l'adresse.

4. Marithé a dit qu'elle avait téléphoné à Pierre.

5. Christelle s'était fait mal au pied en marchant.

6. Le film avait déjà commencé quand nous sommes arrivés.

7. Géraldine était allée au café avant d'aller à la piscine.

C For each of the sentences below, put the verb in parentheses in the plus-que-parfait.

1. Tu savais qu'il _____ **était parti** _____ au Canada? (partir)

2. On m'a dit que Brigitte et Jean _____! (se marier)

3. Je ne savais pas que tu _____ un accident. (avoir)

4. Vous saviez que Didier _____ une moto? (acheter)

5. Nous _____ des photos, puis on a perdu l'appareil photo. (prendre)

6. Maman m'a demandé si j'_____ la vaisselle. (faire)

7. Tu _____ ton bac avant ton séjour en Angleterre, n'est-ce pas? (passer)

8. Pauline et Xavier _____ bien avant 1995. (se rencontrer)

9. Tu savais que Félix _____ le bras, toi? (se casser)

10. Quand Alex avait trois ans, il _____ à nager. (apprendre)

D Compare the meanings of the two sentences below. Then, in your own words, explain how the two tenses are formed differently.

Vous êtes sortis.   **Vous étiez sortis.**

_____

_____

_____

_____

Sequence of tenses in indirect discourse   CHAPITRE 3

In English When you're reporting what someone said, you can use direct quotation (*The king said, "We will defeat them."*), or you can use **indirect discourse** *(The king said that we would defeat them.)* In indirect discourse, you have a main clause *(the king said)* and a dependent clause *(that we would defeat them)*. The tense in the main clause determines the tense in the dependent clause. Observing the **sequence of tenses** means that the tense of the verbs in the main clause and the dependent clause agree. There are several possibilities for combinations of tense.

> The king **says** that he **wants** peace.
> The king **says** that he **will travel** far.
> The king **says** that a battle **has started**.
> The king **said** that he **wanted** peace.
> The king **said** that he **would travel** far.
> The king **said** that a battle **had started**.

A Circle the verbs in the main and dependent clauses. Determine the tense of the verbs and write them in the table.

1. She says that she is going to the movie.

2. Thomas said that he had already seen the film.

3. Louis says that they will have fun.

4. They said that they would meet after class.

5. I said that I was too busy.

6. They say that they will go for ice cream.

main	dependent
present	p. progressive

In French The **sequence of tenses** also means that the tense of the verb in the dependent clause is determined by the tense of the verb in the main clause. If the main clause verb is in the **présent,** the dependent clause verb may be in the **présent, futur, passé composé,** or **imparfait.**

> Le roi **dit** qu'il **travaille**. (at the present time)
> Le roi **dit** qu'il **travaillera**. (at some time in the future)
> Le roi **dit** qu'il **a travaillé**/qu'il **travaillait**. (at some time in the past)

If the main clause verb is in the **passé composé,** the dependent clause verb may be in the **imparfait, conditionnel,** or **plus-que-parfait.**

> Le roi **a dit** qu'il **travaillait**. (at some time in the past)
> Le roi **a dit** qu'il **travaillerait**. (at some time in the future)
> Le roi **a dit** qu'il **avait travaillé**. (at some time further in the past)

SEQUENCE OF TENSES IN INDIRECT DISCOURSE CHAPITRE 3

B Circle the verbs in the main and dependent clauses. Determine the tense of the verbs and write them in the table.

1. Elle dit qu'elle combattra l'ennemi.

2. Ils disent qu'ils veulent l'indépendance.

3. Le prince a dit qu'il explorerait le Maroc.

4. Le peuple dit que le conflit a commencé.

5. Vous avez dit que vous aviez vu un tapis volant?

6. Le président dit que la guerre se terminera.

main	dependent
présent	futur

C Circle the correct form of the verb to complete each sentence.

1. Le professeur a dit que nous (lisons / lirions) l'histoire de la monarchie.

2. Mon amie dit qu'elle (a / aurait) un livre d'histoire très intéressant.

3. Son frère a dit que le livre (est / était) dans sa chambre.

4. Je lui ai dit que nous l' (avons trouvé / avions trouvé) dans la salle.

5. Vous dites que nous (devons / devrions) finir le livre avant jeudi.

6. Mes copains ont dit que l'examen (aura / aurait) lieu dans une semaine.

D Rewrite the following sentences changing the verb **dire** to the **passé composé** and changing the verb in the dependent clause to the correct tense.

1. Monique dit que Frédéric est à la bibliothèque.

   Monique a dit que Frédéric était à la bibliothèque. _____

2. Tu dis qu'Agnès sortira du lycée à 4 heures.

   _____

3. Eugénie dit qu'elle a besoin de tes notes de chimie.

   _____

4. Vous dites que nous adorerons le nouveau roman.

   _____

5. Jean-Paul dit que tu n'as pas reçu mes lettres.

   _____

6. Je dis qu'il aura lieu après le coup d'état.

   _____

The past infinitive

In English The **past infinitive** is made up of the verb **have** in its infinitive form and the **past participle** of the verb: **to have come, to have seen**.

The past infinitive is used when infinitive constructions express an action that was complete at the time of the main verb.

> It is better **to have made** mistakes than **to not have tried** at all.
> Mozart is said **to have written** his first symphony when he was a young boy.
> The kingdom was mistakenly reported **to have been** peaceful.

A Fill in the blanks with the past infinitives of the verbs in parentheses.

1. They claimed ___to have been___ too tired to run. (be)

2. It was a good idea _____ some water with us. (bring)

3. It was said _____ the hottest day of the year. (be)

4. Do you think it was better _____ in the race even though we lost? (participate)

5. It was impossible _____ in under two hours. (finish)

6. The winner was finally shown _____. (cheat)

7. He was believed _____ a shortcut. (take)

In French The **past infinitive** is formed with the infinitive of the helping verbs **avoir** or **être** and the **past participle** of the main verb: **avoir terminé, être venu**.

The past infinitive indicates an action that occurred before the action of the main verb, but only when the subject of both verbs are the same. Notice that the rules for agreement with past participles are the same as for the **passé composé**.

> Après **être rentrée** chez elle, la princesse s'est couchée.
> Le prince est parti après l'**avoir vue**.
> L'armée a célébré sa victoire après **avoir gagné** le conflit.

THE PAST INFINITIVE CHAPITRE **3**

B Fill in the blanks with the past infinitives of the verbs in parentheses.

1. Excusez-moi d'__**être arrivé(e)**_____ en retard. (arriver)

2. Après _____ mes études, je veux devenir architecte. (finir)

3. Après _____ amoureux, ils se sont mariés. (tomber)

4. Tu ne peux pas aller à l'université sans _____ au bac. (réussir)

5. Les Martin ont acheté leur maison après _____ à Chartres. (arriver)

6. Félix a vendu sa moto après _____ un accident. (avoir)

C Combine these actions into a sentence, by using one verb in the **passé composé** and the one that logically came before it in the past infinitive.

1. mes sœurs: se réveiller / faire leurs lits

   Après s'être réveillées, mes sœurs ont fait leurs lits. _____

2. je: prendre le bus / prendre le petit-déjeuner

3. Christelle: se baigner / s'habiller

   _____

4. nous: aller au cinéma / finir nos devoirs

   _____

D Compare the following sentences. How are **avoir** and **être** translated into English? What can you conclude about the usage of the past infinitive in French and English?

Je suis content de les avoir vus. *I am happy to have seen them.*
J'ai fait du jogging après m'être levé. *I exercised after having woken up.*

_____

_____

_____

_____

Reciprocal verbs

In English Actions that involve two or more people doing something for each other are reciprocal actions. These mutual actions can be seen in the expressions **each other** and **one another**.

> Sean and Lori like **each other**.
> Randy and Madison help **one another** with their homework.

If the meaning is clear enough, you don't have to say **each other**. In the sentence below, who will speak to whom is obvious, so you could leave out *to each other*.

> Let's talk (**to each other**) on the phone tonight.

Because the reciprocity of action verbs takes place between several people or things, these verbs are necessarily plural.

A Underline the reciprocal expression in each sentence.

1. Manuel and Robert help <u>each other</u> study for the test.

2. Elisa and Anne argue with each other all the time.

3. Now the girls aren't speaking to one another.

4. They finally made up with each other.

5. We trust one another with our deepest secrets.

6. The students told one another about their vacations.

7. You and your classmate have a lot of respect for each other.

In French Reciprocal verbs use some of the same pronouns as reflexive verbs: **se, nous,** and **vous.** These pronouns are plural and generally mean *each other*.

Nous **nous** aimons.	*We love each other.*
Il **se** sont rencontrés hier.	*They met each other yesterday.*

In the **passé composé,** reciprocal verbs take the helping verb **être.** When a verb takes a direct object, the past participle agrees with the pronoun.

> Elles **se sont vues** à la gare.

When a verb takes an indirect object, the past participle does not agree with the pronoun. Some verbs that take indirect objects are **conseiller, demander, dire, écrire, offrir, parler, plaire,** and **téléphoner.**

> Elles **se sont téléphoné** hier.
> Nous **nous sommes parlé** la semaine dernière.

B Underline the reciprocal pronoun in each sentence.

1. Nous <u>nous</u> sommes vus ce matin.

2. Vous vous disputez trop souvent.

3. Elles se sont offert des cadeaux.

4. Nous nous parlions rarement au lycée.

5. Ils se sont regardés et tout de suite, ils se sont plu.

6. Vous vous êtes rencontrés où?

7. Pourquoi Fatima et Alice se sont disputées?

C Rewrite the following sentences in the **passé composé.** Remember to make the past participles agree with their direct objects.

1. Nous nous voyons dimanche.

   Nous nous sommes vu(e)s dimanche. _____

2. Julie et Jean se retrouvent à la piscine.

   _____

3. Carole et Charlotte se réconcilient.

   _____

4. Est-ce que Georges et toi, vous vous aimez beaucoup?

   _____

5. Nous nous disons la vérité.

   _____

6. Elles se conseillent souvent.

   _____

D How do you know when the plural pronoun **se** expresses the reciprocal idea of *each other* and when it does not? Explain your answer using the following sentences as examples.

1. Louis et Rose **se** promènent.

2. Louis et Rose **se** téléphonent tous les jours.

   _____

   _____

   _____

   _____

The past conditional

In English The **past conditional** consists of **would** plus the past infinitive (**have** + past participle). It serves to express missed opportunities and hypothetical situations.

> He told me that he **would have liked** to come to the party.
> In your place, I **would have done** the same thing.

The past conditional is often found in hypothetical sentences with **if**. When **if** is followed by the **past perfect**, the conditional past is used in the other clause that states the result.

> If I **had had** the time, I **would have done** my homework.
> **Would** you **have stayed** at home if it **had rained** yesterday?

A Circle the correct verbs to complete the following sentences.

1. I (would have invited / had invited) Karim if he had been free.

2. If I (would have won / had won) the lottery, I would have bought a car.

3. I would have told you if I (would have known / had known).

4. In your position, I (would have lent / had lent) him some money.

5. If Zahra (would have finished / had finished) her homework, she would have played soccer with us.

6. The teacher (would have been / had been) sad if her students had not passed their exam.

7. Victor would have responded to your e-mail if he (would have received / had received) it.

In French The **past conditional** consists of the conditional of the helping verb (**avoir** or **être**) and the past participle of the main verb. The past conditional is used to talk about conditions in the past that could have taken place in the past, but did not.

> Tu **aurais pu** m'aider!

The past conditional is also used to state the result in a hypothetical situation taking place in the past. The **past perfect** is used in the **si** clause, and the **past conditional** is used in the result clause.

> Si nous **avions vu** les Renaud, nous leur **aurions parlé**.
> J'**aurais finis** mes devoirs si j'**avais eu** le temps.
> Ils se **seraient réconciliés** s'ils **s'étaient parlé**.

THE PAST CONDITIONAL   CHAPITRE **4**

B Circle the correct verbs to complete the following sentences.

1. S'il avait été riche, il (aurait acheté / avait acheté) une maison.

2. Si tu (serais venu / étais venu) hier soir, tu aurais vu tes amis chez nous.

3. Il aurait répondu à ta lettre s'il (aurait eu / avait eu) le temps.

4. Si tu avais voulu, je t'(aurais apporté / avais apporté) mon cahier.

5. Si vous me l'aviez demandé, je vous (aurais prêté / avais prêté) mon stylo.

6. Il a cru hier qu'il (aurait plu / avait plu) ce matin.

7. Si vous (étiez tombé / seriez tombé), il vous serait venu en aide.

C Say what would have happened if the situations were different, using a si clause in the past perfect and a result clause in the past conditional.

1. Pascal ne m'a pas téléphoné. Il était trop occupé.

   Pascal m'aurait téléphoné s'il n'avait pas été trop occupé.

2. Maryse n'a pas étudié. Elle a eu une mauvaise note.

   _____

   _____

3. Je n'ai pas fait le ménage. Je n'ai pas eu le temps.

   _____

   _____

4. Nathalie n'a pas joué au foot. Elle s'est foulé la cheville.

   _____

   _____

5. Honoré était fatigué. Il avait mal dormi.

   _____

   _____

6. Nous étions de mauvaise humeur. Nous avions perdu le match.

   _____

   _____

7. Vous ne m'avez pas parlé au café. Vous ne m'avez pas vu.

   _____

   _____

Subjunctive with necessity, desire, and emotions   CHAPITRE 4

In English The **subjunctive mood** is sometimes used in a dependent clause following a verb of necessity. It is also used to express a wish that is contrary to fact.

It is important that you **be** ambitious.

I wish that you **were** here.

Verbs of desire (*to hope, to want*) and of emotion (*to be happy*) usually take the indicative or infinitive form.

I hope the weather **is** good.

They want you **to be** happy.

A Write whether each underlined verb is in the indicative, subjunctive, or infinitive form.

1. It's a good idea for us <u>to wake</u> up early.   _____infinitive_____

2. I wish that <u>were</u> a true story.   _____

3. The teacher wants all of us to <u>learn</u>.   _____

4. It is important that she <u>follow</u> my advice.   _____

5. My parents hope that I <u>will become</u> a doctor.   _____

6. I'm glad that you <u>know</u> how to swim.   _____

In French The **subjunctive mood** is required when the main clause expresses **necessity, desire,** or **emotion** regarding another person.

Expressions of necessity:
Il faut que
Il est essentiel que
Il faudrait que
Il est nécessaire que
Il vaudrait mieux que
Il est important que

Expressions of desire:
Je désire que
Je souhaite que
Je veux que
Je voudrais que

Expressions of emotion:
Je suis désolé(e) que   **Je suis content(e)/heureux(-se) que**
C'est dommage que   **Je suis ravi(e) que**

Il faut que tu **lises** ce roman.

Je veux que nous **partions** en vacances.

Nous sommes désolés que vous **deviez** déménager.

When the subject of the main clause and the dependent clause is the same, the infinitive is used in the dependent clause.

Nous sommes désolés d'**avoir** déménagé.

Je veux **rester**.

SUBJUNCTIVE WITH NECESSITY, DESIRE, AND EMOTIONS CHAPITRE 4

B Write whether each underlined verb is in the subjunctive or infinitive form.

1. Ils désirent <u>rester</u> ici.   **infinitive**

2. C'est dommage qu'il <u>soit</u> malade. _____

3. Il faut que tu <u>fasses</u> tes devoirs. _____

4. Je suis content d'<u>avoir</u> de bons amis. _____

5. Nous voulons <u>voyager</u> en Angleterre. _____

6. Je ne veux pas que tu te <u>fâches</u>. _____

C Complete each sentence with the subjunctive of the verb in parentheses.

1. Je suis heureuse que vous le _____**rencontriez**_____. (rencontrer)

2. Je suis fâché qu'il ne vous _____ pas. (reconnaître)

3. Il est nécessaire que tu _____ l'anglais. (apprendre)

4. Il vaudrait mieux que nous _____ encore une année à Nice. (rester)

5. Je souhaite que vous _____ voir cette exposition. (aller)

6. C'est dommage qu'ils ne _____ pas de progrès. (faire)

7. Il faudrait que je _____ demain. (partir)

D Complete the following sentences with what you wish, hope, feel, and think is necessary. Use the subjunctive or the infinitive as necessary.

1. Il est essentiel que **nous fassions un apprentissage.** _____

2. Je suis ravi(e) de _____

   _____

3. Je voudrais que mes amis et moi, nous _____

   _____

   _____

4. Je suis désolé(e) de _____

   _____

5. Il est important que le président _____

   _____

6. Je souhaite que les jeunes _____

   _____

Subjunctive with expressions of fear CHAPITRE 5

> **In English** To express fear, you can use the expressions **to be afraid that** and **to fear that**. The tense that follows these expressions depends on the context, but it is always in the **indicative** mood.
>
> > **We are afraid that** they **are** lost.
> > **I fear that** more animals **will become** extinct.
>
> After the expression **afraid of**, the **gerund** (verb ending in **-ing**) is used.
>
> > **I'm afraid of touching** the iguana.

A Underline the expression of fear and circle the verb that follows it. Then write whether the verb is in the indicative mood or whether it is a gerund.

1. Their team <u>was afraid of</u> [losing].   _____gerund_____

2. If I tell you, I fear that you will get angry.   _____

3. Anne was afraid of falling down the cliff.   _____

4. We're afraid that Robert knows the secret.   _____

5. Do you fear that the climate is changing?   _____

6. Are you afraid of trying new things?   _____

> **In French** To express fear, you can use the expressions **avoir peur que** and **craindre que**. Since fear is an emotion, use the **subjunctive** in the clause that follows **que**.
>
> > **J'ai peur qu'il y ait** des crocodiles.
> > **Je crains que** nous nous **perdions** dans le parc.
>
> The subjunctive is only used if there are two different subjects in the two clauses linked by **que**. If the subjects are the same person, then the **infinitive** is used.
>
> > **J'ai peur que** vous vous **blessiez.**
> > **J'ai peur de** me **blesser.**

B Underline the expression of fear and circle the verb that follows it. Then write whether the verb is in the subjunctive or is an infinitive.

1. <u>J'ai peur que</u> le dauphin [soit] blessé.   _____subjunctive_____

2. Je crains de rencontrer un requin.   _____

3. Vous avez peur de nager dans la mer?   _____

4. J'ai peur qu'une guêpe me pique.   _____

5. Nous craignons qu'il n'y ait plus de corail.   _____

SUBJUNCTIVE WITH EXPRESSIONS OF FEAR

C Write complete sentences summarizing what each person fears.

1. Robert: Nous sommes en retard.

   Robert craint que nous soyons en retard. _____

2. Je: Jean-Marc nous attend.

   _____

3. Jean-Marc: Vous avez un accident.

   _____

4. Tu: Le restaurant ferme à 10h.

   _____

5. Christine: Nous ne nous rencontrons pas.

   _____

6. André: Tu perds les clés.

   _____

7. Nous: Il est interdit de s'arrêter ici.

   _____

D Write a sentence saying that you also fear that for yourself.

1. Michel a peur qu'ils se perdent.

   Moi aussi, j'ai peur de me perdre. _____

2. Philippe a peur que nous ne sachions pas monter la tente.

   _____

3. Vous avez peur qu'ils oublient l'ouvre-boîte.

   _____

4. Mon père a peur que nous voyons des serpents.

   _____

5. Barbara a peur que vous ayez mal partout.

   _____

6. Édouard a peur qu'elles tombent en faisant de l'escalade.

   _____

146

Subjunctive with doubt and uncertainty CHAPITRE 6

> **In English** When the main clause of a sentence contains an expression of **certainty** or **possibility,** the indicative is used in the dependent clause.
>
> **It's true that** the report is reliable.
> **It's possible that** the president will talk tonight.
>
> When the main clause of a sentence expressess **doubt** or **disbelief,** the indicative is also used in the dependent clause. Often a modal such as would or could is used with the verb.
>
> **I doubt that** the journalist is trustworthy.
> **I can't believe that** anyone would write such nonsense.

A In the following sentences, underline the expression that shows doubt, possibility, or certainty. Then circle the verb in the dependent clause.

   1. <u>I don't believe that</u> Stephen is reading the comics.

   2. It is true that the press knows everything.

   3. Tammy doubts that you interviewed the movie star.

   4. It's possible that this is a real classified ad.

   5. I can't believe that someone would collect broken buttons.

   6. It is clear that you actually believe the articles in those tabloids.

> **In French** When the main clause of a sentence contains an expression of **certainty,** the **indicative** is used in the dependent clause.
>
> **Je suis sûr que** le kiosque **vend** ce journal.
>
> However, when the main clause of a sentence expresses **uncertainty,** the subjunctive is used in the dependent clause.
>
> **Je ne suis pas sûr que** le kiosque **vende** ce journal.
>
> The subjunctive is also used in the dependent clause when the main clause of a sentence expresses **doubt** or **disbelief.**
>
> **Je doute que** ce film **ait** du succès.
> **Ça m'étonnerait que** ces articles **soient** publiés.
>
> With most expressions of **possibility,** such as **il se peut que** and **il est possible que,** the subjunctive is used. However, with **il me semble que,** the indicative is used.
>
> **Il est possible que** nous **allions** au cinéma ce soir.
> **Il me semble que** nous **passerons** une soirée amusante!

SUBJUNCTIVE WITH DOUBT AND UNCERTAINTY CHAPITRE **6**

B In the following sentences, underline the expression that shows doubt, possibility, or certainty. Then circle the verb in the dependent clause and indicate whether it is in the indicative (I) or the subjunctive (S).

	I	S
1. Je doute que ce magazine soit gratuit.		✓
2. Je ne crois pas qu'il lise la presse à sensation.		
3. Il se peut que l'article soit vrai.		
4. Il est persuadé que nous nous sommes abonnés à ce journal.		
5. Je suis sûre que c'est en première page.		
6. Ça m'étonnerait que vous fassiez du parachutisme.		
7. Je ne pense pas que ce dessin humoristique soit drôle.		

C Respond to the following sentences using an expression from the box.

il se peut que	il me semble que	je doute que
je suis certain(e) que	je ne crois pas que	ça m'étonnerait que

1. Les médias savent tout.

_____

2. Beaucoup de gens lisent les informations sur Internet.

_____

3. Un garçon de six ans est rédacteur en chef.

_____

4. La météo est toujours exacte.

_____

5. Le président des États-Unis va en Chine cette année.

_____

D You have learned several expressions that take the subjunctive in French. List the types of expressions here. Then circle the ones that also take the subjunctive in English.

_____

_____

_____

Negative expressions

In English Most **negative expressions** contain the word **not**.

He is **not** going.   I haven't read it **yet**.

Sometimes there is more than one way to express a negative concept.

I do **not** see **anybody**.   I see **no one**.

Nobody, no one, and **nothing** can be the subject of a sentence.

Nobody came to the party.   **Nothing** happened.

The elements of the expression **neither . . . nor** immediately precede the words they modify.

I like **neither** pretzels **nor** potato chips.

Neither Bob **nor** Ted called yesterday.

A Underline the negative expressions in the following sentences.

1. Don does <u>not</u> go <u>anywhere</u> during the week.

2. Nobody brought anything to drink.

3. I like neither spiders nor snakes.

4. I am not going anywhere this weekend.

5. Tina has nothing to give him for his birthday.

6. We don't have any good ideas.

In French Like ne... pas, other **negative expressions** have at least two parts: ne and another word or expression.

ne... pas encore	*not yet*
ne... jamais	*never*
ne... plus	*not anymore / no longer*
ne... personne	*no one / not anyone*
ne... rien	*nothing*
ne... ni... ni	*neither... nor*
ne... aucun(e)	*no / not any*
ne... nulle part	*nowhere*

The negative expressions are placed around the conjugated verb. In the **passé composé,** however, **personne, aucun(e),** and **nulle part** go after the past participle. If there is a direct object, **nulle part** will follow it.

Nous n'avons **jamais** lu ce livre.

Il n'a écrit **aucun** article intéressant.

Je n'ai trouvé tes clés **nulle part.**

When **aucun(e)** modifies the subject, it is followed by **ne** and precedes the verb which is always in the singular.

Aucun journal **ne** parle de cette histoire.

B Underline the negative expressions in the following sentences.

1. Je <u>ne</u> fais <u>rien</u> cet après-midi.

2. Elle n'est allée nulle part pendant les vacances.

3. Personne ne sait jouer aux cartes?

4. Délia n'est pas encore arrivée?

5. On ne passe rien à la télé ce soir.

6. Je n'aime ni la chimie ni la biologie.

7. Vous n'avez lu aucun livre de Saint-Exupéry?

C Unscramble the following sentences that contain negative expressions.

1. fais / jamais / vaisselle / tu / la / ne

   Tu ne fais jamais la vaisselle. _____

2. le / qui / donne / professeur / aucun / c'est / devoir / ne

   _____

3. leurs / encore / devoirs / fini / ont / pas / ils / n'

   _____

4. n' / aller / nous / voulu / nulle part / avons

   _____

5. la / est / ministre / dernière / n' / aucun / semaine / arrivé

   _____

6. sur / ai / personne / vu / n' / autoroute / je / l'

   _____

D Explain the difference in the placement of **ne... aucun** in the following sentences.

Aucun journal n'est arrivé. Je n'ai reçu aucun journal.

_____

_____

_____

_____

The passive voice

> **In English** There are two voices: active and passive. In the **active voice**, the subject of a sentence is the *agent*, that is, the person or thing doing something. In the **passive voice**, the subject *receives* the action. The passive is used to say that something *is being done* to someone or something.
>
> ACTIVE: The hurricane **destroyed** our home.
> PASSIVE: Our home **was destroyed** by the hurricane.
>
> To express a passive action, use a form of **to be** and the **past participle** of the main verb. The agent can be expressed through a **by** + noun clause *(by the hurricane)*. Often in a passive sentence, the agent is not even mentioned.
> Our house **was built** last year.

A Circle the form of the verb *to be* and underline the past participle in the following passive sentences. The indicate who or what the agent is. If the sentence lacks one, write **no agent.**

		AGENT
1. This dam was built by my grandfather.		_____ my grandfather _____
2. The same book was read by all students.		_____
3. Your voice could be heard across the room.		_____
4. The thief was arrested by the police.		_____
5. The injured were taken to the hospital.		_____
6. Ten roads will be built next year.		_____
7. The tree was struck by lightning.		_____
8. The information is found in my blog.		_____

> **In French** There are also **active** and **passive** voices. To form a sentence in the passive voice, use a form of **être** and the **past participle** of the main verb.
>
> Cette maison **a été construite** en 1965.
>
> The past participle (**construite**) must agree in number and gender with the recipient of the action (**cette maison**).
>
> To tell who or what is doing the action, use **par** + the agent.
> La maison **a été détruite par** un cyclone.
> Le livre **a été lu par** les étudiants.

THE PASSIVE VOICE

B Circle the form of the verb **être** and underline the past participle in the following passive sentences. On the right, write who or what the agent is. If the sentence lacks one, write **no agent.**

AGENT

1. Ce pont a été construit par mon oncle.   **mon oncle**

2. Tous les appartements sont loués. _____

3. Le mur a été détruit par un raz-de-marée. _____

4. Je suis invitée par mon ami. _____

5. Le lycée a été évacué ce matin. _____

6. Le président est interviewé par ton frère? _____

7. Deux alligators ont été attrapés en Floride. _____

8. Je crains que tu sois mordu par ce chien. _____

C Rewrite these active sentences as passive sentences.

1. Beaucoup de gens lisent les journaux.

   Les journaux sont lus par beaucoup de gens.

2. Les voisins décorent les maisons du quartier.

   _____

3. Les enfants vont nettoyer les rues après la fête.

   _____

4. Trois hommes ont monté le piano.

   _____

5. Geneviève va acheter le gâteau.

   _____

D The passive voice is used less frequently in French than in English, because the same idea can be expressed two different ways: **Une tornade est prévue. On prévoit une tornade.** For the following sentences, express the same idea a different way.

1. Le français est parlé à Lausanne.

   _____

2. On passe des films français dans ce cinéma.

   _____

Quand, lorsque, and dès que

In English After the conjunction **when** or **as soon as**, you use the present tense when discussing a situation in general.

> **As soon as** the sun **rises**, Peter gets up.
> We're always glad **when** we **see** you.

You also use the present tense to talk about future events after **when** or **as soon as**.

> **As soon as** the train **arrives**, we will find our seats.
> **When** Billy **is** twenty-five, he will have a good job.

A In each of the following sentences, underline any verbs that are in the present tense and circle any verbs that are in the future tense.

1. When I <u>finish</u> high school, I will travel.
2. As soon as the guests leave, we will get some sleep.
3. Martin gets angry when people do not carpool.
4. The ship will depart as soon as everyone is on board.
5. Candace will return to work when she recovers from the accident.
6. As soon as it starts to rain, we will turn off the sprinklers.

In French After the conjunctions **quand** *(when)* and **lorsque** *(when, at the moment of)*, you use the present tense when discussing a situation in general.

> **Quand** j'**ai** des sacs en plastique, je les recycle.
> **Lorsqu**'il **fait** beau, je vais en ville à vélo.

You use the future tense after **quand** *(when)*, **lorsque** *(when, at the moment of)*, and **dès que** *(as soon as)* when the event will occur in the future.

> Les écologistes seront contents **quand** tout le monde **recyclera**.
> **Dès que** les usines **arrêteront** de polluer, l'environnement s'améliorera.
> **Lorsque** l'énergie solaire **sera** plus populaire, on utilisera moins de gaz.

B In each of the following sentences, underline any verbs that are in the present tense and circle any verbs that are in the future tense.

1. Quand tu iras aux Jeux olympiques, tu seras content.
2. Je serai heureuse lorsque je serai enfin à la maison.
3. Dès que Christophe rentre à la maison, il surfe sur Internet.
4. Dès que tu auras le temps, tu viendras nous voir.
5. Quand il neige, les enfants construisent un bonhomme de neige.
6. Sophie cherchera un emploi quand elle aura son diplôme.

153

C Complete the following sentences by conjugating the verbs in parentheses either in the present or future tense.

1. Quand tu _____ **seras** _____ (être) en France, tu verras beaucoup de petites voitures.

2. Je vous _____ (écrire) dès que j'arriverai là-bas.

3. Nous _____ (aller) au café quand nous avons le temps.

4. Lorsque Janine _____ (apprendre) la nouvelle, elle nous téléphonera.

5. Dès qu'ils _____ (savoir) que je suis ici, ils viendront me voir.

6. Qu'est-ce que vous _____ (faire) quand vous aurez 25 ans?

7. Est-ce que tu consommes trop d'eau quand tu _____ (prendre) une douche?

D Complete the sentences below with a logical ending.

1. Quand je serai en vacances, **je partirai en France**. _____

2. Quand j'aurai vingt et un ans, _____
   _____

3. Dès que j'aurai mon diplôme, _____
   _____

4. Lorsque j'ai de l'argent, _____
   _____

5. Dès que j'aurai une nouvelle voiture, _____
   _____

E Consider why French speakers use the future tense after **quand, lorsque,** and **dès que.** Does this make sense to you? Why or why not?

_____
_____
_____
_____
_____
_____

Contractions with lequel

In English An **interrogative pronoun** is a pronoun used to ask a question. There are five interrogative pronouns: **what, which, who, whom,** and **whose**.

> To whom are you referring?
> **Whose** car is in the driveway?

What, which, who, whom, and **whose** may also be used as **relative pronouns**. A relative pronouns relates to another noun preceding it in the sentence. It sometimes functions as an object of a preposition within a dependent clause.

> The man <u>with</u> whom I spoke is from Marseilles.
> The people <u>on</u> whose behalf I speak could not be here.

A In each sentence, underline the interrogative or relative pronoun. Then indicate which type of pronoun it is.

	Interrogative	Relative
1. <u>What</u> are you thinking?	✓	
2. This is the student for whom I voted.		
3. Mandy likes the candidate who is energetic.		
4. Which of the posters do you prefer?		
5. The mayor, whose name I forget, is here.		
6. On whose behalf are you speaking?		
7. The article which I wrote is on the front page.		

In French **Lequel** and its forms **lesquels, laquelle, lesquelles** can be used as interrogative pronouns. They can also function as objects of a preposition.

> **Lesquels** sont pour toi?
> C'est une personne <u>à</u> **laquelle** je parle souvent.

The forms of **lequel** contract with the prepositions **à** and **de**.

	Singular	**Plural**
Masculine	auquel, duquel	auxquels, desquels
Feminine	à laquelle, de laquelle	auxquelles, desquelles

> **Auxquelles** de ces manifestations as-tu assisté?
> Le candidat **auquel** je m'intéresse est artiste.
> Le parti politique **duquel** il fait partie est nouveau.

CONTRACTIONS WITH LEQUEL · CHAPITRE 8

B In each sentence, underline the interrogative or relative pronoun. Then indicate which type of pronoun it is.

	Interrogative	Relative
1.		✓
2.		
3.		
4.		
5.		
6.		

1. Voilà le monsieur <u>auquel</u> tu as parlé.

2. Duquel de ces députés tu parles?

3. La table sur laquelle j'écris est cassée.

4. De toutes ces affiches, laquelle tu préfères?

5. Auquel de ces débats mes copains ont pris part?

6. Auxquels as-tu participé?

C Respond to the following sentences with an appropriate contraction of the interrogative pronoun **lequel**.

1. Nous allons au bureau de vote. _____**Auquel?**_____

2. Je parle d'un nouveau candidat. _____

3. Nous avons assisté à une manifestation. _____

4. Elle a téléphoné aux sénateurs. _____

5. Je me souviens de ces candidates. _____

6. Le député joue de plusieurs instruments. _____

D Combine the sentences below using an appropriate form of the relative pronoun **lequel**.

1. La candidate est sympa. + Tu m'as parlé de la candidate.

   La candidate de laquelle tu m'as parlé est sympa.

2. Où sont les bureaux de vote? + Les électeurs vont aux bureaux de vote.

   _____

3. C'est l'effet de serre. + Le premier ministre s'intéresse à l'effet de serre.

   _____

4. Voilà les immigrants. + Je t'ai parlé des immigrants.

   _____

5. Les candidates ont été élues. + J'ai le plus entendu parlé de ces candidates.

   _____

The past subjunctive

In English The **past subjunctive** is used in *if* clauses in sentences that are contrary to fact or unlikely to happen. The conditional *(would + verb)* is used in the main clause.

> If I **were** a doctor, I *would volunteer* at the hospital.
> If he **could**, my boss *would pay* me more.

The past subjunctive also appears in some hypothetical sentences.

> I wish I **were** the president.
> Suppose the senator **were** to resign. What would happen?

For all verbs, except *be*, the form of the past subjunctive is the same as the simple past tense. For *be,* the past subjunctive is always **were**, even in the first and third person singular forms.

A In the following sentences, underline the verbs in the past subjunctive.

1. Imagine that you <u>lived</u> in a dictatorship.

2. Joseph wishes he were the minister of sports.

3. If I could vote, I would vote for you.

4. Suppose that you held a seat in the senate.

5. If Laura had her way, we would go on strike.

6. We would have more holidays if the bill went into law.

In French The **past subjunctive** is used to refer to actions and situations that took place in the past, after the same expressions and conjunctions that use the present subjunctive. The past subjunctive is formed with the subjunctive of the helping verb **avoir** or **être** and the **past participle** of the main verb.

que j'	**aie choisi**	**sois rentré(e)**
que tu	**aies choisi**	**sois rentré(e)**
qu'il/elle/on	**ait choisi**	**soit rentré(e)(s)**
que nous	**ayons choisi**	**soyons rentré(e)s**
que vous	**ayez choisi**	**soyez rentré(e)(s)**
qu'ils/elles	**aient choisi**	**soient rentré(e)s**

Il est possible que notre candidat **ait perdu** l'élection.
Je suis heureux que le président **soit venu** nous rendre visite.

THE PAST SUBJUNCTIVE

B In the following sentences, underline the verbs in the past subjunctive.

1. Je suis désolé que ta candidate ait perdu.

2. Nous sommes heureux que vous soyez venus.

3. Je ne crois pas que le président ait joué au foot avec vous.

4. Il y a peu de chance qu'il ait démissionné.

5. Je suis content que le gouvernement ait aidé les victimes.

6. Je doute que le ministre soit allé en prison.

C Use the following elements to write complete sentences in the past subjunctive.

1. être possible / le roi revenir de Chine hier

Il est possible que le roi soit revenu de Chine hier.

2. je / avoir peur / la campagne ne pas réussir

_____

_____

3. nous / être désolés / les étudiants ne pas participer aux élections

_____

_____

4. je / ne pas être sûr(e) / tu lire la bonne rubrique

_____

_____

5. tu / craindre / le député ne pas recevoir ta lettre

_____

_____

6. vous / être triste / le président tomber malade

_____

_____

D Explain the difference in meaning between the two sentences below.

Il est content que nous venions.   **Il est content que nous soyons venus.**

_____

_____

_____

Present participles used as adjectives CHAPITRE 9

In English Verbs have a form called the **present participle**, which can be used as an adjective. The present participle is formed by adding **-ing** to the verb.

  interest → **interesting**   intrigue → **intriguing**   cry → **crying**

When participles are used as adjectives, they are usually placed in front of the nouns they describe.

  Have you seen my **painting** gloves?
  Mr. Watson bought a **touching** painting of a mother and child.

A In each of the following sentences, underline the present participle used as an adjective. Then write the verb from which it is derived.

  1. The mural honors the <u>working</u> man.   __to work__

  2. This is an exciting book about Mars.   _____

  3. I found the art exhibit fascinating!   _____

  4. There is a growing number of digital artists.   _____

  5. The sculpture depicts a dying flower.   _____

  6. The landscape on the etching is haunting.   _____

  7. The relaxing sound of water filled the gallery.   _____

  8. I liked the painting with the dancing girls.   _____

In French The **present participle** can also be used as an adjective. To form the present participle of most verbs, replace the **-ons** ending of the present tense **nous** form with **-ant**.

  passionner →   passionnons →   **passionnant**
  impressionner →   impressionnons →   **impressionnant**
  émouvoir →   émouvons →   **émouvant**

When a participle is used as an adjective, it usually follows the noun it modifies and, like all adjectives, it must agree in gender and number with the noun.

  À Paris, je suis allé à une exposition **passionnant<u>e</u>**.
  Ce sont des statues **impressionnant<u>es</u>**.
  Van Gogh a peint des tableaux **émouvant<u>s</u>**.

PRESENT PARTICIPLES USED AS ADJECTIVES CHAPITRE **9**

B In each of the following sentences, underline the present participle used as an adjective. Then write the verb from which it is derived.

1. C'est une gravure impressionnante. _____**impressionner**_____

2. Je trouve l'autoportrait charmant. _____

3. J'aime les eaux dormantes de ce paysage. _____

4. Regarde les cheveux tombants du modèle. _____

5. Le chien est obéissant et il ne bouge pas. _____

6. Ce sculpteur est un artiste très passionnant. _____

C Complete each sentence using the present participle of the verb in parentheses as an adjective.

1. J'aime bien les soirées _____**dansantes**_____. (danser)

2. La chauve-souris est un mammifère _____. (voler)

3. Ils se rencontreront à la nuit _____. (tomber)

4. Cette peinture à l'huile utilise des couleurs _____. (briller)

5. À mon avis, c'était une exposition _____, même choquante. (surprendre)

6. Je trouve les critiques d'art _____. (énerver)

D Based on the following description, write three more sentences summarizing what is on the painting. Use il y a + noun + past participle used as an adjective.

> C'est un beau paysage. La couleur du ciel est rouge car le soleil se couche. Un oiseau qui chante est sur un arbre. Sous l'arbre, quatre filles dansent et rient. Deux chiens dorment près d'elles.

1. **Il y a un soleil couchant.** _____

2. _____

3. _____

4. _____

Si and oui

> **In English** To respond affirmatively to an affirmative question, you use **yes**.
>
> —Did you go to the art fair?
> —**Yes**, I went yesterday.
>
> To contradict a negative statement or question, you change the pitch of your voice and stress the modal verbs, such as **do** and **is**.
>
> —You don't like the Van Gogh painting?
> —Yes, I <u>do</u>!
>
> —She's not wearing the blue dress, is she?
> —Oh, but she <u>is</u>!

A In each of the following conversations, indicate whether the second sentence affirms or contradicts the first sentence.

	AFFIRM	CONTRADICT
1. —Is he going to the museum? —Yes, he is.	✓	
2. —They don't have the right answer. —Yes, they do.		
3. —Is the last day of school June 1st? —Yes, it is.		
4. —We aren't going skiing? —Oh, but we are!		
5. —She isn't going with him, is she? —Yes, she is.		
6. —You've done ceramics this year? —Yes, I have.		

> **In French** To respond affirmatively to an affirmative question, you use **oui**.
>
> —Tu es allée au musée?
> —Oui, j'y suis allée hier.
>
> To contradict a negative statement or question, you use the word **si** instead of **oui** in your response.
>
> —Tu n'aimais pas les tableaux de van Gogh que tu as vus?
> —Si! Je les aimais beaucoup!

SI AND OUI

B In each of the following conversations, indicate whether the second sentence affirms or contradicts the first sentence.

	AFFIRM	**CONTRADICT**
1. —Est-ce que tu as seize ans?		
—Oui, j'ai seize ans.	✓	
2. —Elle n'aime pas dessiner?		
—Si, elle aime bien.	_____	_____
3. —Vous n'aimez pas les escargots?		
—Si, j'adore!	_____	_____
4. —Nous avons arts plastiques à onze heures?		
—Oui.	_____	_____
5. —Tu n'as pas de peintures à l'huile?		
—Si, j'en ai.	_____	_____

C Answer the following questions with **non**, **oui**, or **si**.

1. Vous aimez l'art contemporain?

   Oui, j'aime beaucoup l'art contemporain. _____

2. Tu n'aimes pas voyager?

   _____

3. Tes amis et toi, vous aimez aller aux concerts?

   _____

4. Tes amis ne vont jamais au cinéma?

   _____

5. Tu n'as jamais vu de statue?

D How is contradicting a negative statement different in English and in French?

_____

_____

_____

_____

Adverb placement

In English Adverbs are usually formed by adding **-ly** to an adjective: careful →
carefully, quick → **quickly**. Some common adverbs that do not end in **-ly** are:
almost, a lot, just, now, often, soon, very, well.

When an adverb is modifying an adjective or another adverb, it is placed in front of
the word it is modifying.
    The hotel is **very** close to the airport.

When an adverb is modifying a verb, it is usually placed after the verb or at the end
of the sentence.
    The tour group walked **slowly** around the plaza.
    We visited France **last year**.

Adverbs of frequency, however, are generally placed before the conjugated verb.
And adverbs that give an opinion are usually placed at the beginning of a sentence.
    Do you **sometimes** travel by train?
    Luckily, the museum was still open.

A Circle the adverb in each sentence and underline the word it modifies.

    1. He left yesterday on the five o'clock train.

    2. The baggage claim area is almost empty.

    3. The plane from New York has apparently landed.

    4. Unfortunately, I don't have a video camera.

    5. They rarely travel abroad.

In French Most **adverbs** are formed by adding **-ment** to the feminine form of the
adjective: actuelle → **actuellement**, sérieuse → **sérieusement**. Some common
adverbs that do not end in **-ment** are: **beaucoup, bien, mal, déjà, quelquefois,
d'habitude, souvent, tard.**

As in English, adverbs go directly in front of the adjective or adverb they modify.
    Nous avons passé la douane **très** vite!

Adverbs that modify a verb usually go directly after the conjugated verb. In the
passé composé that means they go after the helping verb.
    Notre vol arrivera **tard**.
    Est-ce que vous avez **déjà** confirmé votre vol?

Longer adverbs and adverb of time can be placed at the beginning or end of the
sentence.
    D'habitude, on embarque dans l'avion juste avant le départ.
    Mes cousins arriveront **demain**.

B Circle the adverb in each sentence and underline the word it modifies.

1. J'<u>aime</u> beaucoup voyager.

2. Il faut arriver tôt à l'aéroport.

3. Heureusement, les petits chiens peuvent aller en cabine.

4. Notre vol était absolument horrible.

5. Vous avez peu dormi dans l'avion.

6. Je préfère que nous nous rencontrions ici.

7. Quand elles voyagent, elles se disputent régulièrement.

C Complete each sentence with an adverb from the box.

quelquefois	malheureusement	mal
rapidement	très	près

1. Tu trouves qu'on mange _____mal_____ dans l'avion?

2. Pour sortir vite de l'avion, assieds-toi_____ de la porte.

3. Si nous ne marchons pas _____, nous manquerons le vol.

4. Nous logeons _____ chez des amis mais pas toujours.

5. _____, on n'a pas assez d'argent pour voyager.

6. Mon oncle est pilote depuis _____ longtemps.

D Write the adverb in parentheses in the correct space. Then, explain why you chose that position.

1. Le train est _____ confortable _____. (assez)

   _____

   _____

2. Nous avons _____ dormi _____. (bien)

   _____

   _____

3. Ils sont _____ partis _____. (hier)

   _____

   _____

Answer Key

Answer Key

Answer Key: Level 1

CHAPITRE 1
Subjects and verbs

A Nicole Hello, I am Nicole.

Paul Hi, my name is Paul. Are you the new student?

Nicole Yes, I am from Belgium.

Paul Who is your English teacher?

Nicole Mrs. Paterson is my teacher. I like her a lot. She is very funny.

Paul Yes, she makes me laugh too.

Nicole But, we have a lot of homework in her class.

Paul Would you like to study together?

Nicole Sure, you can help me with English grammar.

B Laurent Salut, je m'appelle Laurent Humbert.

Corinne Salut, je m'appelle Corinne Thibaut. Je te présente Nathalie.

Nathalie Tu as quel âge, Laurent?

Laurent Moi, j'ai quatorze ans.

Corinne Nathalie a dix-sept ans!

Laurent Et bien, mon ami s'appelle Marcel. Il a vingt ans!

C 1. Je (pronoun)
2. Marine (noun)
3. professeur (noun)
4. vous (pronoun)
5. Tu (pronoun)
6. Elle (pronoun)
7. ami (noun)
8. M. Lemaire (noun)

D 1. Il **va** bien?
2. Je te **présente** mon ami.
3. Lucas **est** mon ami.
4. Comment elle **s'appelle**?
5. Eva **a** quel âge?
6. Tu **as** seize ans.

Subject pronouns

A 1. Yolanda plays tennis, but **she** prefers to skate.
2. Henry and I like pizza. **We** eat it every day.
3. My parents wake up very early because **they** both work.
4. Marie looks great today! Did **she** get a haircut?
5. Mr. Mallet is very happy. **He** just got a promotion.
6. Tom, Arthur, Alice, and you are invited to my party. **You** don't need to bring anything.

B 1. Comment **tu** t'appelles?
2. Monsieur Guillaud, comment allez-**vous**?
3. C'est un ami. **Il** s'appelle Mathieu.
4. Sarah et Laura? **Elles** ont quel âge?
5. J'ai quinze ans.
6. En France, **on** parle français.
7. Et toi? **Tu** as quel âge?
8. Bonjour, mademoiselle. **Je** m'appelle Alexis.

C 1. Michel est mon ami. **Il**
2. Valentin et moi parlons français. **Nous**
3. Le professeur s'appelle M. Cartier. **Il**
4. Charlotte a dix-huit ans. **Elle**
5. Mme Lambert et Mme Gidon sont professeurs. **Elles**
6. Nicolas et Benjamin adorent le tennis. **Ils**
7. Nathan et Amandine ont vingt ans. **Ils**

D 1. Mme Lambert et Mme Gidon: **Elles** is the pronoun that stands for two or more females.
2. Nicolas et Benjamin: **Ils** is the subject pronoun that stands for two or more males.
3. Nathan et Amandine: **Ils** is the subject pronoun that stands for a mixed group of males and females.

Indefinite articles

A 1. Lucy is carrying a heavy suitcase.

2. Did you mail a card to Aunt Ruthie?

3. I don't have a calculator in my backpack.

4. Victor has an iguana in his bedroom.

5. I want a new mp3 player for my birthday.

6. Do you have an e-mail address?

7. My friends and I bought a DVD and some CDs.

B 1. Oui, il y a des CD. (P, M)

2. Est-ce qu'il y a des posters? (P, M)

3. Il n'y a pas de lecteur de DVD. (S, M)

4. Est-ce qu'il y a une fenêtre? (S, F)

5. Non, il n'y a pas de filles. (P, F)

6. Il y a des ordinateurs. (P, M)

7. Il y a un tableau dans la classe. (S, M)

C 1. Je te présente Axel. C'est un ami.

2. Il y a des bureaux dans la classe.

3. Il n'y a pas de tableaux dans ma classe.

4. Est-ce qu'il y a une carte?

5. Je te présente Jade. C'est une amie.

6. Il y a des élèves et des professeurs.

7. Non, il n'y a pas de télé dans la classe.

D 1. Il y a des cahiers.

2. Il y a des garçons.

3. Il y a un bureau.

4. Il y a des livres.

5. Il y a une fenêtre.

Avoir and negation

A 1. My cousins don't have a DVD player. (negative)

2. Beatrice has a French uncle. (affirmative)

3. I don't have your e-mail address. (negative)

4. Our classroom has four computers. (affirmative)

5. My friends and I don't have a car. (negative)

6. Sarah has not called yet. (negative)

7. We have too many things to do. (affirmative)

B 1. Je n'ai pas quinze ans. (negative)

2. Vous avez un lecteur de DVD. (affirmative)

3. Mon ami Romain a dix-sept ans. (affirmative)

4. Nous n'avons pas de carte. (negative)

5. Pauline n'a pas de ordinateur. (negative)

6. Jeanne et moi, nous avons dix livres. (affirmative)

7. Tu n'as pas de cahiers? (negative)

C 1. Le prof de maths a vingt-neuf ans.

2. Tu n'as pas seize ans?

3. Nous avons un ami français: Jean-François Rivière.

4. Je n'ai pas de bureau.

5. Thomas et Claude ont l'adresse e-mail d'Agathe.

6. Vous avez une télévision et un lecteur de DVD?

7. Le professeur a vingt-trois élèves.

D 1. Ça ne s'écrit pas d-i-x.

2. Lucas n'a pas vingt-deux ans.

3. Je ne présente pas l'élève.

4. Nous n'avons pas quatorze ans.

5. Ça ne va pas?

CHAPITRE 2
Definite articles

A 1. They bought the house next door. (S, no gender)

2. She made a chocolate cake for the boys. (P, M)

3. The businesswoman is wearing a wig. (S, F)

4. The ship sailed to Martinique. (S, no gender)

5. John painted the chairs in one day. (P, no gender)

6. The girls love to play with my cat. (P, F)

B 1. Sophie adore la glace. (S, F)

2. Ils aiment bien l'école. (S, F)

3. Tu n'aimes pas les mathématiques? (P, F)

4. Je déteste le chocolat. (S, M)

5. J'aime bien les animaux. (P, M)

6. Vous aimez la voiture de sport? (S, F)

7. Alexandre adore les romans. (P, M)

C Antoine Tu aimes l'école?

Monique J'aime les maths mais je n'aime pas l'anglais. Et toi?

Antoine Moi, j'adore la classe de musique. M. Panier est le professeur et il est super.

Monique Moi aussi, j'aime bien la musique mais je préfère les vacances!

D Answers will vary. Sample answers:

1. **J'aime regarder la télé. Télé is a singular, feminine noun.**

2. J'aime la glace. **Glace** is a singular, feminine noun.

3. J'aime les mathématiques. **Mathématiques** is a plural, feminine noun.

4. J'aime les animaux. **Animaux** is a plural, masculine noun.

5. J'aime la classe de français. **Classe** is a singular, feminine noun.

-er verbs

A 1. We ride our bikes to school sometimes.

2. Gary rides his bike to school always.

3. Jeannette and Sandra like football.

4. Sandra likes tennis, too.

5. You and Peter go to the movies on Fridays.

6. I play sports after school.

B 1. Tu aimes bien l'ecole?

2. Micheline adore l'anglais.

3. Les amis surfent sur Internet.

4. J'étudie les maths.

5. Nous adorons les vacances.

6. M. et Mme Blanchard, vous regardez la télé?

C 1. (Tu / Elle / Nous) adore surfer sur Internet.

2. (Paul / Vous / Ils) aimez étudier le français?

3. (J' / Tu / Nous) écoute de la musique moderne.

4. (Mathieu / Elles / Tu) détestes la glace?

5. (Je / Marie et Jade / Nous) préfère lire des magazines.

6. (Mes amis / Vous / Agnès) aiment écouter la radio.

7. (Je / Nous / Elles) parlons anglais et français.

8. (Tu / Claudie / Vous) dessines aussi.

D 1. Oui, j'adore les maths.

2. Ils regardent la télé.

3. Tu écoutes de la musique classique?

4. Nous téléphonons à des amis.

5. Paul et Sandrine, vous étudiez le français.

6. Mme Bertrand aime envoyer des e-mails.

7. Tu adores dessiner?

8. Elle déteste dormir.

9. Tu préfères les romans?

10. Non, je ne travaille pas.

11. Est-ce que vous aimez la musique moderne?

12. Hélène et moi, nous chantons bien.

E You follow its pattern with the new verb. For example, for **penser** and **nous,** you drop the **-er** (pens-) and add the ending for **nous** (-ons): **pensons.**

Irregular plurals

A 1. The firemen came fast. (irregular)

2. How many scarves do you have? (irregular)

3. The school will buy new computers. (regular)

4. Canadian geese migrate every year. (irregular)

5. Please buy two loaves of bread. (irregular)

6. I am reading about pioneer women. (irregular)

7. Do you recycle newspapers? (regular)

8. Gray wolves are still endangered. (irregular)

B 1. Il y a deux tableaux dans la classe. (irregular)

2. J'aime lire les journaux. (irregular)

3. Georges préfère lire des magazines. (regular)

4. Est-ce que tu aimes les animaux? (irregular)

5. Nous n'aimons pas les bandes dessinées. (regular)

6. J'ai trente-six DVD. (irregular)

7. Il n'y a pas de bureaux dans la classe? (irregular)

8. Mon ami a des CD de musique classique. (irregular)

C 1. Les garçons aiment les **jeux**.

2. Vous avez des **bureaux** dans la classe?

3. Samir n'a pas de **journaux**. Moi non plus.

4. Est-ce qu'il y a des **animaux**?

5. Moi, j'aime bien les **CD** de musique classique.

6. Il y a des cartes et des **tableaux** dans la classe.

D 1. **Il y a dix-neuf élèves dans la classe.**

2. Il y a trois animaux dans la classe.

3. Il y a deux bureaux dans la classe.

4. Il y a vingt journaux dans la classe.

5. Il y a un tableau dans la classe.

Contractions with à

A 1. This isn't my backpack. (is not)

2. You don't you like to dance? (do not)

3. How come she's always late? (she is)

4. How's it going, Bob? (How is)

5. We've come a long way. (We have)

6. Sam, you're a great friend. (you are)

7. I haven't done my homework. (have not)

B 1. M. Baubeau travaille à l'école. (à + l')

2. Jacques adore aller au cinéma. (à + le)

3. Abdul n'aime pas aller au café. (à + le)

4. Tu aimes jouer aux cartes? (à + les)

5. Nous allons au parc souvent. (à + le)

C 1. Mes amis jouent **au** base-ball.

2. Nous aimons aller à **la** piscine.

3. Zoe travaille **au** café.

4. Tu étudies à **l'**école.

5. Je n'aime pas jouer **aux** échecs.

6. Vous allez **au** stade?

7. Jean et Célia dansent à **la** MJC.

D Answers may vary. Possible answers:

1. **J'aime aller à la piscine.**

2. Tu manges au café.

3. Nous aimons aller au parc.

4. Camille travaille à l'école.

5. Mes amis jouent aux échecs.

E Answers will vary. Possible answer:

English contractions are optional, but French contractions are required. English contractions consist of an apostrophe in place of the missing letters. French contractions may consist of new words, such as **aux**.

Est-ce que

A 1. **Are you going to lunch at noon?**

2. Does Bernard like ice skating and skiing?

3. Is it cold outside?

4. Do they live in Miami, Florida?

5. Will you play tennis with me?

6. Does Simone like to go to the movies?

B 1. **Est-ce que tu aimes lire?**

2. Est-ce qu'Océane aime faire du sport?

3. Est-ce que Lucie joue au golf?

4. Est-ce qu'ils écoutent de la musique?

5. Est-ce que vous aimez faire la fête?

6. Est-ce que tu préfères discuter avec des amis?

7. Est-ce qu'elles regardent la télé?

8. Est-ce que Bruno parle anglais?

C Answers will vary. Possible answer:

Similarities: In both languages, you can raise the pitch of your voice to change a statement into a question.

Differences: In French, you can add **est-ce que**; in English, you can add **do** or **does.**

CHAPITRE 3
Adjective agreement

A 1. Donna has a cute brother with big, blue eyes.
2. The huge locomotive made a loud noise.
3. The server spilled icy beverages on the clean floor.
4. Does Sophie know the secret code?
5. He reads a lot of exciting mysteries.
6. The campers were tired and hungry after the long hike.

B 1. Thérèse est une bonne amie.
2. J'ai les yeux verts.
3. Est-ce que tu aimes les grands magasins?
4. Didier a un long nez et une petite bouche.
5. D'après moi, elle est mignonne et marrante.
6. Vous préférez les vieux films?
7. Émile déteste les animaux méchants.

C 1. Mon ami Frédéric est (sérieux / sérieuse).
2. Tristan et Robert sont (marrant / marrants).
3. Monique a une voiture (blanc / blanche).
4. Mme Pendraud est une (bon / bonne) professeur.
5. J'aime mieux les cahiers (noirs / noires).
6. Lorraine est très (gentil / gentille).
7. Mes amis sont super (sportifs / sportives).
8. Florence est (créatif / créative) et (timide / timides).

D 1. **Luc est assez grand.**
2. Pascal est très généreux.
3. La porte est noire.
4. Julie et Edith sont gentilles.
5. Les filles sont mignonnes.

Irregular adjectives

A 1. Patricia is brown-haired. (**S**)
2. I bought a very cool shirt. (S)
3. These shoes are old. (P)
4. We went to a chic restaurant. (S)
5. The Hinaults live in a beautiful house. (S)
6. Have you met my new neighbors? (P)

B 1. Élisabeth est belle. (**S, F**)
2. Il n'y a pas de nouveaux élèves. (P, M)
3. J'aime bien les vieilles fenêtres. (P, F)
4. Olivier a une voiture marron. (S, F)
5. C'est un vieux stade. (S, M)
6. Tu trouves le magasin chic? (S, M)

C 1. Jules a de **beaux** posters.
2. Je te présente un **nouveau** professeur.
3. Il y a de **nouvelles** chaises dans la classe.
4. Isaac est mon **nouvel** ami.
5. J'ai trois crayons **marron.**
6. Constance a une **vieille** voiture.
7. C'est un **bel** animal!

D 1. Colette est une belle fille et Gaston est un beau garçon.
2. J'ai les yeux marron et une voiture marron.
3. The adjective beautiful does not change forms; the adjective *beau* does. Both beautiful and *beau* come before the noun they describe. The adjective brown comes before the noun it describes, but *marron* comes after the noun. Both brown and *marron* are invariable; they never change forms.

ANSWER KEY

Irregular adjectives

A 1. The Smiths bought their first house last month.

2. His hamster is sleeping in its nest.

3. My parents have their 25th wedding anniversary tomorrow.

4. Where did I put my keys?

5. It's great to hear that our soccer team won.

6. Your sister left her backpack on the playground.

B 1. Sa tante est très chic.

2. Leurs enfants sont pénibles.

3. Quel âge a ton frère?

4. Votre fils est super gentil.

5. C'est une photo de ma grand-mère.

6. Il n'a pas son cahier.

C **Madeleine** Comment s'appelle **ton** demi-frère?

Étienne **Mon** demi-frère s'appelle André. Il est sympa mais **ses** amis sont pénibles.

Madeleine Et **tes/vos** parents, ils sont comment?

Étienne **Mes/Nos** parents s'appellent Lucie et Georges. Ils sont marrants. Ils ont deux petits chiens. **Leurs** chiens s'appellent Plif et Plouf. Et toi, tu as un chien, n'est-ce pas?

Madeleine Oui. **Mon** chien s'appelle Puce.

D Answers will vary. Possible answer:

Son frère can mean his brother or her brother. **Sa sœur** can mean his sister or her sister. **Ses cousins** can mean his cousins or her cousins. In the third person, English possessive adjectives match the gender of the possessor. In French, they match the gender of the person or object possessed.

Contractions with de

A 1. doesn't
2. can't
3. I'm
4. They're
5. Mary's
6. didn't

B 1. du
2. des
3. —
4. du
5. du
6. —
7. des

C 1. de l'
2. des
3. du
4. de l'
5. du
6. des
7. de la
8. du

D **Arnaud** Qui c'est, ça?

Laetitia C'est le père **du** mari de ma tante. Il est sympa.

Arnaud Et la fille brune?

Laetitia C'est la nièce **de la** cousine de mon demi-frère.

Arnaud Qui c'est le garçon roux?

Laetitia C'est le fils unique **des** cousins de ma mère. Il s'appelle Amaury.

Arnaud Et la madame rousse? C'est la tante d'Amaury?

Laetitia Non, non. C'est la femme **de** l'oncle de ma tante Sylvie.

Arnaud Et le monsieur mince? C'est qui?

Laetitia Thierry? C'est le frère **du** mari **de la** demi-sœur de ma mère.

Arnaud Oh, là, là! C'est une grande famille!

C'est versus il/elle est

A
1. **These** are my parents, Henry and Lucille.
2. Edith? **She** is a very nice girl.
3. **This/That** is my French teacher, Mme Duquenne.
4. **Those** are my cousins who live in Québec.
5. Let me introduce to you my brother. **He** is a college student.
6. Who's the blond girl? **That** is Josette, a good friend of mine.
7. **This/That** is Vincent, the new student.

B
1. C'est mon oncle.
2. Ça, c'est Roger. Il est génial.
3. Elle est créative, a mon avis.
4. Il est assez jeune et il a les yeux marron.
5. Éléonore? C'est une copine.
6. Elle n'est ni petite ni grande.
7. C'est un garçon pénible.

C
1. **C'est** ma tante Virgine.
2. **C'est** le fils de M. Lagaffe.
3. **Elle est** rousse.
4. **C'est** un gros chat.
5. **Il est** très paresseux.
6. **Il est** vieux et méchant.
7. **C'est** un monsieur fort.
8. **C'est** le beau-père d'Arnaud.

D Answers will vary. Possible answer:

She's an athletic girl can be translated into **C'est une fille sportive**, and She's athletic into **Elle est sportive**. **C'est** is used in the first sentence because it is followed by a noun phrase. **Elle est** is used in the second sentence because it is with an adjective by itself.

CHAPITRE 4
Days of the week

A
1. one specific day
2. regularly
3. regularly
4. one specific day
5. regularly
6. one specific day
7. one specific day
8. regularly

B
1. one specific day
2. regularly
3. one specific day
4. regularly
5. one specific day
6. regularly
7. regularly

C
1. **Serge joue au base-ball le lundi et le mercredi.**
2. Serge nage à la piscine le mardi.
3. Serge étudie à la bibliothèque le jeudi.
4. Serge a cours de musique le vendredi.
5. Serge rend visite à sa grand-mère le samedi.

D Answers will vary. Possible answer: In French, the days of the week are not capitalized.

Adjectives as nouns

A
1. I cannot see the brick building, but I can see the glass one.
2. This backpack isn't mine; give me the black one.
3. The gold necklace is more expensive than the silver one.
4. We don't have to do all the exercises, only the important ones.
5. I'd rather go to the good affordable university than the overpriced one.
6. Tanasha is wearing her corduroy pants today, not the cotton ones.
7. Do you like this small dog or the big one?

B
1. Tu préfères le sac à dos vert ou le bleu?
2. Avez-vous les cahiers bleus ou les rouges?
3. Je n'aime pas le tee-shirt jaune mais j'aime bien l'orange.
4. Est-ce que j'achète les baskets blanches ou les noires?
5. C'est qui ton amie, la fille rousse ou la blonde?

6. Est-ce que vous aimez le <u>portable</u> noir ou le gris?
7. Yves aime les <u>shorts</u> bleus mais Xavier préfère les verts.
8. Est-ce que Marguerite achète le <u>sweat-shirt</u> rose ou le violet?

C 1. Est-ce que Pierre vend le vieil ordinateur ou (la nouvelle / le nouvel)?
2. Prenez-vous les stylos bleus ou (le rouge / les rouges)?
3. Le tee-shirt blanc, ça va, mais je préfère (le noir / les noirs).
4. Qu'est-ce que j'achète? Le grand dictionnaire ou (la petite / le petit)?
5. Qui est la sœur de Jean Baptiste? La fille brune ou (la blonde / le blond)?
6. J'aime la voiture rouge mais je préfère (le blanc / la blanche).

D 1. **Non, j'aime les bleus.**
2. Non, j'aime les vieilles.
3. Non, il préfère le blanc.
4. Non, j'achète la petite.
5. Non, elle n'aime pas les ennuyeuses.
6. Non, les grises sont belles.

E Answers will vary. Possible answers:

The French uses the definite article and an adjective in place of the absent noun. Keeping gender and number in agreement in French is important because it is the only way for the speaker to understand what deleted noun the article refers to.

CHAPITRE 5
The verb faire

A 1. What do you **do** for fun?
2. Tara **makes** most of her clothes.
3. When are we **going** swimming?
4. What sports do you **play**?
5. I like to **go** jogging every evening.
6. My friends **do** community theater.
7. What are you **doing** this weekend?
8. Can Sam **make** a cake for tomorrow?

B 1. Je préfère <u>faire du ski</u>. (**ski**)
2. Nous <u>faisons du vélo</u>. (bike)

3. Est-ce que tu <u>fais du jogging</u>? (jog/go jogging)
4. Jeanne <u>fait du patin à glace</u>. (ice-skates)
5. Ignace adore <u>faire du surf</u>. (to surf)
6. Est-ce que vous <u>faites du skate</u>? (skateboard)

C 1. c
2. e
3. a
4. b
5. d
6. f

D 1. fais
2. faire
3. fais
4. faisons
5. font
6. fait

E Answers will vary. Possible answer:

The answer to a question containing the verb **faire** may or may not contain a form of **faire**.

Question words

A 1. (Where / Who) do you live?
2. (What / When) does summer vacation begin?
3. (How / What) time is it?
4. (What / Where) do you like to do after school?
5. (How / Who) did you do that?
6. (What / Where) are you from?
7. (Why / How) doesn't she call me back?
8. (Who / When) is the science teacher?

B 1. (Quand / Qui) est-ce que on va à la bibliothèque?
2. (Qu' / Quand) est-ce que tu fais demain?
3. (Comment / Pourquoi) est ton amie?
4. (Qui / Avec qui) est-ce que tu vas au cinéma?
5. (Pourquoi / Où) est-ce qu'elle n'aime pas la télé?
6. (Où / Qu') est-ce que vous faites en été?

7. (Qui / Où) est-ce que tu nages?

8. (Quand / Qui) est la fille blonde?

C **Camille** Qu'est-ce que tu fais ce week-end?

Enzo Je ne fais rien.

Camille On va au théâtre ce week-end.

Enzo Quand?

Camille Samedi soir.

Enzo Où?

Camille Au théâtre Molière.

Enzo Avec qui?

Camille Avec Hugo et Irène.

D Answers will vary. Possible answers:

1. Quand est-ce que tu vas faire du surf?

2. Qui est le monsieur?

3. Comment est-ce qu'il s'appelle?

4. Où est-ce que tu étudies?

5. Avec qui est-ce que tu manges?

Adverbs

A 1. She quietly tiptoed up the stairs.

2. I will buy new shoes tomorrow.

3. He was really surprised about the party.

4. You can truly imagine what life was like in the 1800s.

5. I always read the newspaper.

6. The thief answered the questions nervously.

7. The alarm clock rang softly.

B 1. Tu joues régulièrement au football?

2. Pourquoi est-ce qu'il va rarement au cinéma?

3. Nous faisons nos devoirs facilement.

4. Elle joue mal au basket.

5. Les élèves mangent rapidement.

6. Tu chantes bien!

C 1. Le garçon sportif nage rapidement.

2. Heureusement, c'est le week-end.

3. Est-ce que tu joues régulièrement à des jeux vidéo?

4. Mon frère parle rarement au téléphone.

5. Francis joue bien de la guitare.

6. Jade prête généreusement ses fournitures scolaires.

7. J'entends mal la musique.

8. Madeleine et Jean dansent facilement.

D 1. The French words that end in –ment are adverbs; the ones that don't are adjectives.

2. In French, adverbs are usually placed after the verb. In English, the same adverb can go at the beginning of a sentence, at the end, or before the word it modifies.

Aller and the near future

A 1. near future

2. near future

3. where

4. where

5. near future

6. near future

7. where

B 1. where

2. where

3. near future

4. near future

5. near future

6. where

7. where

C 1. Michèle ne va pas aller au lac.

2. Tu vas avoir beaucoup de devoirs.

3. Vendredi, ils vont aller au musée.

4. Vous allez faire les magasins dimanche?

5. Nous allons regarder un film samedi.

6. Je ne vais pas jouer au tennis.

7. Guillaume ne va pas manger avec nous.

D Answers will vary. Possible answers:

1. Je vais nager à la plage.

2. Mes amis et moi, nous allons étudier à la bibliothèque.

3. Marc et Brigitte vont manger au café.

4. Claude va surfer sur Internet au cybercafé.

5. Vous **allez faire du ski** à la montagne.

6. Je **vais chanter** à la Maison des jeunes et de la culture.

7. Tu **vas faire du vélo** au parc.

8. Mes parents **vont faire un pique-nique** à la campagne.

CHAPITRE 6
The partitive

A 1. Bring us some water, please. (mass)

2. Does Casey have a car? (count)

3. We don't have any milk. (mass)

4. She ate a large sandwich. (count)

5. Marie brought some cheese. (mass)

B 1. Je veux du pain, s'il vous plaît. (partitive)

2. Vous avez des pommes? (indefinite)

3. J'aimerais un croissant. (indefinite)

4. Tu veux du poivre? (partitive)

5. Vous voulez de la glace? (partitive)

6. Je mange des céréales. (partitive)

7. Nous avons de la tarte. (partitive)

C 1. J'achète **des** bananes.

2. Est-ce qu'il y a **du** jus de pomme?

3. Elle prend **une** tartine avec **de la** confiture.

4. Vous prenez **du** beurre?

5. Tu veux **de l'**omelette?

6. J'aimerais **un/du** chocolat chaud.

7. Elle prend **un** toast ou **des** céréales.

8. Dans le jus, il y a **des** oranges, **des** bananes.

9. J'aime manger **des** œufs et **du** bacon.

D Answers will vary. Possible answers:

Il mange une tarte means that he eats the whole pie. **Il mange de la tarte** means that he eats some pie.

The imperative

A 1. Don't eat that! (I)

2. This is my little brother. (S)

3. Have some pie. (I)

4. Don't forget the milk! (I)

5. Please pass the potatoes. (I)

6. He is watching television again. (S)

7. We don't need to wake up early. (S)

8. Read this newspaper article. (I)

B 1. Écoute ce CD!

2. Prenez une pizza!

3. On va au café.

4. Ne choisis pas le porc!

5. Nous faisons du ski.

6. Allons au cinéma ce soir!

7. J'ai envie de manger des légumes.

C 1. Vous avez faim? **Mangez!**

2. Tu veux t'amuser? **Fais du vélo!**

3. Allons au parc et **jouons au volley!**

4. Tu aimes faire les magasins? **Va au centre commercial!**

5. Vous voulez maigrir? **Faites du sport!**

6. Vous avez de la limonade? **Donnez-moi un verre, s'il vous plaît.**

D Answers will vary. Possible answers:

1. **Prends un sandwich!**

2. Écoute la radio!

3. Joue au football!

4. Bois de l'eau!

5. Regarde la télé!

CHAPITRE 7
Demonstrative adjectives

A 1. This backpack is not mine. (S)

2. Did you make that pie? (S)

3. How much are those socks? (P)

4. These toys belong to Katie. (P)

5. I bought that little red hat. (S)

6. Did you write these stories? (P)

7. This black shirt is very stylish. (S)

B 1. Elle aime bien ce stylo rouge. (S, M)

2. Tu n'aimes pas cette chemise? (S, F)

3. Nous préférons ces tee-shirts bleus. (P, M)

4. Pauline adore ce manteau-là. (S, M)

5. Il n'achète pas ce short gris. (S, M)

6. Vous aimez ces lunettes de soleil? (P, F)

7. Je préfère cet anorak-ci. (S, M)

C 1. Élodie préfère **ce** jean.

2. Tu n'aimes pas **ce** costume?

3. Mon père achète **ce** CD de Céline Dion.

4. Je voudrais **ces** chaussettes-là.

5. Lisette n'aime pas **cette** écharpe horrible.

6. Marc adore **cet** ordinateur!

7. Je n'aime pas **cette** cravate violette.

8. C'est combien, **ces** bottes-là?

D Answers will vary. Possible answers:

1. **Je vais acheter ces baskets**.

2. Tu vas acheter cette jupe.

3. Hélène va acheter ce pantalon.

4. Hortense et Joseph vont acheter ces lunettes.

5. Nous allons acheter cet anorak.

Interrogative adjectives

A 1. <u>What</u> fell off the shelf?

2. <u>What</u> is the problem, sir?

3. <u>What</u> ugly shoes!

4. <u>Which</u> course is Lola taking?

5. <u>Which</u> scarf do you like best?

B 1. <u>Quel</u> est le numéro de téléphone de Sophie?

2. <u>Quelle</u> couleur!

3. <u>Quel</u> jean est-ce que tu prends?

4. <u>Quels</u> sont tes magasins préférés?

5. <u>Quelle</u> pointure faites-vous?

6. <u>Quel</u> beau manteau!

C 1. **Quels** magasins est-ce que tu préfères?

2. **Quelle** pizza est-ce que tu prends?

3. **Quelles** sont ses couleurs préférées?

4. **Quel** chemisier est-ce que Florence porte ce soir?

5. **Quelle** longue jupe!

6. **Quel** chat méchant!

7. **Quelles** chaussures est-ce que tu achètes?

8. **Quel** est ton pantalon préféré?

D M. Roux **Quel** est votre nom, mademoiselle?

Sabine Sabine Nicoud.

M. Roux **Qu'est-ce que** vous faites?

Sabine Je fais les magasins!

M. Roux **Qu'est-ce que** vous aimez acheter?

Sabine Des vêtements.

M. Roux **Quels** vêtements est-ce que vous cherchez?

Sabine Une jupe en jean et un chemisier.

M. Roux **Quel** est votre magasin préféré?

Sabine J'aime bien Maryse.

M. Roux Merci beaucoup.

Sabine Pas tu tout.

M. Roux Eh... **Qu'est-ce que** vous pensez de ma cravate?

Sabine Franchement, elle est un peu tape-à-l'œil.

M. Roux **Qu'est-ce que** vous dites? Elle est tout à fait chic!

The passé composé of -er verbs

A 1. Rita <u>ordered</u> soup and salad.

2. Marion <u>worked</u> at the ice cream stand.

3. Edwin <u>talked</u> to Susanne all afternoon.

4. Marianne <u>hasn't cleaned</u> her room.

5. I <u>didn't finish</u> the book last night.

6. Gabriel <u>lived</u> in Senegal for ten years.

B 1. Qu'est-ce que tu |as| acheté ce week-end?

2. Nous |avons| trouvé ces jeans.

3. J'|ai| mangé de la pizza.

4. Claire |a| étudié à la bibiothèque.

5. Les éleves n'|ont| pas visité le musée.

C 1. Philippine **a essayé** trois jeans.

2. Nous **avons acheté** un cerf-volant.

3. Est-ce que tu **as parlé** au téléphone avec Emmanuelle?

4. Dominique **n'a pas trouvé** de canne à pêche.

5. Je **n'ai pas écouté** la nouvelle chanson.

6. Jérôme et Isaac **ont nagé** ce matin.

7. Vous **n'avez pas décidé**?

D Paul Tu vas étudier aujourd'hui?

Lorraine **Non, j'ai étudié hier.**

Paul Les parents achètent une voiture?

Lorraine Non, ils ont acheté une voiture hier.

Paul Toi et tes amis, vous allez jouer au tennis cet après-midi?

Lorraine Non, nous avons joué au tennis hier.

Paul Tu vas téléphoner à Éric?

Lorraine Non, j'ai téléphoné à Éric hier.

Paul Tes frères regardent le film maintenant?

Lorraine Non, ils ont regardé le film hier.

Paul Tu vas surfer sur Internet aujourd'hui?

Lorraine Non, j'ai surfé sur Internet hier.

The passé composé of irregular verbs

A 1. My uncle <u>fought</u> in the war. (to fight)
2. Her older brother <u>drove</u> to school. (to drive)
3. I <u>ate</u> the whole pizza. (to eat)
4. My aunt <u>came</u> to visit. (to come)
5. We <u>haven't caught</u> any fish. (to catch)
6. The kitten <u>hid</u> inside the sack. (to hide)
7. She <u>has told</u> us everything. (to tell)
8. Joseph <u>sat</u> patiently for hours. (to sit)

B 1. Ils <u>ont voulu</u> manger au café. (vouloir)
2. Vous <u>avez lu</u> un bon livre? (lire)
3. J'<u>ai fait</u> du ski en hiver. (faire)
4. Pourquoi tu n'<u>as pas voulu</u> aller? (vouloir)
5. J'<u>ai été</u> à la bibliothèque. (être)
6. Est-ce qu'il <u>a plu</u> hier? (pleuvoir)
7. Elle <u>a mis</u> son maillot de bain. (mettre)
8. Nous <u>avons eu</u> un accident. (avoir)

C 1. **Vous avez vu un film super.**

2. Séverine a pris le déjeuner.
3. Tu as lu un magazine en français.
4. Ils ont fait un pique-nique au parc.
5. J'ai mis des chaussures de randonnée.
6. Nous n'avons pas bu de café.

D Answers will vary. Possible answers:
1. J'**ai vu un film** au cinéma.
2. Il **a mangé** un croque-monsieur.
3. Mes amis **ont fait** un pique-nique au parc.
4. Tu **as mis** un manteau?
5. Nous **avons lu** les bandes dessinées.

CHAPITRE 8
Negative expressions

A 1. I <u>never</u> go swimming in the evenings.
2. I have <u>not</u> seen anybody around today.
3. I am hungry because I ate <u>nothing</u> this morning.
4. <u>Nobody</u> goes there anymore.
5. There is <u>none</u> left.
6. I am <u>not</u> going to watch any movies tonight.
7. We <u>no longer</u> eat red meat.

B 1. Étienne <u>ne</u> va <u>jamais</u> à la plage.
2. Il <u>n'</u>a <u>plus</u> d'amis.
3. <u>Personne ne</u> joue au football.
4. Il <u>ne</u> fait <u>rien</u> le week-end.
5. Nous <u>n'</u>avons <u>pas encore</u> parlé avec ses parents.
6. <u>Rien n'</u>est intéressant.
7. Il <u>n'</u>aime <u>ni</u> le cinéma <u>ni</u> les jeux vidéo.

C **Honoré** Je ne peux **pas** sortir? Et pourquoi?

Maman Tu n'as **pas encore** fait des corvées.

Honoré Mais si. J'ai débarrassé la table.

Maman Et la vaisselle? **Personne n'a** fait la vaisselle.

Honoré La lave-vaisselle peut faire la vaisselle.

Maman Désolée, mais on **n'a plus** de lave-vaisselle.

Honoré Ah, maman. C'est pénible faire la vaisselle.

Maman Rien n'est facile, Honoré.

D 1. **Nous ne déjeunons jamais au café.**

2. Personne n'a fait du patin à glace.

3. Je n'ai rien étudié au cybercafé.

4. Tu n'as plus faim?

5. Vous ne nagez jamais au lac?

The passé composé with être

A 1. Carl has written a letter to his congressman.

2. I have seen this movie before.

3. Cheryl hasn't received her invitation yet.

4. He has come to fix the dishwasher.

5. My cousins have lived in that house for many years.

6. You have read *The Little Prince*, right?

B 1. Francine est née à Avignon.

2. Nanette est tombée dans l'escalier.

3. Les Granger sont partis en vacances.

4. Nous sommes restés chez Tante Huguette.

5. Est-ce que tu es sorti avec ma sœur?

6. Je suis arrivé hier soir.

C 1. Monsieur, quand est-ce que vous **êtes arrivé**?

2. Louise **est allée** en Afrique.

3. Le petit garçon **est tombé** du balcon!

4. Laurent et moi, nous **sommes nés** le même jour.

5. Marie-Thérèse, tu **es devenue** professeur!

6. Mes sœurs **sont restées** chez mamie.

D 1. **Les filles sont descendues à la salle à manger.**

2. Geneviève est sortie à huit heures.

3. Le nouveau tapis est arrivé ce matin.

4. Est-ce que Jules et Olivier sont retournés?

5. Mes grands-parents sont morts l'année dernière.

6. Marc et moi ne sommes pas allés à la MJC.

CHAPITRE 9
Inversion

A 1. Is Henry absent today?

2. He has gone to the party.

3. Is Cafe Paris on this street?

4. Have you found the map?

5. There are too many questions.

6. Am I dressed appropriately?

7. Are your parents home?

8. You are very smart.

B 1. Fait-il chaud?

2. Marie habite chez sa tante.

3. Comment allez-vous?

4. Pierre est tombé du deuxième étage.

5. Tes parents ont-ils téléphoné?

6. Pascal n'a-t-il pas parlé?

7. Vous allez écouter la radio.

8. Ont-elles lu toute la soirée?

C 1. **Êtes-vous allé en métro?**

2. Le taxi est-il déjà parti?

3. Où habites-tu?

4. Tes parents veulent-ils que tu rentres tôt?

5. As-tu pris le bus pour aller au centre-ville?

6. Sabine, a-t-elle acheté des timbres?

D Answers will vary. Possible answer:

In both the French questions **Est-il ton frère?** and **Est-il allé à l'école aujourd'hui?** and the English questions *Is he your brother?* and *Did he go to school today?*, the verbs comes before the subject pronouns. The difference is that in French, there is a hyphen between the verb and subject pronoun.

CHAPITRE 10
Prepositions with countries and cities

A 1. Does he often go **to** Montreal?

2. Why don't we move **to** Texas?

3. I'll call you when I'm **in** Saint Louis.

4. This cheese came **from** France.

5. How often do you go **to** Ireland?

6. Her cousins live **in** Belgium.

7. Our new classmate is **from** Dakar.

8. Is his family originally **from** New York?

B 1. Stéphane voudrait aller <u>au</u> Canada. **(to)**

2. Tu as un frère qui habite <u>à</u> Londres? **(in)**

3. Mes amis ont passé un week-end <u>en</u> Italie. **(in)**

4. Je suis allé <u>à</u> la Martinique. **(to)**

5. Moulay vient <u>du</u> Maroc. **(from)**

6. Nous prenons le train pour aller <u>en</u> Espagne. **(to)**

7. Elle va aller <u>au</u> Japon. **(to)**

8. Son oncle vient <u>des</u> États-Unis. **(from)**

C Feminine countries end in **–e. Le Mexique** also ends in **–e,** but it is masculine.

D 1. Charlotte est maintenant **aux** États-Unis.

2. Les élèves vont **en** Russie.

3. Qu'est-ce qu'on peut acheter **au** Maroc?

4. Lourdes habite à Guadalajara, **au** Mexique.

5. Nous allons passer une semaine **à** New York.

6. Daniel vient **de** Tunisie.

7. Je vais visiter les villages **en** Allemagne et **en** Italie.

8. Est-ce qu'il pleut souvent **au** Brésil?

9. Mes amis sont partis **de** Seattle et ils vont **à** San Francisco.

Level 2

CHAPITRE 1
The adjectives beau, nouveau, vieux

A 1. I want to visit Paris, because everyone says it is a beautiful city.

2. The students loved listening to old records.

3. It is a beautiful house but the plumbing doesn't work.

4. Henry came to school riding his new bicycle.

5. The old part of the city has streets made of bricks.

6. The magician amazed everyone with his new trick.

B 1. Ma tante habite dans une belle ville.

2. Nous avons une vieille voiture.

3. Ce chapeau est très vieux.

4. Derrière la maison il y a un beau jardin.

5. Tu aimes bien ce bel anorak?

6. Mes parents m'ont offert une nouvelle bicyclette.

C 1. Ce sont de (belles / beaux) animaux.

2. On a visité les (vieilles / vieux) églises de la ville.

3. Dans un magasin très chic, j'ai acheté cette (belle / belles) jupe.

4. J'ai besoin d'une (nouvelle / nouveau) valise pour le voyage.

5. Nous sommes restés dans un (vieil / vieux) hôtel.

6. Est-ce que vous habitez dans le (nouvelle / nouvel) appartement?

7. Mes amis adorent les (vieilles / vieux) films français.

8. Tu connais le (nouvel / nouveau) élève, n'est-ce pas?

D 1. **Ma tante est très vieille.**

2. Connaissez-vous notre vieil hôpital?

3. C'est un beau film.

4. Mes copains sont beaux.

5. Nous avons acheté un nouvel ordinateur.

6. Tu aimes mes nouveaux pantalons?

CHAPITRE 2
Direct objects

A 1. The library also lends <u>DVDs</u>.

2. Her parents drive an antique <u>car.</u>

3. We need <u>candles</u> for the birthday cake.

4. I'm meeting <u>George</u> at the park.

5. I take <u>the bus</u> to school on occasion.

6. The dog always obeys his <u>master</u>.

7. She doesn't understand the chemistry <u>lesson</u>.

8. Did you take <u>pictures</u> of the fireworks?

B 1. Tu as ton <u>sac</u>?

2. Monique cherche le <u>livre</u> de maths.

3. Je ne vois pas <u>Jean</u>.

4. J'aime ce <u>chemisier</u> blanc.

5. Delphine veut acheter ce <u>cadeau</u>.

6. Est-ce que tu as invité <u>Magali</u> à la fête?

7. Elle trouve ce <u>bouquet</u> de fleurs très beau.

8. Nous prenons un <u>sandwich</u> au café.

C 1. J'aime bien ⌐les céréales¬ pour le petit-déjeuner.

2. Nous avons trouvé ⌐notre chien¬ au parc.

3. Avez-vous vu ⌐le film¬ allemand?

4. Au magasin, j'ai choisi ⌐un tee-shirt noir¬.

5. Tu as invité ⌐tes cousins¬ à la fête?

6. Mes amis et moi, nous attendons ⌐le bus¬ pour aller à l'école.

D Answers will vary. Possible answer:

J'aime l'école has a direct object, **école**. The other sentence does not have a direct object because the preposition **à** comes between the verb and the noun.

Direct object pronouns

A 1. Finish your <u>homework</u> now and hand ⌐it¬ in tomorrow

2. I bought an <u>apple</u> for later, but I ate ⌐it¬ immediately.

3. If you don't know <u>Russell</u>, let me introduce ⌐him¬ to you!

4. I heard a lot about your <u>brothers</u>, but I never met ⌐them¬.

5. I wanted to see two <u>movies</u>, but my friend had already see ⌐them¬.

6. Did you phone <u>Grandmother</u> or did you email ⌐her¬?

7. Do you like these <u>flowers</u>? I bought ⌐them¬ for my mom.

8. I sent you my first <u>novel</u>. You never read ⌐it¬, did you?

B 1. Elle essaie les <u>robes</u> et ⌐les¬ achète.

2. <u>La jupe</u> est horrible. Elle ne ⌐la¬ prend pas.

3. Est-ce que vous montez les <u>lits</u> ou ⌐les¬ descendez?

4. <u>Marcel</u>, je ⌐te¬ souhaite bon anniversaire!

5. <u>Monsieur et Madame Langlois</u>, je ⌐vous¬ invite chez moi.

6. J'adore les <u>feux d'artifice</u> et je vais ⌐les¬ voir cette année.

7. Cette <u>carte</u> est belle. Tu veux ⌐l'¬envoyer?

C 1. **Non, je ne les aime pas.**

2. Oui, je le prends./Non, je ne le prends pas.

3. Oui, je les invite./Non, je ne les invite pas.

4. Oui, je les achète souvent./Non, je les achète rarement.

5. Oui, je l'attends./Non, je ne l'attends pas.

6. *(Name of person)* la fait.

D Answers will vary. Possible answer:

In the present, **ne... pas** goes around the verb and the pronoun. In the near future, **ne... pas** goes around the first verb (a form of **aller**) and before the pronoun.

Indirect objects

A 1. I wrote ⌐my best friend¬ many e-mails while I was away.

2. Who sent that package to ⌐you¬?

3. I brought ⌐my grandmother¬ a bouquet of daisies.

4. My parents bought ⌐my brother and me¬ a new computer!

5. Let's write ⌐our congresswoman¬ a letter.

6. We gave ⌐the dog¬ a big, juicy bone.

B 1. Tu peux offrir un CD ⌐à Sophie¬.

2. Je dois téléphoner ⌐à mes parents¬.

3. Est-ce que vous pouvez donner ce livre ⌐à Jean-Luc¬?

4. Le prof d'histoire va rendre les devoirs ⌐aux élèves¬.

5. Nous pouvons parler à Mylène et à François à la fête.

6. Ma tante offre toujours des chocolats aux enfants.

C 1. **Nous donnons des cadeaux** à nos amis.

2. J'écris une carte de vœux à mes grands-parents.

3. Les Hébert vendent leur maison aux parents de Martin.

4. Notre chien apporte le journal aux filles.

5. Je vais demander de l'argent à mon père.

6. J'offre un ballon à mon petit ami.

7. Tu n'envoies pas une invitation aux sœurs d'Alice.

D Answers will vary. Possible answer:

English and French verbs meaning the same thing don't necessarily take the same kind of object. Verbs that take direct objects in English may take indirect objects in French.

Indirect object pronouns

A 1. Who gave me this present?

2. He did not know her, but offered it to her anyway.

3. Why did you give him a small tip?

4. Who writes you so many letters?

5. Frank gave it to us last week.

6. She explained everything to me.

7. Could you leave the lights on for them?

B 1. Nous allons te l'acheter.

2. Je ne lui prête pas mes choses.

3. Il vous a dit tout, n'est-ce pas?

4. Son père va la lui prêter.

5. Est-ce que vous allez nous le vendre?

6. Gilles ne veut pas me le montrer.

7. Tu vas la leur envoyer?

C 1. —Tu dois lui écrire une lettre.

2. —Non, je **leur** pose rarement des questions.

3. —Je vais **vous** les montrer demain.

4. —Oui, je vais **lui** acheter celui-ci.

D 1. **Grégoire nous l'envoie.**

2. Lorraine nous les écrit.

3. Sylvie et Maude te les rendent.

4. Mon grand-père va me l'acheter.

5. Sa tante le lui donne.

6. M. Dupuy va les leur prêter.

CHAPITRE 3
The pronoun y

A 1. Mom's at the store.

2. I can't wait to go to Montreal.

3. John and Julie are in the library.

4. Her best friend is moving to Seattle.

5. The State Fair takes place in Dallas.

6. They go to France often.

7. Are you going to the art museum?

B 1. Maman va au supermarché le lundi.

2. Est-ce qu'on peut aller à la piscine cet après-midi?

3. Laure fait de l'athlétisme au stade.

4. Didier et Thomas vont chez ses parents.

5. Cécile est allée à Berlin l'été dernier.

6. Le poivre est sur la table.

7. Nous prenons le bus pour aller au centre commercial.

C 1. Oui, Mylène y habite.

2. Oui, elle y va.

3. Oui, nous y prenons un sandwich.

4. Oui, mes copains y étudient.

5. Oui, je vais y aller.

6. Oui, les filles y parlent.

7. Oui, elle va y aller.

8. Oui, j'y mange.

D Answers will vary. Possible answers:

J'y vais. / Je l'achète.

Je vais y aller. / Je vais l'acheter.

The pronoun en

A 1. I love chocolate so I eat a lot of it.

2. Juice? No, I don't want any.

3. I haven't read my e-mails because there are too many of them.

4. I made homemade ice-cream. Do you want some?

5. I would like to buy your CDs, but not all of them.

6. Yes, this is my popcorn and you can grab some.

7. I bought a box of candy but I don't have any left.

8. I love horror movies so I watch all of them.

B 1. —Avez-vous un frère? —Oui, j'en ai un.

2. —Est-ce que tu as de l'argent? —Non, je n'en ai pas.

3. —Veux-tu de la soupe? —Oui, j'en veux.

4. —As-tu beaucoup de temps? —Non, je n'en ai pas beaucoup.

5. —Combien d'œufs est-ce qu'il y a? —Il y en a plusieurs.

6. —Connaissez-vous des professeurs ici? —Oui, j'en connais deux.

7. —As-tu assez de café? —Oui, j'en ai assez.

8. —Il n'a pas d'amis? —Mais si, il en a beaucoup.

C 1. **Non, il y en a vingt-six.**

2. Non, Karine en a dix-sept.

3. Non, les élèves en ont cinquante à lire. (50)

4. Non, il y en a deux.

5. Non, je vais en acheter huit.

6. Non, nous en avons douze.

7. Non, Ignace en parle trois.

8. Non, cette maison en a quatre.

Placement of object pronouns

A 1. **Anne always offers it to them.**

2. Why did you lend it to him?

3. I plan to give them to you.

4. Olivia is baking it for her.

5. Victor bought it for them.

6. We haven't told it to him.

B 1. **Il ne me la prête jamais.**

2. Tu vas les leur donner.

3. Nous pouvons leur en envoyer.

4. Tu peux les y trouver.

5. Vous y en achetez souvent.

6. Je t'en offre beaucoup.

7. Maurice ne les y voit pas.

C 1. **J'y en achète.**

2. Je la lui donne.

3. Marie-France va nous les prêter.

4. Les parents doivent leur en lire.

5. Tu ne leur en envoies jamais.

6. Nous allons y en acheter.

7. Je ne veux pas te le donner.

CHAPITRE 4
Object pronouns with the passé composé

A 1. **I have not bought it yet.**

2. Have I shown you my collection?

3. We will have finished them.

4. I had bought this shirt for her.

5. Has she phoned him?

6. My friends have given it to me.

B 1. **Je les ai jetées à la poubelle.**

2. Est-ce que tu ne les as pas trouvés?

3. Je lui ai préparé un sandwich.

4. Il ne nous a pas donné l'adresse.

5. Nous les avons achetés au marché.

C 1. Corinne n'a pas écrit à ses parents, mais elle **leur a téléphoné.**

2. Tu n'as pas encore envoyé la lettre, mais tu **l'as écrite.**

3. Eugénie n'offre jamais de cadeaux à ses sœurs, mais elle **leur a prêté** ses choses.

4. Je n'ai pas vu Serge, mais je **lui ai parlé** au téléphone.

5. Frédéric n'aime pas sa cousine, mais il **l'a choisie** pour son équipe de volley.

6. Nous n'avons pas fini nos devoirs, mais nous **les avons rendus** au professeur.

D Answers will vary. Possible answers:

1. The past participle **invités** agrees with the direct object **les** because **les** precedes the verb.

2. The past participle **vu** doesn't agree with the direct object **sœur** because the object goes after the verb.

3. The past participle **parlé** doesn't agree with **cousine** because the pronoun **lui** is an indirect object.

Quelqu'un, quelque chose

A
1. I didn't see (anyone / nobody) at the park.
2. Are you doing (anything / nothing) Friday night?
3. (Anyone / Someone) is calling your name.
4. There is (anything / nothing) to eat.
5. She says she doesn't have (anything / nothing) to wear.
6. There must be (anyone / someone) here.
7. (Anything / Nothing) interesting has happened.

B
1. Je n'ai (quelque chose / rien) mangé.
2. (Quelqu'un / Personne) n'est sorti hier soir.
3. J'ai acheté (quelque chose / rien) pour toi.
4. Est-ce que tu connais quelqu'un / personne) d'intelligent?
5. Je ne vois (quelqu'un / personne) ici.
6. Il n'y a (quelque chose / rien) de nouveau.
7. Est-ce qu'il y a (quelqu'un / quelque chose) qui parle allemand?

C
1. Il n'y a personne dans le laboratoire.
2. Personne ne veut parler avec vous.
3. Rien n'est arrivé.
4. Je ne voudrais rien boire.
5. Nous n'avons invité personne d'important.
6. Guy n'a rien acheté de bon.
7. Personne n'a gagné la compétition.

D Answers will vary. Sample answers:

English: I can't see anything.
French: Je ne vois rien.

English: Can I do anything?
French: Est-ce que je peux faire quelque chose?

CHAPITRE 5
Reflexive verbs

A
1. non-reflexive
2. reflexive
3. reflexive
4. non-reflexive
5. reflexive
6. non-reflexive
7. reflexive

B
1. reflexive
2. non-reflexive
3. reflexive
4. reflexive
5. non-reflexive
6. non-reflexive
7. reflexive

C
1. Ma cousine se lève à 6h.
2. Tu ne te dépêches pas?
3. Nous nous réveillons tôt.
4. Gilles et Claire ne s'habillent pas avant midi.
5. On se baigne tous les jours.
6. Vous vous rasez avant de prendre une douche?
7. Je me lave les mains avant de manger.
8. Combien de fois par jour est-ce qu'il se brosse les dents?

D Answers will vary. Possible answer:

The French sentences always have a reflexive pronoun with the reflexive verbs (**me, se**), but in English the reflexive pronouns myself, herself are not necessary. Also, in French, the definite article is used with a body part that receives the action of a reflexive verb (**les**) whereas in English, a possessive pronoun is used (my, her).

Reflexive verbs in the passé composé and in commands

A
1. Children, enjoy (yourself / yourselves) at the amusement park.
2. We have often asked (ourselves / themselves) that question.

Holt French   **184**   Grammar Tutor

3. Frank heard (yourself / himself) on the radio.

4. They treated (ourselves / themselves) to a banana split.

5. I have already helped (myself / himself) to some salad.

6. Patricia has never burnt (herself / yourself) ironing.

7. Have you ever made (yourself / themselves) a foot-long sandwich?

B 1. Adèle, tu (t'es lavé / s'est lavé) la figure?

2. Pierre et Henri, ne (couchez-vous / vous couchez) pas tard!

3. Chantal, (dépêche-toi / te dépêche)!

4. Est-ce que les enfants (s'est habillé / se sont habillés)?

5. Élise (s'est réveillé / s'est réveillée) de bonne heure.

6. Moi, je (me suis séché / t'es séché) les cheveux.

7. Alfred, (coiffe-toi / coiffe-nous)!

C 1. Olivier et moi, nous **nous sommes réveillés** tôt.

2. Constance **s'est lavé** la figure.

3. Monique et Corinne **se sont maquillées**.

4. Tous les copains **se sont préparés** rapidement.

5. Tu **t'es séché** les cheveux.

6. Odile et Claude, vous **vous êtes couchés** trop tard.

D 1. **Lève-toi!**

2. Déshabillez-vous!

3. Ne vous dépêchez pas!

4. Réveille-toi!

5. Brossons-nous les dents!

6. Ne te rase pas!

CHAPITRE 6
The imparfait

A 1. Present

2. Past

3. Past

4. Present

5. Past

6. Present

7. Past

B 1. Past

2. Past

3. Present

4. Past

5. Present

6. Past

7. Past

C 1. Je lisais des bandes dessinées.

2. Nous allions au supermarché le dimanche.

3. Bruno et Sylvie habitaient à la campagne.

4. Tu promenais ton chien après l'école?

5. Quand j'étais petit, je mangeais des escargots.

6. Ma sœur sortait la poubelle le vendredi.

7. Mes frères et moi, nous voulions toujours nager dans le lac.

D Quand j'avais six ans, ma famille et moi, nous habitions à la campagne. Nous n'avions pas beaucoup d'argent mais nous étions heureux. J'aimais grimper aux arbres et ma petite sœur jouait toujours avec les animaux. Mes parents travaillaient au marché le samedi. Ils vendaient des légumes et des œufs.

E Answers will vary. Possible answer: In the first sentence, the verb stem has the same spelling change as the present-tense **nous** form. In the second sentence, it doesn't because the **imparfait** ending doesn't begin with **a.**

The passé composé and the imparfait

A 1. Completed event

2. Ongoing event or condition

3. Completed event

4. Ongoing event or condition

5. Ongoing event or condition

6. Completed event

7. Ongoing event or condition

B 1. Ongoing event or condition
2. Ongoing event or condition
3. Ongoing event or condition
4. Completed event
5. Completed event
6. Completed event
7. Ongoing event or condition

C 1. Ce matin, il **est allé** chez ses grands-parents.
2. Normalement, elle **avait** de bonnes idées.
3. Il **faisait** toujours chaud en été.
4. D'abord, nous **avons pris** le train.
5. De temps en temps, Patricia **arrivait** en retard.
6. Vous **alliez** souvent au cirque?
7. Nous jouions aux dames quand tu **as téléphoné**.
8. Quand Henri **était** jeune, il **aimait** jouer au train électrique.

D 1. **Passé composé**, because it talks about a completed action in the past.
2. **Imparfait**, because it refers to an action that happened habitually in the past.

The comparative with adjectives and nouns

A 1. My suitcase is heavier than yours. (adjectives)
2. This poster is as colorful as that one. (adjectives)
3. John ate as much pizza as Rachid. (nouns)
4. A boulevard is wider than a street. (adjectives)
5. There are fewer houses than here. (nouns)
6. Are movies less interesting than books? (adjectives)

B 1. Julie est moins courageuse que Chloé. (adjectives)
2. Il y a plus d'animaux qu'en ville. (nouns)
3. L'histoire, c'est plus intéressant que les maths. (adjectives)
4. J'ai autant de livres que Michèle. (nouns)

5. Les rues sont plus propres qu'à New York. (adjectives)
6. Ma vie est aussi stressante qu'à Paris. (adjectives)

C 1. La prairie est aussi belle que la montagne.
2. Le village est plus tranquille que la ville.
3. Les chèvres sont moins gros que les chevaux.
4. L'eau ici est aussi propre qu'à la campagne.
5. Les cochons sont plus sales que les canards.
6. Les bicyclettes sont aussi dangereuses que les patins.

D Answers will vary. Possible answers:
1. Les poules sont **aussi** mignonnes **que** les lapins.
2. À la ferme, il y a **plus de** moutons **que** d'ânes.
3. On a **moins de** théâtres **que** de cinémas.
4. Le musée d'art reçoit **autant de** visiteurs **que** le musée d'histoire.
5. Les chats sont **plus** marrants **que** les chiens.
6. J'ai **moins de** CD **que** mes amis.
7. Faire un pique-nique, c'est **moins** ennuyeux **que** faire les magasins.

The superlative with adjectives

A 1. Frieda is the kindest person I know.
2. It is Paul who writes the most beautiful letters.
3. Of all my friends, Jack is the most talkative.
4. Barbara is the least timid among all of us.
5. Rowena is the smartest girl in the class.
6. The snake is the least appealing animal I can imagine.

B 1. François est le plus grand de mes amis.
2. Amélie est la fille la plus créative de notre famille.

3. Dorothée est l'élève la moins préparée de la classe.
4. Les Salines est la plus belle plage du monde.
5. Chez Yves est le magasin le plus élégant du pays.
6. Où se trouve le restaurant le plus cher du quartier?

C 1. Le TGV est le train le plus rapide de France.
2. La chimie est la classe la moins facile du lycée.
3. C'est la ville la moins intéressante du pays.
4. Vous avez la plus jolie maison de la rue.
5. C'est l'église la plus vieille de la ville.
6. J'ai acheté l'anorak le moins cher du magasin.

D 1. Louise est l'élève la plus généreuse de l'école.
2. Lise est l'élève la plus intelligente de l'école.
3. Jérôme est l'élève le moins obéissant de l'école.
4. Jacques est l'élève le plus fort de l'école.
5. Anne-Marie est l'élève la plus gentille de l'école.
6. Olivia est l'élève la moins sérieuse de l'école.
7. Jean-Paul est l'élève le moins sportif de l'école.

CHAPITRE 7
The passé composé and the imparfait

A 1. Travis used to climb trees as a kid. (habitual action)
2. I read that book and it made me cry. (end of action, reaction)
3. We played soccer, talked, and went home. (sequence of events)
4. Ian used to climb a different hill every month. (habitual action)

5. You were sleeping when the fire alarm rang. (ongoing action, interruption)
6. Samantha had a big dog when she was a kid. (ongoing states)
7. We ignored Frankie so he got angry. (end of action, reaction)

B 1. J'ai lu ce livre et j'ai pleuré. (PC, PC)
2. Louise avait dix ans et elle habitait à Paris. (I, I)
3. On a couru, on s'est baigné et on a dîné. (PC, PC, PC)
4. D'habitude, nous allions à la plage. (I)
5. Je dormais quand soudain je suis tombé. (I, PC)
6. Il faisait beau. Les oiseaux chantait. (I, I)
7. Nous sommes rentrés chez nous à minuit. (PC)

C J'ai passé un très bon week-end! Dimanche, c'était mon anniversaire. Quand j'étais petite, on allait toujours au parc zoologique pour mon anniversaire. Pas cette année. Dimanche matin, mes parents ont préparé un petit-déjeuner délicieux. Ensuite, nous sommes partis en voiture pour la montagne. Il faisait beau. Nous avons fait du ski toute la journée. Quand nous sommes rentrés, nous étions fatigués mais heureux. Plus tard, pendant que je me mettais en pyjama, j'ai entendu quelqu'un à la porte. C'était ma meilleure amie. Elle a apporté un gros gâteau d'anniversaire!

D 1. D'abord, nous sommes allés à la pêche.
2. D'habitude, nous allions à la pêche.

Verbs with être or avoir in the passé composé

A 1. Of course we have finished our homework!
2. Who has brought in the milk?
3. Doreen hasn't taken her driving test.
4. We have forgotten our canteens!
5. Which movies have you seen lately?

6. Scott hasn't published his poems.

7. I haven't entered the data yet.

8. The bellhop has taken our luggage to the room.

B 1. Ils ont passé une année en France.

2. Vous avez monté nos bagages?

3. Nous les avons descendus ce matin.

4. J'ai sorti mes lunettes de mon sac.

5. Est-ce qu'elle te l'a passée?

6. Nous avons descendu les tentes de la voiture.

7. Bien sûr, je les ai déjà montés.

C 1. Thérèse est sortie de sa maison.

2. Michel et moi, nous sommes montés au troisième étage.

3. Ils ont montéX les tentes près du lac.

4. Mme Kléber, vous êtes descendue par l'escalier?

5. Les allumettes? Elle nous les ont passées.

6. Elles ont montéX les journaux.

7. Ma cousine a descenduX sa valise.

D Mme Vallée a sorti sa voiture du garage de bonne heure. Ensuite, elle a descendu la rue Marbeuf. Comme d'habitude, elle est passée chez Mme Allard. À 8 heures du matin, Mme Vallée et Mme Allard ont descendu l'escalier de l'immeuble. Elles sont sorties par la porte d'entrée et elles sont montées dans la voiture. Vingt minutes plus tard, elles sont arrivées au lac. Ensuite, les deux amies ont sorti deux fauteuils pliants. Et la crème solaire? Elles l'ont sortie aussi.

The future

A 1. We will do the dishes after the movie.

2. Dad will be pleased with your grades.

3. We won't stay here past Saturday.

4. The couple will have a baby this fall.

5. Martin won't hesitate to help us.

6. Our team will win the game.

B 1. Les amis se baigneront après le petit-déjeuner.

2. Quand nous arriverons au café, nous boirons.

3. Christine attrapera un grand poisson.

4. Je voyagerai beaucoup l'été prochain.

5. La prochaine fois, tu emporteras une lampe de poche.

6. Vous camperez en Bretagne.

C 1. Je ne travaillerai pas aujourd'hui.

2. Nous choisirons une université.

3. Tu écriras une lettre à une école technique.

4. Vous vivrez dans une ferme.

5. Tes enfants grimperont aux arbres.

6. Tout le monde se couchera de bonne heure.

D

j'ai	nous avons
tu as	vous avez
il a	ils ont

je jouerai	nous jouerons
tu joueras	vous jouerez
il jouera	ils joueront

Answers will vary. Possible answer:

The endings of the future tense are the same as the forms of avoir in the present tense, except for nous and vous. Because I know the forms of avoir, the future tense endings should be easy to remember.

The future (irregular verbs)

A 1. will have

2. will see

3. will have

4. will give

5. will buy

6. will drive

7. will take

8. will be

B 1. voir

2. faire

3. devoir

4. être

5. venir

6. aller

7. pouvoir

C
1. La semaine prochaine, nous **irons** à la forêt.
2. Nous **verrons** beaucoup d'oiseaux.
3. J'**irai** à la pêche.
4. Il **fera** beau, j'y pense.
5. Mon frère **voudra** grimper aux arbres.
6. Mes parents **diront** que c'est trop dangereux.
7. Tu **pourras** voir les photos quand nous **reviendrons**.

D
1. **Non, elle reviendra demain.**
2. Non, j'irai au lycée demain.
3. Non, je ferai les magasins demain.
4. Non, il voudra jouer avec moi demain.
5. Non, les élèves verront le film demain.
6. Non, tu devras l'acheter demain.

CHAPITRE 8
The subjunctive

A
1. Indicative
2. Subjunctive
3. Subjunctive
4. Indicative
5. Subjunctive
6. Indicative

B
1. Subjunctive
2. Indicative
3. Subjunctive
4. Subjunctive
5. Indicative
6. Subjunctive

C
1. Il faut que nous **nous levions** de bonne heure.
2. Il est important qu'on **prenne** le petit-déjeuner tous les jours.
3. Marc, il faut que tu **ailles** chez le docteur.
4. Il faut que j' **étudie** ce soir.
5. Il est nécessaire que tu **sois** en forme.
6. Il est important qu'ils **achètent** les médicaments.
7. Simone et Sophie, il faut que vous **ayez** une trousse de premiers soins.

8. Il est important que nous **mettions** de la crème solaire.
9. Il faut que Mamie **soit** patiente.
10. Allez les enfants, il faut que vous **buviez** du lait.

Uses of the subjunctive

A
1. I wish that your friend were nicer to me.
2. It is important that you be on time.
3. Lauren wishes that she were taller.
4. I recommend that he bring a compass.
5. They prefer that Jack work the late shift.
6. Can the doctor demand that her patient undergo surgery?

B
1. Il est bon que nous mangions beaucoup de légumes.
2. Je suis contente que tu aimes ce livre.
3. Il est nécessaire que vous lui disiez la vérité.
4. Mes parents veulent que j'aille à l'université.
5. Il faut que nous rentrions à la maison.
6. Je suis triste que tu sois malade.

C
1. **Je veux que** nous invitions les frères Pépin.
2. Il n'y a pas des boissons. **Il faut que** tu en achètes.
3. **Je suis triste que** Claire ne vienne pas. C'est dommage!
4. **Je ne veux pas que** tes cousins viennent. Ils sont pénibles!
5. Nous serons beaucoup ce soir. **Il est bon que** nous ayons un gros gâteau.

D Chère Corinne,
Mes parents et moi, nous **sommes** en bonne santé. Je suis triste que tu ne **viennes** pas nous voir pendant les vacances. Je sais que tu **es** toujours occupée mais je veux que tu **changes** d'avis. Il faut que nous nous **voyions**! Dis que tu viendras!

E Answers will vary. Sample answers:

1. Madame, vous êtes fatiguée. Il est important que **vous dormiez un peu.**
2. Mes amis regardent la télé tout le temps. Je veux que **nous fassions autre chose.**
3. Tu as mal aux dents? Il faut que tu **ailles chez le dentiste.**
4. Je me suis coupé le doigt. Il est nécessaire que **je le désinfecte.**

The conditional

A
1. She <u>would help</u> you if you asked her to.
2. Joe <u>would buy</u> this bike if it were less expensive.
3. <u>Would</u> you <u>turn</u> in your own girlfriend to the principal?
4. In that situation, I <u>would ask</u> my family's advice.
5. I <u>would love</u> to meet your friends.
6. He <u>would</u> never <u>go</u> on a safari.
7. You <u>would look</u> handsome in that suit.

B
1. S'il faisait beau, je <u>jouerais</u> au tennis.
2. Tu <u>pourrais</u> me passer du sel?
3. J'<u>aimerais</u> être dentiste.
4. Ça <u>serait</u> super si tu venais cet été.
5. Est-ce que vous <u>voudriez</u> visiter le musée d'art?
6. Qu'est-ce que tu <u>ferais</u> à ma place?
7. Tu <u>devrais</u> faire du yoga tous les jours.

C
1. J'écouterais les élèves et les professeurs.
2. Je voudrais organiser un bal.
3. Tous les élèves auraient un ordinateur.
4. Je parlerais avec le directeur.
5. Nous pourrions sortir plus tôt.
6. La classe de français ferait un voyage en France.
7. Je serais un bon président.

D Answers will vary. Sample answers:

Je <u>irais</u> en Europe. J'achèterais un château en France. J'inviterais tous mes amis à vivre avec moi et nous <u>serions</u> heureux.

Si clauses

A
1. If I <u>had</u> the money, I <u>would buy</u> the latest mobile phone.
2. I <u>would help</u> you if I <u>had</u> the time.
3. If Gisela <u>spoke</u> French, she <u>would live</u> in France.
4. If you <u>wanted</u> to lose weight, you <u>would exercise</u> more.
5. If I <u>were</u> you, I <u>would call</u> your parents.
6. Peter <u>would know</u> more about current events if he <u>read</u> the newspaper.

B
1. Mes cousins <u>viendraient</u> plus souvent si on <u>avait</u> une grande maison.
2. Si tu <u>voulais</u>, tu <u>pourrais</u> jouer aux cartes avec nous.
3. Ça <u>serait</u> magnifique si nous <u>gagnions</u>.
4. J'<u>aimerais</u> bien l'inviter si je <u>savais</u> danser.
5. Si Henri <u>pouvait</u>, il <u>irait</u> à Dakar.
6. Si vous <u>aviez</u> un long week-end, vous <u>auriez</u> le temps de camper.

C
1. Si j'(<u>habitais</u> / habiterais) au Méxique, je (parlais / <u>parlerais</u>) espagnol.
2. Nous (cherchions / <u>chercherions</u>) un emploi si nous (<u>voulions</u> / voudrions) de l'argent.
3. Si mes parents (<u>gagnaient</u> / gagneraient) plus d'argent, nous (voyagions / <u>voyagerions</u>).
4. S'ils (<u>avaient</u> / auraient) un enfant, ils (avaient / <u>auraient</u>) beaucoup de responsabilités.
5. J'/Je (étais / <u>serais</u>) dans un groupe de rock si je (<u>jouais</u> / jouerais) de la guitare.
6. Si elle (<u>allait</u> / irait) voir le médecin, elle (arrêtait / <u>arrêterait</u>) de tousser.
7. Vous me (téléphoniez / <u>téléphoneriez</u>) si vous (<u>vouliez</u> / voudriez) me parler.

8. Si tu (comprenais / comprendrais)
l'anglais, tu (pourrais / pouvais) lire
cette lettre.

D Answers will vary. Sample answers:

1. **Si je me sentais malade, j'irais
chez le médecin.**

2. Si tu avais mal à la tête, tu prendrais
des médicaments.

3. Si nous voulions maigrir, nous
ferions un régime.

4. Si j'étais stressé(e), j'écouterais de la
musique.

5. Si vous fumiez, vous devriez arrêter.

6. Si mes amis faisaient de la
musculation, ils seraient forts.

CHAPITRE 9
The relative pronouns qui, que, dont

A 1. Linda is a friend <u>whom</u> I trust.
(object, person)

2. Billy read from a book <u>that</u> he wrote.
(object, thing)

3. They gave me a toy <u>that</u> glows in the
dark. (subject, thing)

4. The bulb <u>which</u> was flickering
burned out. (subject, thing)

5. We visited Mrs. Franklin <u>who</u> is sick.
(subject, person)

B 1. C'est un film <u>que</u> je n'aime pas.
(object, thing)

2. Louise est une amie <u>qui</u> est sincère.
(subject, person)

3. Elle est la dame <u>que</u> j'ai connue à
Paris. (object, person)

4. C'est l'histoire d'une fille <u>qui</u> est
pilote. (subject, person)

5. C'est un auteur <u>dont</u> j'ai lu tous ses
livres. (object, person)

6. Voici l'arbre <u>qui</u> est tombé sur sa
maison. (subject, thing)

7. Je veux voir le film <u>dont</u> je t'ai parlé.
(object, thing)

C 1. La chanson **qu**'il a chantée est très
belle.

2. C'est une histoire **qui** finit bien.

3. Le musée **dont** je t'ai parlé est très
intéressant.

4. Chris et Cécile sont les copains **que**
j'ai rencontrés au cinéma.

5. Ça parle de deux jeunes filles **qui**
vont à Québec.

6. Le film **dont** nous avons envie de
voir passe au cinéma Max.

7. Maman parle à un monsieur **qui** a
fait le tour du monde.

8. Juliette Binoche est l'actrice **que**
mon père préfère.

9. Le chien **dont** ma sœur a peur habite
juste à côté.

10. Nous aimons les films **qui** ont
beaucoup de suspense.

D Answers will vary. Sample answers:

Lues end in **-es** because when the **passé
composé** is used, the past participle
agrees with the direct object that comes
before the verb. In this case, the object is
que and **que** stands for **bandes
dessinées**, which feminine and plural.

The interrogative pronoun lequel

A Nina Hi, Paul. Do you want to catch a
<u>movie</u>?

Paul Which one? The new horror
movie?

Nina No, the one with those two
comedians.

Paul Two <u>comedians</u>? Which ones?

Nina Those two guys that appear on a
commercial together.

Paul A <u>commercial</u>? Which one?

Nina You know, the one with the new
computer.

Paul Oh, yeah. They're real funny.
Where is the movie showing?

Nina At the Plaza <u>Theater</u> and at the
Gothic <u>Theater</u>. Which one do
you prefer?

Paul Let's go to the Plaza Theater!

B Maya Tu veux regarder un <u>film</u>?

Pierrot Lequel?

Maya Le nouveau film de guerre avec
ton actrice préférée.

Pierrot Mon <u>actrice</u> préférée? Laquelle? Catherine Deneuve?

Maya Non. On la voit à la télé, tu sais, dans les <u>émissions</u> de télé.

Pierrot Lesquelles?

Maya Je ne sais pas! Mais alors, tu veux voir le film? Ça passe au deux <u>cinémas</u> près d'ici.

Pierrot Lesquels?

Maya Tu es impossible, Pierrot!

C 1. Lequel?
2. Laquelle?
3. Lequel?
4. Lesquels?
5. Lesquelles?
6. Laquelle?
7. Lequel?
8. Lesquelles?

D Answers will vary. Sample answers:

Lequel? In this sentence, the interrogative pronoun stands for a noun that is masculine and singular, **chat**. The words **il, ce, petit,** and **mignon** are all in the masculine singular form. The verb **est** shows that it is singular.

The demonstrative pronoun celui

A 1. <u>This one</u> is my favorite sitcom. (singular)
2. I really prefer <u>that one</u>. (singular)
3. <u>These</u> are his favorite actors. (plural)
4. Mary raved about <u>that one</u>. (singular)
5. I thought <u>those</u> were great. (plural)
6. Did you already listen to <u>these</u>? (plural)
7. I never miss <u>this one</u>. (singular)

B 1. Je prends <u>celui-là</u>. (S, M)
2. Tu n'aimes pas <u>celles-là</u>? (P, F)
3. Nous préférons <u>celui</u> qui passe à 20h. (S, M)
4. Pauline déteste <u>ceux-là</u>. (P, M)
5. Je ne regarde jamais <u>ceux</u> qui sont déprimants. (P, M)
6. Vous aimez <u>celle-ci</u>? (S, F)
7. <u>Ceux-là</u> sont très drôles! (P, M)

C 1. Mes films préférés sont **ceux** qui me font rire.
2. Ton jeu favori est **celui** qui passe sur TF1?
3. La présentatrice dont je parle est **celle** qui a les yeux verts.
4. Les bons documentaires sont **ceux** qui nous intéressent.
5. Ma chaîne préférée est **celle** qui a les informations.
6. Les actrices que j'aime sont **celles** qui font du théâtre.
7. Les reportages que je regarde sont **ceux** qui valent le coup.

D 1. **Non, pas celle-ci.**
2. Non, pas celles-là.
3. Non, pas celui-ci.
4. Non, pas ceux-ci.
5. Non, pas celle-là.

CHAPITRE 10
Review of the subjunctive

A 1. I recommend that he (visit / visits) Paris.
2. I think that Paris (be / is) a beautiful city.
3. It is important that your friend (make / makes) a hotel reservation.
4. It's not necessary that you (be / are) with the tour group.
5. It is obvious that the guide (know / knows) a lot about history.
6. I've read that the museum (have / has) a great gift shop.
7. It is especially important that everyone (have / has) a passport.

B 1. Il faut que nous (allions / allons) au centre commercial.
2. Le magasin Passeport (ait / a) des valises à bon prix.
3. Il faut que j' (achète / achèterais) deux valises.
4. Il n'est pas nécessaire que les valises (soient / sont) grandes.
5. Je trouve que le prix (soit / est) plus important que la couleur.
6. Il n'est pas nécessaire que mes parents y (alliez / aillent) avec nous.

7. Il faut que tu m' (emmenais / **emmènes**) au centre commercial.

C 1. Il faut que tu m'**écrives** des cartes postales.

2. Il est nécessaire que ton chien **soit** avec quelqu'un gentil pendant les vacances.

3. Il faut absolument qu'il se **fasse** vacciner.

4. Il n'est pas nécessaire que nous **allions** à la plage.

5. Il ne faut pas que tu **oublies** le plan.

6. Est-ce qu'il est nécessaire que j'**aie** une trousse de toilette?

D 1. **Il faut que nous visitions le Louvre.**

2. Il faut que vous alliez à l'Arc de Triomphe.

3. Il faut que je prenne beaucoup de photos.

4. Il faut que tu montes à Montmartre.

5. Il faut qu'Hélène n'oublie pas son permis de conduire.

6. Il faut que tes amis visitent les Tuileries.

Answer Key: Level 3

CHAPITRE 1
Verbs followed by the infinitive

A 1. He agreed to study with us.

2. Our class is going to visit the art museum.

3. Amy finally decided to study chemistry.

4. I wanted to be the captain of the ski team.

5. We are going to meet at the library at 4 o'clock.

6. The students tried to understand the lesson.

7. I intend to finish the book even though it's 700 pages long.

B 1. Je vais faire du skate au parc.

2. On peut aller au cinéma si vous voulez.

3. Mathilde veut monter à cheval.

4. Nous venons de jouer au basket.

5. Où est-ce que vous allez voir un film d'horreur?

6. On doit prendre le bus ou le métro.

C 1. Je **viens** de faire les magasins.

2. Est-ce que tu **veux** aller au cinéma vendredi?

3. Je ne **peux** pas jouer aux échecs avec vous.

4. Nous **venons** de regarder un film super!

5. Vous **voulez** faire de la vidéo amateur?

6. Hélène **peut** jouer de la guitare.

7. Mes amis **doivent** étudier pour leur examen.

8. Je **vais** parler avec le conseiller d'éducation.

D 1. Luc vient de nager à la piscine.

2. Luc vient de ranger sa chambre.

3. Luc va manger chez ses grands-parents.

4. Luc va faire ses devoirs.

5. Luc va emprunter des DVD.

CHAPITRE 2
Feminine form of nouns

A 1. d
2. c
3. e
4. f
5. a
6. b

B 1. c
2. f
3. a
4. b
5. d
6. e

C 1. Clara est devenue **architecte**.

2. La **maîtresse** et son mari sont très gentils.

3. Ma cousine est une **artiste** formidable.

4. Leur fille est **informaticienne**.

5. Tu connais l'**avocate**? Elle est allemande.

6. Ma sœur aimerait être **pâtissière**.

7. Emma va devenir **vétérinaire** parce qu'elle adore les animaux.

D 1. **Sarah est architecte aussi.**
2. Son mari est coiffeur aussi.
3. Amélie est auteur aussi.
4. Sa femme est couturière aussi
5. Sa sœur est agricultrice aussi.

The future perfect

A 1. By the time you get back, I will have cleaned my room.
2. By this time next year, I will have graduated.
3. My cousin will have visited every state by the time she's forty.
4. By the time we get there, everybody will have left.
5. If he keeps it up, he will have changed jobs four times in one year.
6. In June, my parents will have been married 25 years.
7. We will have driven more than 500 miles by the time we get to Montreal.
8. They will have moved in before the month of August.

B 1. Je te téléphonerai quand j'aurai trouvé un travail.
2. Vous sortirez quand vous aurez terminé vos devoirs.
3. Que feras-tu quand tu auras dépensé tout ton argent?
4. Nous nous lèverons quand le président aura fini son discours.
5. Je vous répondrai quand j'aurai reçu votre lettre.
6. Dans quinze jours, tu seras déjà arrivé en Afrique.
7. Elle construira notre maison quand elle sera devenue architecte.
8. Quand ils auront dîné, ils partiront tout de suite.

C 1. Tu arriveras quand je **serai sorti(e)**.
2. Elle apportera les boissons quand nous **aurons fini** de manger.
3. Il vous téléphonera quand vous **vous serez couchés**.
4. Nous arriverons sûrement quand ils **auront fermé** le restaurant.

5. Vous prendrez le métro quand nous **serons venus** vous emprunter votre voiture.

D 1. **Quand Julien aura étudié à l'étranger, il deviendra professeur.**
2. Quand Julien sera devenu professeur, il connaîtra un pilote.
3. Quand Julien aura connu un pilote, il voyagera partout.
4. Quand Julien aura voyagé partout, il écrira un roman.

Present participles

A 1. Tamasha told me a depressing story. (adjective)
2. Mr. Brown was looking for a job. (verb)
3. Nobody was hiring at the time. (verb)
4. He was very cold during the freezing winter. (adjective)
5. The smell of burning tires was unpleasant. (adjective)
6. The family is now living in Happy Canyon. (verb)

B 1. En partant à 7 heures, tu arriveras à l'heure. (verb)
2. Son travail est vraiment déprimant. (adjective)
3. Il gagne beaucoup d'argent en faisant des heures supplémentaires. (verb)
4. On parle des employés étant licenciés. (verb)
5. En lisant, j'ai beaucoup appris. (verb)
6. Il m'a raconté une histoire intéressante. (adjective)

C 1. En **sortant** du lycée, j'ai vu mon cousin Olivier.
2. Nous avons discuté en **allant** au café.
3. **Étant** passionné d'art, Olivier étudie l'histoire de l'art moderne.
4. Il apprend beaucoup en **visitant** les musées.
5. Moi, je trouve les musées d'art peu **intéressants**.
6. À mon avis, cette comédie est plus **amusante**.
7. **Sachant** ma passion, je deviendrai acteur ou directeur.

D 1. **En suivant des cours de langues, tu seras interprète.**

2. En faisant un séjour au Mexique, tu apprendras l'espagnol plus vite.

3. Tu réussiras ton examen oral en écoutant des émissions en espagnol.

4. Tu pourras travailler à Barcelone en parlant bien espagnol.

5. En étant interprète, tu connaîtras des personnes intéressantes.

CHAPITRE 3
Relative pronouns with ce

A 1. I don't know <u>what</u> you're talking about. (object)

2. They liked <u>what</u> they saw in Rome. (object)

3. <u>What</u>'s interesting is the color of this house. (subject)

4. They don't know <u>what</u>'s best for them. (subject)

5. I'll tell you <u>what</u> the princess likes. (object)

6. No one knows <u>what</u> will happen next. (subject)

B 1. <u>Ce que</u> je lis, c'est une légende. (object)

2. Je ne sais pas <u>ce qu</u>'on met dans la potion. (object)

3. <u>Ce qui</u> m'intéresse, c'est le Moyen-Orient. (subject)

4. <u>Ce qu</u>'on raconte n'est pas vrai. (object)

5. Dis-moi vite <u>ce qui</u> est arrivé! (subject)

6. Le géant mangea tout <u>ce qu</u>'il trouva. (object)

C 1. Tu ne nous a pas dit **ce que** tu as lu hier soir.

2. **Ce qui** ne me plaît pas dans cette maison, c'est les fantômes.

3. Tu veux faire disparaître **ce dont** tu as peur?

4. Tu sais **ce qui** est arrivé à l'héroïne?

5. **Ce qu**'elle n'aime pas du tout, c'est les monstres.

6. Avec sa baguette magique, le magicien faisait apparaître **ce dont** il avait besoin.

7. La marraine ne savait pas **ce que** la fille avait souhaité.

8. **Ce qui** prend beaucoup de temps, c'est de préparer une potion magique.

9. **Ce dont** j'ai envie, c'est un tapis volant!

10. Le prince n'a pas accepté **ce que** le sorcier lui avait offert.

D Answers will vary. Possible answer: In the first sentence, **qui** is used because it refers to a noun (**une fille**) that is previously mentioned. In the second sentence, **ce qui** is used because it refers to something that hasn't been mentioned.

Adjective placement and meaning

A 1. It is an ancient legend from Africa.

2. People say that it is a true story.

3. There was a great king whom everyone respected.

4. He had a daughter who loved expensive jewelry.

5. One day, a poor farmer finds a necklace.

6. It is the only necklace in the world that sings.

B 1. C'est une légende ancienne d'Afrique.

2. On dit que c'est une histoire vraie.

3. Il y avait un grand roi que tout le monde respectait.

4. Il avait une fille qui aimait les bijoux chers.

5. Un jour, un fermier pauvre trouva un collier.

6. C'était le seul collier du monde qui chantait.

C 1. —Tu ne partages plus une chambre avec ton frère?
   —Non. J'ai ma **propre** chambre maintenant.

2. —Ton nouvel ordinateur a coûté beaucoup d'argent?
   —Oui, c'est un ordinateur **cher**.

3. —Henri est un bon ami, n'est-ce pas?

—Oui, c'est un **cher** ami.

4. —Véronique nettoie toujours sa chambre?

—Oui, c'est une chambre **propre**.

5. —Combien mesure ton père?

—C'est un homme **grand** qui mesure 2 mètres.

6. —Est-ce que les Archambault sont riches?

—Pas du tout! C'est une famille **pauvre**.

D Answers will vary. Possible answer: **Nicole était la seule étudiante dans la classe.** If the adjective **seule** would be after the noun, then it would mean that Nicole was the lonely student.

The plus-que-parfait

A 1. She <u>had</u> always <u>considered</u> Lois a close friend.

2. They <u>had</u> not <u>forgotten</u> us after all.

3. When we drove up to the farm, we saw that everybody <u>had left</u>.

4. We <u>had</u> just <u>started</u> to eat when the phone rang.

5. They <u>had drunk</u> some water before starting the race.

6. Charlene <u>had</u> never <u>been</u> to a circus before.

7. In truth, I barely recognized it, since it <u>had changed</u> so much.

B 1. Nous <u>avions déménagé</u> l'année d'avant.

2. Ils <u>avaient voyagé</u> en France.

3. Je n'y suis pas allé parce que j'<u>avais oublié</u> l'adresse.

4. Marithé a dit qu'elle <u>avait téléphoné</u> à Pierre.

5. Christelle <u>s'était fait</u> mal au pied en marchant.

6. Le film <u>avait</u> déjà <u>commencé</u> quand nous sommes arrivés.

7. Géraldine <u>était allée</u> au café avant d'aller à la piscine.

C 1. Tu savais qu'il **était parti** au Canada?

2. On m'a dit que Brigitte et Jean **s'étaient mariés**.

3. Je ne savais pas que tu **avais eu** un accident.

4. Vous saviez que Didier **avait acheté** une moto?

5. Nous **avions pris** des photos, puis on a perdu l'appareil photo.

6. Maman m'a demandé si j'**avais fait** la vaisselle.

7. Tu **avais passé** ton bac avant ton séjour en Angleterre, n'est-ce pas?

8. Pauline et Xavier **s'étaient rencontrés** bien avant 1995.

9. Tu savais que Félix **s'était cassé** le bras, toi?

10. Quand Alex avait trois ans, il **avait appris** à nager.

D Answers will vary. Possible answer: The first sentence means *you left*. It is in the **passé composé** and it is made up of the present tense of the helping verb and a past participle. The second sentence means *you had left (before something else happened)*. It is in the **plus-que-parfait** and it is made up of the imperfect of the helping verb and a past participle.

Sequence of tenses in indirect discourse

A 1. She [says] that she [is going] to the movie. (present, present progressive)

2. Thomas [said] that he [had] already [seen] the film. (past, past perfect)

3. Louis [says] that they [will have] fun. (present, future)

4. They [said] that they [would meet] after class. (past, conditional)

5. I [said] that I [was] too busy. (past, past)

6. They [say] that they [will go] for ice cream. (present, future)

B 1. Elle [dit] qu'elle [combattra] l'ennemi. (présent, futur)

2. Ils [disent] qu'ils [veulent] l'indépendance. (présent, présent)

3. Le prince [a dit] qu'il [explorerait] le Maroc. (passé composé, conditionnel)

4. Le peuple dit que le conflit a commencé. (présent, passé composé)
5. Vous avez dit que vous aviez vu un tapis volant? (passé composé, plus-que-parfait)
6. Le président dit que la guerre se terminera. (présent, futur)

C 1. Le professeur a dit que nous (lisons / lirions) l'histoire de la monarchie.
2. Mon amie dit qu'elle (a / aurait) un livre d'histoire très intéressant.
3. Son frère a dit que le livre (est / était) dans sa chambre.
4. Je lui ai dit que nous l' (avons trouvé / avions trouvé) dans la salle.
5. Vous dites que nous (devons / devrions) finir le livre avant jeudi.
6. Mes copains ont dit que l'examen (aura / aurait) lieu dans une semaine.

D 1. **Monique a dit que Frédéric était à la bibliothèque.**
2. Tu as dit que Agnès sortirait du lycée à 4 heures.
3. Eugénie a dit qu'elle avait besoin de tes notes de chimie.
4. Vous avez dit que nous adorerions le nouveau roman.
5. Jean-Paul a dit que tu n'avais pas reçu mes lettres.
6. J'ai dit qu'il aurait lieu après le coup d'état.

The past infinitive

A 1. They claimed to have been too tired to run.
2. It was a good idea to have brought some water with us.
3. It was said to have been the hottest day of the year.
4. Do you think it was better to have participated in the race even though we lost?
5. It was impossible to have finished in under two hours.
6. The winner was finally shown to have cheated.

7. He was believed to have taken a shortcut.

B 1. Excusez-moi d'être arrivé(e) en retard.
2. Après avoir fini mes études, je veux devenir architecte.
3. Après être tombés amoureux, ils se sont mariés.
4. Tu ne peux pas aller à l'université sans avoir réussi au bac.
5. Les Martin ont acheté leur maison après être arrivés à Chartres.
6. Félix a vendu sa moto après avoir eu un accident.

C 1. **Après s'être réveillées, mes sœurs ont fait leurs lits.**
2. J'ai pris le bus après avoir pris le petit-déjeuner.
3. Après s'être baignée, Christelle s'est habillée.
4. Nous sommes allés au cinéma après avoir fini nos devoirs.

D Answers will vary. Possible answer: **Avoir** and **être** are translated into English as *having*. Sentences that take the past infinitive in French do not in English.

CHAPITRE 4
Reciprocal verbs

A 1. Manuel and Robert help each other study for the test.
2. Elisa and Anne argue with each other all the time.
3. Now the girls aren't speaking to one another.
4. They finally made up with each other.
5. We trust one another with our deepest secrets.
6. The students told one another about their vacations.
7. You and your classmate have a lot of respect for each other.

B 1. Nous nous sommes vus ce matin.
2. Vous vous disputez trop souvent.
3. Elles se sont offert des cadeaux.

4. Nous <u>nous</u> parlions rarement au lycée.

5. Ils <u>se</u> sont regardés et tout de suite, ils <u>se</u> sont plu.

6. Vous <u>vous</u> êtes rencontrés où?

7. Pourquoi Fatima et Alice <u>se</u> sont disputées?

C 1. **Nous nous sommes vu(e)s dimanche**.

2. Julie et Jean se sont retrouvés à la piscine.

3. Carole et Charlotte se sont réconciliées.

4. Est-ce que Georges et toi, vous vous êtes beaucoup aimés?

5. Nous nous sommes dit la vérité.

6. Elles se sont souvent conseillées.

D Answers will vary. Possible answer: **Se promener** (taking a walk) is something people usually do for themselves. **Se téléphoner** (to phone) is something people usually do to others, so we interpret the second sentence as reciprocal: *Louis and Rose phone each other every day.*

The past conditional

A 1. I would have invited / had invited) Karim if he had been free.

2. If I (would have won / had won) the lottery, I would have bought a car.

3. I would have told you if I (would have known / had known).

4. In your position, I (would have lent / had lent) him some money.

5. If Zahra (would have finished / had finished) her homework, she would have played soccer with us.

6. The teacher (would have been / had been) sad if they had not passed their exam.

7. Victor would have responded to your e-mail if he (would have received / had received) it.

B 1. S'il avait été riche, il (aurait acheté / avait acheté) une maison.

2. Si tu (serais venu / étais venu) hier soir, tu aurais vu tes amis chez nous.

3. Il aurait répondu à ta lettre s'il (aurait eu / avait eu) le temps.

4. Si tu avais voulu, je t'(aurais apporté / avais apporté) mon cahier.

5. Si vous me l'aviez demandé, je vous (aurais prêté / avais prêté) mon stylo.

6. Il a cru hier qu'il (aurait plu / avait plu) ce matin.

7. Si vous (étiez tombé / seriez tombé), il vous serait venu en aide.

C 1. **Pascal m'aurait téléphoné s'il n'avait pas été trop occupé**.

2. Si Maryse avait étudié, elle n'aurait pas eu de mauvaise note.

3. J'aurais fait le ménage si j'avais eu le temps.

4. Nathalie aurait joué au foot si elle ne s'était pas foulé la cheville.

5. Honoré n'aurait pas été fatigué s'il avait bien dormi.

6. Nous n'aurions pas été de mauvaise humeur si nous n'avions pas perdu le match.

7. Vous m'auriez parlé au café si vous m'aviez vu.

Subjunctive with necessity, desire, and emotions

A 1. It's a good idea for us to <u>wake</u> up early. (infinitive)

2. I wish that <u>were</u> a true story. (subjunctive)

3. The teacher wants all of us to <u>learn</u>. (infinitive)

4. It is important that she <u>follow</u> my advice. (subjunctive)

5. My parents hope that I <u>will become</u> a doctor. (indicative)

6. I'm glad that you <u>know</u> how to swim. (indicative)

B 1. Ils désirent <u>rester</u> ici. (infinitive)

2. C'est dommage qu'il <u>soit</u> malade. (subjunctive)

3. Il faut que tu <u>fasses</u> tes devoirs. (subjunctive)

4. Je suis content d'<u>avoir</u> de bons amis. (infinitive)

5. Nous voulons <u>voyager</u> en Angleterre. (infinitive)

6. Je ne veux pas que tu te <u>fâches</u>. (subjunctive)

C 1. Je suis heureuse que vous le **rencontriez**.

2. Je suis fâché qu'il ne vous **reconnaisse** pas.

3. Il est nécessaire que tu **apprennes** l'anglais.

4. Il vaudrait mieux que nous **restions** encore une année à Nice.

5. Je souhaite que vous **alliez** voir cette exposition.

6. C'est dommage qu'ils ne **fassent** pas de progrès.

7. Il faudrait que je **parte** demain.

D Answers will vary. Sample answers:

1. Il est essentiel que **nous fassions un apprentissage**.

2. Je suis ravi(e) de **connaître un auteur célèbre**.

3. Je voudrais que mes amis et moi, nous **trouvions du travail**.

4. Je suis désolé(e) de **me disputer avec ma sœur**.

5. Il est important que le président **aille au Moyen-Orient**.

6. Je souhaite que les jeunes **lisent les journaux**.

CHAPITRE 5
Subjunctive with expressions of fear

A 1. Their team <u>was afraid of</u> [losing]. (gerund)

2. If I tell you, I <u>fear that</u> you [will get] angry. (indicative)

3. Anne <u>was afraid of</u> [falling] down the cliff. (gerund)

4. We're <u>afraid that</u> Robert [knows] the secret. (indicative)

5. Do you <u>fear that</u> the climate [is] [changing]? (indicative)

6. Are you <u>afraid of</u> [trying] new things? (gerund)

B 1. J'ai <u>peur que</u> le dauphin [soit] blessé. (subjunctive)

2. Je <u>crains de</u> [rencontrer] un requin. (infinitive)

3. <u>Vous avez peur de</u> [nager] dans la mer? (infinitive)

4. J'ai <u>peur qu'</u>une guêpe me [pique]. (subjunctive)

5. <u>Nous craignons qu'</u>il n'y [ait] plus de corail. (subjunctive)

C 1. **Robert craint que nous soyons en retard.**

2. Je crains que Jean-Marc nous attende.

3. Jean-Marc craint que vous ayez un accident.

4. Tu crains que le restaurant ferme à 10h.

5. Christine craint que nous ne nous rencontrions pas.

6. André craint que tu perdes les clés.

7. Nous craignons qu'il soit interdit de s'arrêter ici.

D 1. **Moi aussi, j'ai peur de me perdre.**

2. Moi aussi, j'ai peur de ne pas savoir monter la tente.

3. Moi aussi, j'ai peur d'oublier l'ouvre-boîte.

4. Moi aussi, j'ai peur de voir des serpents.

5. Moi aussi, j'ai peur d'avoir mal partout.

6. Moi aussi, j'ai peur de tomber en faisant de l'escalade.

CHAPITRE 6
Subjunctive with doubt and uncertainty

A 1. <u>I don't believe that</u> Stephen [is] [reading] the comics.

2. <u>It is true that</u> the press [knows] everything.

3. Tammy <u>doubts that</u> you [interviewed] the movie star.

4. <u>It's possible that</u> this [is] a real classified ad.

5. <u>I can't believe that</u> someone [would] [collect] broken buttons.

6. <u>It is clear that</u> you actually [believe] the articles in those tabloids.

B 1. Je doute que ce magazine soit gratuit. (S)

2. Je ne crois pas qu'il lise la presse à sensation. (S)

3. Il se peut que l'article soit vrai. (S)

4. Il est persuadé que nous nous sommes abonnés à ce journal. (I)

5. Je suis sûre que c'est en première page. (I)

6. Ça m'étonnerait que vous fassiez du parachutisme. (S)

7. Je ne pense pas que ce dessin humoristique soit drôle. (S)

C Answers will vary. Sample answers:

1. Je doute que les médias sachent tout.

2. Je suis certain(e) que beaucoup de gens lisent les informations sur Internet.

3. Ça m'étonnerait qu'un garçon de six ans soit rédacteur en chef.

4. Je ne crois pas que la météo soit toujours exacte.

5. Il se peut que le président des États-Unis aille en Chine cette année.

D Answers will vary. Possible answer: expressions of necessity, expressions of desire, expressions of emotions, expressions of doubt and uncertainty

Negative expressions

A 1. Don does not go anywhere during the week.

2. Nobody brought anything to drink.

3. I like neither spiders nor snakes.

4. I am not going anywhere this weekend.

5. Tina has nothing to give him for his birthday.

6. We don't have any good ideas.

B 1. Je ne fais rien cet après-midi.

2. Elle n'est allée nulle part pendant les vacances.

3. Personne ne sait jouer aux cartes?

4. Délia n'est pas encore arrivée?

5. On ne passe rien à la télé ce soir.

6. Je n'aime ni la chimie ni la biologie.

7. Vous n'avez lu aucun livre de Saint-Exupéry?

C 1. Tu ne fais jamais la vaisselle.

2. C'est le professeur qui ne donne aucun devoir.

3. Ils n'ont pas encore fini leurs devoirs.

4. Nous n'avons voulu aller nulle part.

5. Aucun ministre n'est arrivé la semaine dernière.

6. Je n'ai vu personne sur l'autoroute.

D Answers will vary. Possible answer:

Aucun... ne goes at the beginning of the sentence because it describes the subject. **Ne... aucun** goes around the verb because it describes the direct object.

CHAPITRE 7
The passive voice

A 1. This dam was built by my grandfather. (my grandfather)

2. The same book was read by all students. (all students)

3. Your voice could be heard across the room. (no agent)

4. The thief was arrested by the police. (the police)

5. The injured were taken to the hospital. (no agent)

6. Ten roads will be built next year. (no agent)

7. The tree was struck by lightning. (lightning)

8. The information is found in my blog. (no agent)

B 1. Ce pont a été construit par mon oncle. (mon oncle)

2. Tous les appartements sont loués. (no agent)

3. Le mur a été détruit par un raz-de-marée. (un raz-de-marée)

4. Je suis invitée par mon ami. (mon ami)

5. Le lycée a été évacué ce matin. (no agent)

6. Le président est interviewé par ton frère? (ton frère)

7. Deux alligators ont été attrapés en Floride. (no agent)

8. Je crains que tu sois mordu par ce chien. (ce chien)

C 1. **Les journaux sont lus par beaucoup de gens.**

2. Les maisons du quartier sont décorées par les voisins.

3. Les rues seront nettoyées par les enfants après la fête.

4. Le piano a été monté par trois hommes.

5. Le gâteau sera acheté par Geneviève.

D 1. Le français se parle à Lausanne./On parle français à Lausanne.

2. Des films français sont passés dans ce cinéma./Des films français se passent dans ce cinéma.

Quand, lorsque, and dès que

A 1. When I finish high school, I will travel.

2. As soon as the guests leave, we will get some sleep.

3. Martin gets angry when people do not carpool.

4. The ship will depart as soon as everyone is on board.

5. Candace will return to work when she recovers from the accident.

6. As soon as it starts to rain, we will turn off the sprinklers.

B 1. Quand tu iras aux Jeux olympiques, tu seras content.

2. Je serai heureuse lorsque je serai enfin à la maison

3. Dès que Christophe rentre à la maison, il surfe sur Internet.

4. Dès qu tu auras le temps, tu viendras nous voir.

5. Quand il neige, les enfants construisent un bonhomme de neige.

6. Sophie cherchera un emploi quand elle aura son diplôme.

C 1. Quand tu seras en France, tu verras beaucoup de petites voitures.

2. Je vous écrirai dès que j'arriverai là-bas.

3. Nous allons au café quand nous avons le temps.

4. Lorsque Janine apprendra la nouvelle, elle nous téléphonera.

5. Dès qu'ils sauront que je suis ici, ils viendront me voir.

6. Qu'est-ce que vous ferez quand vous aurez 25 ans?

7. Est-ce que tu consommes beaucoup d'eau quand tu prends une douche?

D Answers will vary. Sample answers:

1. Quand je serai en vacances, je partirai en France.

2. Quand j'aurai vingt et un ans, je trouverai un appartement.

3. Dès que j'aurai mon diplôme, j'irai à l'université.

4. Lorsque j'ai de l'argent, j'achète des CD.

5. Dès que j'aurai une nouvelle voiture, je sortirai plus souvent.

E Answers will vary. Possible answer:
It makes sense to have both clauses in the future since both events are going to happen in the future.

CHAPITRE 8
Contractions with lequel

A 1. What are you thinking? (interrogative)

2. This is the student for whom I voted. (relative)

3. Mandy likes the candidate who is energetic. (relative)

4. Which of the posters do you prefer? (interrogative)

5. The mayor, whose name I forget, is here. (relative)

6. On whose behalf are you speaking? (interrogative)

7. The article which I wrote is on the front page. (relative)

B 1. Voilà le monsieur auquel tu as parlé. (relative)

2. Duquel de ces députés tu parles? (interrogative)

3. La table sur laquelle j'écris est cassée. (relative)

4. De toutes ces affiches, <u>laquelle</u> tu préfères? (interrogative)

5. <u>Auquel</u> de ces débats mes copains ont pris part? (relative)

6. <u>Auxquels</u> as-tu participé? (interrogative)

C 1. Auquel?

2. Duquel?

3. À laquelle?

4. Auxquels?

5. Desquelles?

6. Desquels?

D 1. **La candidate de laquelle tu m'as parlé est sympa.**

2. Où sont les bureaux de vote auxquels les électeurs vont?

3. C'est l'effet de serre auquel le premier ministre s'intéresse.

4. Voilà les immigrants desquels je t'ai parlé.

5. Les candidates duquelles j'ai le plus entendu parlé ont été élues.

The past subjunctive

A 1. Imagine that you <u>lived</u> in a dictatorship.

2. Joseph wishes he <u>were</u> the minister of sports.

3. If I <u>could</u> vote, I would vote for you.

4. Suppose that you <u>held</u> a seat in the senate.

5. If Laura <u>had</u> her way, we would go on strike.

6. We would have more holidays if the bill <u>went</u> into law.

B 1. Je suis désolé que ta candidate <u>ait perdu.</u>

2. Nous sommes heureux que vous <u>soyez venus</u>.

3. Je ne crois pas que le président <u>ait joué</u> au foot avec vous.

4. Il y a peu de chance qu'il <u>ait démissionné.</u>

5. Je suis content que le gouvernement <u>ait aidé</u> les victimes.

6. Je doute que le ministre <u>soit allé</u> en prison.

C 1. Il est possible que le roi soit revenu de Chine hier.

2. J'ai peur que la campagne n'ait pas réussi.

3. Nous sommes désolés que les étudiants n'aient pas participé aux élections.

4. Je ne suis pas sûr(e) que tu aies lu la bonne rubrique.

5. Tu crains que le député n'ait pas reçu ta lettre.

6. Vous êtes triste que le président soit tombé malade.

D Answers will vary. Possible answer: **Il est content que nous venions** means that he is happy that we're coming. **Il est content que nous soyons venus** means that he is happy that we've come.

CHAPITRE 9
Present participles used as adjectives

A 1. The mural honors the <u>working</u> man. (to work)

2. This is an <u>exciting</u> book about Mars. (to excite)

3. I found the art exhibit <u>fascinating</u>! (to fascinate)

4. There is a <u>growing</u> number of digital artists. (to grow)

5. The sculpture depicts a <u>dying</u> flower. (to die)

6. The landscape on the etching is <u>haunting</u>. (to haunt)

7. The <u>relaxing</u> sound of water filled the gallery. (to relax)

8. I liked the painting with the <u>dancing</u> girls. (to dance)

B 1. C'est une gravure <u>impressionnante</u>. (impressioner)

2. Je trouve l'autoportrait <u>charmant</u>. (charmer)

3. J'aime les eaux <u>dormantes</u> de ce paysage. (dormir)

4. Regarde les cheveux <u>tombants</u> du modèle. (tomber)

5. Le chien est <u>obéissant</u> il et ne bouge pas. (obéir)

7. Ce sculpteur est un artiste très
   <u>passionnant</u>. (passionner)

C 1. J'aime bien les soirées **dansantes**.
   2. La chauve-souris est un mammifère
      volant.
   3. Ils se rencontrerons à la nuit
      tombante.
   4. Cette peinture à l'huile utilise des
      couleurs **brillantes**.
   5. À mon avis, c'était une exposition
      surprenante, même choquante.
   6. Je trouve les critiques d'art
      énervants.

D Answers may vary. Possible answers:
   1. **Il y a un soleil couchant.**
   2. Il y a un oiseau chantant.
   3. Il y a quatre filles dansantes et
      riantes.
   4. Il y a deux chiens dormants.

Si and oui

A 1. affirm
   2. contradict
   3. affirm
   4. contradict
   5. contradict
   6. affirm

B 1. affirm
   2. contradict
   3. contradict
   4. affirm
   5. contradict

C Answers will vary. Possible answers:
   1. **Oui, j'aime beaucoup l'art
      contemporain.**
   2. Si, j'aime voyager!
   3. Oui, nous aimons aller aux concerts.
   4. Si, ils y vont!
   5. Si, j'ai vu des statues!

D Answers will vary. Possible answer:
   In English, you contradict a negative
   statement by using the pitch of your
   voice and stressing the modal verbs. In
   French, you use the word **si**.

CHAPITRE 10
Adverb placement

A 1. He <u>left</u> yesterday on the five o'clock
      train.
   2. The baggage claim area is almost
      empty.
   3. The plane from New York has
      apparently <u>landed</u>.
   4. Unfortunately, I <u>don't have</u> a video
      camera.
   5. They rarely <u>travel</u> abroad.

B 1. J'<u>aime</u> beaucoup voyager.
   2. Il faut <u>arriver</u> tôt à l'aéroport.
   3. Heureusement, les petits chiens
      <u>peuvent aller</u> en cabine.
   4. Notre vol était absolument <u>horrible</u>.
   5. Vous <u>avez</u> peu <u>dormi</u> dans l'avion.
   6. Je préfère que nous <u>nous
      rencontrions</u> ici.
   7. Quand elles voyagent, elles <u>se
      disputent</u> régulièrement.

C 1. Tu trouves qu'on mange **mal** en
      avion?
   2. Pour sortir vite de l'avion, assieds-toi
      près de la porte.
   3. Si nous ne marchons pas
      rapidement, nous manquerons le
      vol.
   4. Nous logeons **quelquefois** chez des
      amis mais pas toujours.
   5. **Malheureusement**, on n'a pas assez
      d'argent pour voyager.
   6. Mon oncle est pilote depuis **très**
      longtemps.

D 1. Le train est **assez** confortable.
      Adverbs generally go before the
      adjective they modify.
   2. Nous avons **bien** dormi.
      In a sentence with a compound tense,
      adverbs generally go after the
      helping verb and before the past
      participle.
   3. Ils sont partis **hier**.
      Adverbs of time can be placed at the
      end of the sentence.